Awakening Words

Awakening Words

John Bunyan
and the Language of Community

Edited by
David Gay, James G. Randall,
and Arlette Zinck

Newark: University of Delaware Press
London: Associated University Presses

© 2000 by Associated University Presses, Inc.

All rights reserved. Authorization to photocopy items for internal or personal use, or the internal or personal use of specific clients, is granted by the copyright owner, provided that a base fee of $10.00, plus eight cents per page, per copy is paid directly to the Copyright Clearance Center, 222 Rosewood Drive, Danvers, Massachusetts 01923. [0-87413-702-0/00 $10.00 + 8¢ pp, pc.] Other than as indicated in the foregoing, this book may not be reproduced, in whole or in part, in any form (except as permitted by Sections 107 and 108 of the U.S. Copyright Law, and except for brief quotes appearing in reviews in the public press).

Associated University Presses
440 Forsgate Drive
Cranbury, NJ 08512

Associated University Presses
16 Barter Street
London WC1A 2AH, England

Associated University Presses
P.O. Box 338, Port Credit
Mississauga, Ontario
Canada L5G 4L8

The paper used in this publication meets the requirements of the American National Standard for Permanence of Paper for Printed Library Materials Z39.48-1984.

Library of Congress Cataloging-in-Publication Data

Awakening words : John Bunyan and the language of community / edited by David Gay, James G. Randall, and Arlette Zinck.
    p. cm.
  Includes bibliographical references (p.   ) and index.
  ISBN 0-87413-702-0
  1. Bunyan, John, 1628–1688—Political and social views. 2. Dissenters, Religious—Political activity—England—History—17th century. 3. Christian literature, English—Puritan authors—History and criticism. 4. Christianity and politics—Great Britain—History—17th century. 5. Literature and society—England—History—17th century. 6. Great Britain—Politics and government—1660–1688. 7. Radicalism—Great Britain—History—17th century. 8. Great Britain—Social conditions—17th century. 9. Dissenters, Religious, in literature. 10. Community in literature. I. Gay, David, 1955– . II. Randall, James G., 1955– . III. Zinck, Arlette.
PR3332.A96 2000
828'.407—dc21   99-43144
                                                                              CIP

PRINTED IN THE UNITED STATES OF AMERICA

Contents

Introduction: Bunyan, the Shadow of Persecution, and the
Power of Awakening Words
    RICHARD L. GREAVES   9

Abbreviations   23

"Till one greater man / Restore us . . .": Restoration Images
in Bunyan and Milton
    N. H. KEEBLE   27

Bunyan and the Cry of Blood
    JOHN R. KNOTT   51

Honey from the Lion's Carcass: Bunyan, Allegory, and the
Samsonian Moment
    SHARON ACHINSTEIN   68

John Bunyan and English Millenarianism
    W. R. OWENS   81

Bunyan's Exceeding Maze: *Grace Abounding* and the
Labyrinth of Predestination
    MICHAEL DAVIES   97

"For the Best Improvement of Time": *Pilgrim's Progress*
and the Liturgies of Nonconformity
    KEN SIMPSON   113

"For then I should be a Ranter or a Quaker": John Bunyan
and Radical Religion
    T. L. UNDERWOOD   127

Bunyan's Sisters: "Unfolding of [their] Secret Things"
    PATRICIA DEMERS   141

"Baffled, and Befooled": Misogyny in the Work of
John Bunyan
    AILEEN ROSS   153

"Christiana and her train": Bunyan and the Alternative
Society in the Second Part of *The Pilgrim's Progress*
    MELISSA D. AARON   169

Pilgrims' Progresses: Derivative Texts and the Seventeenth-
Century Reader
  Susan Cook   186

Bibliography   202
Contributors   215
Index   218

Acknowledgments

THIS VOLUME REFLECTS THE COMMUNITY OF SCHOLARSHIP FORMED around the International John Bunyan Society, founded earlier in this decade with much encouragement and support from many scholars. With that larger community in mind, we wish to thank James F. Forrest, Richard L. Greaves, Neil Keeble and John Knott for sharing their scholarly experience with us to the immeasurable benefit of this volume, and our contributors for their participation. We are also endebted to the editors of *Bunyan Studies* who kindly permitted us to reproduce in revised form Neil Keeble's essay, which first appeared in number 6 of that journal (1995–96). We are especially grateful to Professor Donald Mell and the staff of the University of Delaware Press, and Julien Yoseloff, Director of Associated University Presses, for their support. We also wish to thank The King's University College for their administrative and financial aid to this project. Finally, we owe a number of debts at the University of Alberta: first, our thanks to John Charles, Janine Greene and the staff of the Bruce Peel Special Collections Library who were infinitely patient with us as we checked and re-checked references in the volumes of their world-class Bunyan collection; next, to Glenn Rollans and his associates at the University of Alberta Press who provided valuable consultations on scholarly publishing in the early stages of this project; and, at last, to Leslie Robertson and Carolyn Ives, two excellent Graduate Research Assistants, whose dedicated work is so greatly appreciated.

Introduction:
Bunyan, the Shadow of Persecution, and the Power of Awakening Words

RICHARD L. GREAVES

NO PERIOD IN THE HISTORY OF BUNYAN SCHOLARSHIP HAS BEEN MORE productive than the last four decades of the twentieth century. Inspired by the towering figure of Roger Sharrock, this period can be fairly characterized as the maturation of modern scholarly interest in Bunyan, though, to be sure, this interest owes much to the pioneering studies of James Blanton Wharey and William York Tindall. The mythic Victorian portrayal of Bunyan as a prototype of Charles Haddon Spurgeon has been laid to rest, at least among academics, and the once standard biography by John Brown has been replaced by Michael A. Mullett's *John Bunyan in Context* (1996). In *A Turbulent, Seditious and Factious People: John Bunyan and His Church* (1988) Christopher Hill has firmly grounded Bunyan in the world of English conventicles without losing sight of his literary genius. Another classic, George Offor's edition of Bunyan's works, has been replaced by the critical Oxford edition, of which Sharrock was the general editor; though meritorious as a bibliographical landmark, the Offor edition should no longer be used by scholars.

The best of the recent, burgeoning Bunyan scholarship is characterized by the almost seamless blending of literary, religious, and historical scholarship, two of the preeminent practitioners of which are Neil Keeble and John Knott. The debate over postmodernism has suggested new ways to interpret Bunyan, though we should be wary of imposing an artificial intellectual construct on an author who consciously wrote for a biblically literate but otherwise relatively unsophisticated audience; most of his intended readers, as Keeble notes, were chiefly vulgar. Bunyan, in fact, wrote for various audiences, ranging from the unconverted, whom, above all others, he was most interested in reaching, to the godly, whom he offered scriptural instruction to fortify their faith and pastoral guidance to overcome the experiences of Doubting Castle, Hill Difficulty, Vanity Fair, and the Valley of the Shadow of Death. He found time, too, to debate fellow sectaries whose principles he found wanting, as in the case of Quakers such as Edward Burrough and William Penn or Baptists such as John Denne and William Kiffin. As Ted L. Underwood indicates, Bunyan was at pains to distinguish himself from various other sectaries, undoubtedly because they were his keenest competitors for those who were not committed Prayer-Book Protestants, Presbyterians, or Independents.

Words were Bunyan's sole means to reach his disparate audiences. He had no traditional liturgy, pageantry, or clerical costume and virtually no material symbolism on which to call for assistance in conveying his message, reinforcing his followers, or combating his rivals. With water-baptism optional in Bunyan's judgment and the Lord's Supper observed in simplicity and rather infrequently, what Ken Simpson provocatively calls "the Nonconformist liturgy" was "the liturgy of the Word." Worship had very little to do with physical symbols—the bread and cup of communion, the water of baptism, and the physical pulpit, itself optional, were the exceptions—and everything to do with language. Apart from these exceptions, symbolism was verbal, as when Bunyan depicted the church as a garden, the Christian life as a pilgrimage, and the Lord's Supper as spiritual nourishment. Although some of Bunyan's writing is pedestrian, he is unquestionably a master of verbal imagery, as reflected most obviously in his epics but also in varying degrees in his other works. In *Grace Abounding to the Chief of Sinners*, words in the form of biblical verses bombard Bunyan like darts or arrows. Elsewhere he likens the Ten Commandments to cannons shooting at the soul. Words are weapons, but they are also means of exhortation, admonition, consolation, and instruction.

To use words effectively, opined Bunyan, was a "Gift," by which he meant the God-given ability to expound the Bible and articulate his personal religious experience, which he believed was firmly rooted in Scripture. He first exercised this gift in exhortations to the gathered congregation in Bedford, following which he accompanied several members as they traveled in the region, occasionally speaking "a word of Admonition" to those on whom they called (GA, 83). In fear and trembling, as he later recalled, he began to preach regularly, exercising his gift with "such a Word as might, if God would bless it, lay hold of and awaken the Conscience" (84). His mission, he believed, was "to carry an awakening Word" (87), a conviction to which he remained faithful throughout his career. Words had awakened him, as when "a voice did suddenly dart from Heaven into [his] Soul" while he played cat, plunging him into "an exceeding maze" (10)—the labyrinth explored with such sensitivity by Michael Davies.

Awakened himself by words, and guided through the labyrinth of Christian experience by the language of Scripture, Bunyan was initially surprised at his ability to awaken others—an ability that rested on his decision to preach what he "smartingly did feel" (*GA*, 85) as well as his alluring use of what he modestly called "a parcel of plain, yet sound, true, and home sayings" (*MW*, 2: 16). Just as he deprecated his education, self-consciously comparing himself to boys who had studied the classics, so he played down his oratorical skills. He consciously modeled himself after Christ, who, the sectaries liked to stress, "was low and contemptible in the world himself," as John Burton noted in his epistle to Bunyan's first book, *Some Gospel-Truths Opened* (1656). Suspecting that this book would not be taken seriously in some quarters because of Bunyan's modest education, Burton pointedly insisted that God had "not chosen [Bunyan] out of an earthly, but out of the heavenly University" (*MW*, 1: 11). Bunyan was sensitive to the fact that he lacked the formal education traditionally expected of religious authors, but he turned this to his advantage, deprecating the "Fantastical expressions" and the "light, vain, whimsical Scholar-like terms" associated with men trained at Oxford and Cambridge (*MW*, 1: 16). Awakening words, for Bunyan, were inspired—and inspiring, not necessarily scholarly. Their purpose was serious, so much so that he hesitated to publish *The Pilgrim's Progress*, fearing that his extended allegory might offend some of the godly. "*Solidity, indeed becomes the Pen / Of him that writeth things Divine to men: / But must I needs want solidness, because / By Metaphors I speak . . . ?*" (*PP*, 4). Words, Bunyan had come to realize, could be fun as long as they conveyed the Gospel. In various ways each essay in this volume explores some facet of Bunyan's use of and fascination with words, the vehicle of his message, whether couched in fiction or biblical exposition, spiritual autobiography or polemic tract, prose or poetry.

Awakening words, Bunyan learned by experience, were most easily remembered when phrased allegorically. "*A dark Similitude / will on the Fancie more it self intrude, / And will stick faster in the Heart and Head, / Then things from Similies not borrowed*" (*PP*, 171). *The Pilgrim's Progress* was intended to convert the unregenerate as well as to instruct and encourage believers. Bunyan's pastoral experience had persuaded him that "*Things that seem to be hid in words obscure, / Do but the Godly mind the more alure*" (171). Clearly, Bunyan wrote with this in mind, seeking to entice his Christian readers to dig below the surface in search of greater insights. "The exegetical key," in Keeble's apt phrase, comprises the typological and emblematic patterns with which Bunyan was so familiar. Increasingly sensitive to the importance of such methodology in understanding Bunyan, scholars have begun to recognize how much can be learned by careful attention to his minor as well as his major works. Recent attention has focused especially on *Seasonable Counsel, or Advice to Sufferers*; *An Exposition of the First Ten Chapters of Genesis*; *I Will Pray with the Spirit*; *A Case of Conscience Resolved*, and the controversial writings in which Bunyan dueled with the Quakers and the Baptists. W. R. Owens's essay on *The Holy City* and *Of Antichrist, and His Ruine* is a particularly good example of what can be learned from a close, historically sensitive examination of Bunyan's lesser works. Other writings have yet to be fully reassessed, among them *Come, & Welcome, to Jesus Christ*, which holds clues to Bunyan's remarkable success as a preacher; *The Advocateship of Jesus Christ*, which may deepen our understanding of Bunyan's legal knowledge; *Israel's Hope Encouraged*, which reveals more about Bunyan's political views; and *Solomon's Temple Spiritualized*, which might be revisited with profit in the context of recent studies of typology.

Our understanding of the England in which Bunyan spent most of his adult life has shifted dramatically as the result of recent studies of the late seventeenth century by such scholars as Tim Harris, Gary De Krey, and Jonathan Scott. Once seen as an era of stability, at least from 1660 until 1679, we now realize that it was one of periodic crises or turbulence primarily because of the legacy of radical discontent inherited from the mid-century upheavals as well as the substantive challenge to the regimes of Charles II and James II posed by those who demanded liberty of conscience, at least for Protestants. Bunyan's *I Will Pray with the Spirit*, with its direct attack on the state's right to impose the *Book of Common Prayer*, was an early salvo in this war. When the great debate over conscience erupted in 1667 and continued until the enactment of the Test Act in 1673, Bunyan at first glance seemingly had little to contribute, but in fact he made a profound point in the Vanity Fair episode in *The Pilgrim's Progress* by indicting the Restoration government and its supporters for its persecutory policy: although the supporters of persecution were law-abiding, ostensibly religious people, their actions, in Bunyan's judgment, allied them with the forces of evil. The persecution was doubly insidious because its practitioners were the neighbors of the godly who in other respects were decent, hard-working citizens. Other indictments of the Stuart regime followed, especially in *The Holy War*. Bunyan was emphatically not the Stuart loyalist portrayed by Offor.

Grasping what Bunyan did say to his readers in this turbulent period requires an intensive threefold investigation to date each work as precisely as possible, thereby providing a more accurate sense of its historical context; to assess Bunyan's remarks in the context of contemporary writings; and to subject Bunyan's language to the close biblical reading likely to have been characteristic of his readers' approach. The essays in this volume by John Knott on the "cry of blood" and Sharon Achinstein on the "Samsonian moment" are excellent examples of the second and third approaches, respectively. If Achinstein is correct, Bunyan's readers may have experienced existential tension, faced with a choice of adhering to his dictates to shun rebellion on the one hand and to emulate Samson on the other. Was this tension deliberate? Did Bunyan intend to hold out to readers the possibility of choosing between rebellion and passive disobedience? Words, we know, were themselves a form of action for Bunyan; they awakened readers and listeners to a message on which he expected them to act, both spiritually and in their daily lives. The images he employed, in both allegory and traditional religious prose, were instruments to incite. Even his passages of comfort were intended to steel the godly's resolve to pursue their missions. In his controversies with such competitors as Edward Burrough, the Baptists Henry Danvers and Thomas Paul, and the Latitudinarian Edward Fowler, words were obviously weapons, but this was also true in a broader sense of all Bunyan's writings, for he was engaged in spiritual and often political conflict with forces he deemed evil. We ignore an essential aspect of Bunyan if we fail to appreciate this fact or neglect to read even his somewhat pedestrian works in this light.

The motive force of Bunyan's awakening words can only be grasped against a background of the historical circumstances in which he wrote. There is space here only to suggest the general context. In the first place, it is important to remember that the experience of defeat, virtually a historiographical commonplace in the aftermath of Christopher Hill's book on this theme, was only relative—a temporary defeat in the midst of an ongoing war in which victory was ultimately a certainty, as reflected, for example, in Bunyan's *The Holy City, The Holy War, Of Antichrist, and His Ruine*, and on a more individual basis in both parts of *The Pilgrim's Progress*. Saints suffer and sinners triumph, but only temporarily. For the most part the Nonconformists' mood was not defeatist but combative, resolved, and hopeful. Examples of retrospective, gloomy, or forlorn rhetoric are exceptions to the norm. For Bunyan the post-1660 nadir came between 1664 and 1666, when he felt "empty, spiritless, and barren" and found himself incapable of speaking "so much as five words of Truth, with Life and Evidence" (*MW*, 3: 69). His psycho-spiritual revival, it should be noted, occurred when he meditated on Revelation 21:11, with its vision of the descending holy city aglow with the brilliance of jasper and crystal. The cause of God would triumph and the saints would be resurrected to enjoy life eternal, the subject of his ensuing works *The Holy City* and *The Resurrection of the Dead*. This was not the literature of defeat but of glorious triumph. Virtually all of Bunyan's subsequent books were in some sense dedicated to reinforcing this belief (as in *The Pilgrim's Progress* and *The Holy War*) or to providing readers with the counsel to ward off attackers on their heavenly pilgrimage, whether the sins of the flesh, the complacency of spiritual formalism, persecuting magistrates, or rival religious challengers. Just as Francis Bacon imaginatively depicted himself as the bell-ringer who called others to the scientific revolution, so Bunyan saw himself as a captain in the forces of Emanuel who awakened and exhorted others to stand fast in the holy war, their ultimate triumph assured no matter how difficult the transitory battles.

It would, of course, be foolhardy to underestimate the pressures confronting Nonconformists between the Restoration in 1660 and the enactment of a degree of religious freedom by Parliament in 1689. Bunyan's twelve years in prison were anything but typical. Most Nonconformist clergy spent little or no time in jail, though the threat of incarceration hung over their heads throughout much of this period. The conditions of Bunyan's imprisonment were relatively good: he sometimes enjoyed the liberty to leave his cell to visit friends in the Bedford area or to travel to London, he had ample time to write, and he enjoyed the company of other Nonconformists. But the psychological stress was considerable as he found himself physically separated from his family, barred from his usual livelihood, under threat of banishment, and, if he returned following exile, subject to capital punishment. Not surprisingly, his works are sprinkled with castigatory remarks about his persecutors, whom he names individually and allegorically, including Giant Grim and Lord Hategood. Knott convincingly argues that Bunyan's employment of symbolic punishments against these allegorical figures was "an effort to take divine justice out of the realm of apocalyptic prophecy and make it seem more immediate and credible to an audience unusually vulnerable to a sense of powerlessness" (66).

The uncertainty of impending punishment must have created *Angst* for dissenters. The interest of magistrates in enforcing penal legislation varied from place to place and from time to time. Reports of radical plotting against the government, whether real or imagined, could trigger renewed repression, as occurred in the aftermath of Thomas Venner's Fifth Monarchist uprising in January 1661, the northern rebellion in the autumn of 1663, and the disclosure of the multifaceted Rye House plotting in the spring of 1683. Conversely, little persecution occurred in the mid-1670s or in 1687–88. Because of their refusal to render oaths and pay tithes or church rates, the Quakers probably suffered the most, but they were the only group that attempted to maintain systematic records of their sufferings. According to the research of Craig Horle, in the period 1660–88 there were 4,855 prosecutions of Friends in London and Middlesex, 4,083 in Cumberland, and 1,841 in Bristol. The actual numbers were probably higher; research on Quaker suffering in Ireland in the late seventeenth century underscores the fact that not all cases were recorded in the Great Book of Sufferings (now preserved in the Friends' Library, London). The Quakers also took a greater interest than did other nonconformists in publishing accounts of their suffering, such as Abraham Fuller and Thomas Holme's *A Brief Relation of Some Part of the Sufferings of the True Christians . . . in Ireland* (1672) or William Pooley's *Part of the Sufferings of Leicestershire & North-hamptonshire* (1683). Members of Bunyan's congregation reported some of their own sufferings in *A True and Impartial Narrative of Some Illegal and Arbitrary Proceedings* (1670).

Apart from presenting evidence of the persecution to which some dissenters were subjected, such accounts were significant because they provided virtually all Nonconformists with examples of what they faced should local magistrates subject them to the penal laws. Whether by reading such pamphlets, by word of mouth, or by legal threats from clerics and magistrates, Nonconformists would have been cognizant of the punishment they risked by frequenting conventicles. In most cases this would have entailed fines or distrained goods rather than incarceration, but financial penalties could be painful. During the time of troubles in Ireland (1689–91), the Friends, for instance, sustained losses that may have been as high as £100,000. Arrested following informers' reports in late 1682 or early 1683, the Baptist William Kiffin faced the possibility of fines totaling £300 for having attended fifteen conventicles. The *True Protestant Mercury* carried a report in September 1682 that 1,200 dissenters in Bristol would be fined £200 apiece, and that more than 500 would be expelled from their homes and banished from the city. Bunyan wrote for readers who had to live in the shadow of such persecution, facing the threat of fines, distrained goods, and imprisonment, all of which could have a disruptive, even ruinous impact on their ability to provide for themselves and their families. Dissenters thus had ample reason to read his statements, with care, on how to face the prospect of persecution.

Reports of prison conditions must also have alarmed dissenters who faced the prospect of incarceration. In places the jails were in fact horrific. In 1682 some 125 prisoners, two thirds of them Quakers, were so cramped in a Bristol prison that some had to stand while others slept, and some were detained in a kennel where the keeper normally kept his dog. The following year Bristol jailers threw the bedding and food of Quaker inmates into the dirt and confined fourteen of them in a dungeon lit only by a candle; they had to "lye Three tire one over another" if they wanted to rest at the same time.[1] In early 1683, sixty-three Friends were incarcerated in Norwich, the women in a cellar and the men in a dungeon without warmth or sanitary facilities beneath the guildhall; the only provision for air and light was a small iron grate reeking with urine and malodorous smells from nearby butchers' shops and fish stalls. In these deplorable conditions some of the female prisoners were breast-feeding their infants. On occasion jailers behaved outrageously, confining male and female prisoners together, confiscating fuel from dissenters to give to common criminals, or even urinating on inmates. Rooms contaminated by excrement or unsealed from icy winds and rain (as experienced by George Fox and Margaret Fell at Lancaster) were physically hazardous; so pervasive was the excrement and urine on the floor of Launceston prison that inmates could not lie down.

Yet the Restoration state was not as powerful as it must have seemed to Nonconformists. It was never able to quash all conventicles, to repress an increasingly daring underground press (whose publications included Bunyan's attack on the Book of Common Prayer), or to eliminate the recurrent plotting. To be sure, there were far more rumors of plots than there were actual conspiracies, though the latter were real enough, and the government could not afford to treat all reports lightly. The government faced rebellions by Fifth Monarchists in January 1661, northern rebels in the fall of 1663, Scottish Covenanters in 1666 and again in 1679, and the Argyll and Monmouth rebellions in 1685. It narrowly quashed a planned rebellion, mostly by Nonconformists, in Dublin and Ulster in early 1663. Covenanter assassins murdered the archbishop of St.

Andrews in May 1679; Charles II and James, duke of York were targets of assassination plots; and dissidents apprehended James, duke of Ormonde and were about to hang him at Tyburn when he escaped. Scottish Covenanters periodically assaulted royalist troops in Scotland, killing some of them, and Presbyterian extremists led by Richard Cameron and Donald Cargill openly denounced the Stuart regime and called for its violent overthrow.

Thanks to newspapers and newsletters, reports of such activities circulated widely, instilling understandable concerns in many magistrates and other supporters of the government. They too experienced tension and fear, not knowing which of the many conventicles included people plotting against the regime and its officers. Just as Bunyan and other Protestants "began to fear cutting of Throats, of being burned in our beds, and of seeing our Children dashed in pieces before our Faces" after the disclosure of the alleged Popish Plot (*MW*, 9: xix), so many Tory-Anglicans were alarmed by reports that the Rye House conspirators had allegedly intended to assassinate not only Charles and James but also Lord Keeper Francis North, the marquis of Halifax, the earl of Rochester, Lord Mayor Sir John Moore, the judges who had condemned Edward Fitzharris, and the pensioners in the Cavalier Parliament, whose stuffed corpses they proposed to hang in the Parliament building. No matter how far-fetched some of the rumors, they fed the tension and concern that gripped much of Charles's domain from 1678 to the end of his reign. Fear God, Bunyan advised, but it was difficult not to worry about one's neighbor. Was he a plotter whose actions would not only threaten magistrates but also endanger dissenters averse to conspiracy? an informer, ready to report illegal religious services in return for the reward promised by the Conventicle Act of 1670? a Catholic prepared to murder Protestants, as in Bohemia, the Palatinate, and Ireland?

For their part, the loyalists who supported the policies of Charles II and the Church of England viewed conventicles as nurseries of sedition and threats to their very way of life. The depth of their fears and hostility is strikingly apparent in an order issued by the grand jury of Devonshire in April 1682. Calling for the rigorous implementation of the laws against dissent, the jurors denounced "those ungratefull monsters (nonconformist Ministers wee meane) who in the late Rebellion preach'd upp sedition and treason, and though the King . . . hath since pleased to pardon them, yett wee have reason to beleeve they take the same Methods and Endeavour to debauch the people with the same doctrines still." If dissenters saw persecuting magistrates as soldiers in the army of Antichrist,

Tory-Anglicans deplored those "schismaticall factious people" as proponents of the tenets responsible for the revolutionary upheavals of the 1640s and 1650s. Those principles, in the words of the Devon jurors, had "lett in upon us a deluge of profaness and irreligion."[2] The intensity of the struggle between conformity and dissent stemmed from the conviction of each side that it alone was waging battle in the name of true religion against the forces of ungodliness. Thus when Bunyan's friend Samuel Fenne challenged Charles's headship of the Church of England, a Bedford jury indicted him in 1669 for seditiously scheming to incite rebellion—to return, in other words, to the revolutionary 1640s. Not surprisingly, the Bedford congregation excommunicated Humphrey Merrill the same year after he accused its members of involvement in regicide. The tendency to intertwine religious convictions and political loyalties further heightened tension.

Incarcerating Bunyan and his fellow dissenters did not produce the desired quietude. In prison, Nonconformists ministered to one another, preached to those who gathered outside the windows, wrote pamphlets and treatises to sustain their cause and recruit new members, and, as in Bunyan's case, established organizational links that enabled conventicles to continue despite attempts to repress them. If modern prisons are schools for criminals, late Stuart jails were often seminaries and settings for enforced spiritual retreats, notwithstanding the suffering they also entailed. In the Leicester jail in July 1685 were housed some forty Nonconformists, including ministers. Every day the inmates heard or preached sermons, prayed, and sang. Of this experience the Congregationalist John Maidwell wrote:

> Did our enemies know what kindness they have shewn us in sending us hither, they would soon release us. . . . I would not change my present Confinement for the world's preferment[,] for indeed such comfortable accommodations have we, & such communion with God and his people that makes our prison a palace to us.[3]

Maidwell went on to enunciate the ethic of suffering in a manner comparable to that of Bunyan in *Seasonable Counsel, or Advice to Sufferers*. Fortunately for Bunyan, who escaped the worst prison conditions and won release before his health was impaired, his time of confinement was ultimately a positive force in his life. His greatest works were either written in the Bedford jail or composed with that experience in mind.

Although the Nonconformists often shared prison cells and faced a common threat of persecution, only Presbyterians and Congregationalists displayed occasional willingness to seek some form of organizational union, as in the Merchants' Lectures at Pinners' Hall, London, in 1672, or the Common Fund between 1690 and 1695. For the most part, Nonconformists battled among themselves for a small part of the population—perhaps 4 percent in England in 1669, rising to approximately 6 percent by 1718. At that point there were roughly 179,000 Presbyterians, 60,000 Congregationalists, 40,000 Particular Baptists, 19,000 General Baptists, and 39,500 Quakers. Open-membership, open-communion Baptists, of which Bunyan was one, probably numbered only in the hundreds. The competition was keenest among the assorted Baptists and Friends, who made up less than a third of the dissenting Protestant population. Indeed, as Underwood has shown, Bunyan was more interested in the Quakers and such extremists as Muggletonians, Ranters, and Familists than he was in Presbyterians. (He had limited but positive associations with Congregationalists such as John Owen.) The intensity of the rivalry between groups and individuals at the radical end of the religious spectrum was ultimately the result of their competition for survival. This accounts for the vehemence of the Baptist–Quaker rhetoric, but the rivalry, characterized by mutual recrimination and denunciation of one another's claims to valid spiritual experience, could only have intensified the tensions that already existed in the Nonconformist community.

As some of the authors in this volume suggest, Bunyan's awakening words furnished his readers with ways to cope with the tensions they confronted. Samson's riddle, as Achinstein avers, provided Bunyan's audience with "an experience of active resistance through reading," though Samson was no less a model of fearless fortitude in the face of a seemingly omnipotent state. Samson fortified the saints in their determination to resist ungodly demands, and Samsonian resolve was consequently an integral component of Bunyan's ethic of suffering. Readers in the shadow of persecution must have found strength and emotional satisfaction too in the apocalyptic violence that fills the pages of *Antichrist, and His Ruine*. Owens underscores the stark contrast between this millenarian work, written during the Tory reaction following the revelation of the Rye House plotting, and the more optimistic treatise, *The Holy City*, composed on the eve of what some thought would be the arrival of the millennium in 1666. Bunyan, of course, eschewed attempts to date apocalyptic events, yet the optimism that is so prominent in *The Holy City* indicates that at the point of its writing he was among those who were excited about the prospect of an imminent millennium. But the world went on, and the images of violence found in his writings, particularly in the early and mid-1680s, reflect the suffering to which the godly were increasingly subjected. Understandably, then, Mercy could resoundingly castigate Simple, Sloth, and Presumption, whose great offense had been derailing pilgrims: *"Let them hang and their Names Rot, and their Crimes live for ever against them"* (PP, 214).

In addition to the deliberate use of violent images and Samsonian fortitude to shore up the ethic of suffering, Bunyan effectively depicted the spiritual life not only as a pilgrimage but also as a labyrinth. As Davies cogently argues, this image dominates *Grace Abounding,* composed in prison in the reflective aftermath of Bunyan's recovery from an unnerving bout of depression, and is also found in *The Pilgrim's Progress,* where the pilgrims experience a host of barriers and digressions—"a labyrinth of hesitations"—on their heavenward trek. Thus Bunyan's greatest allegory could provide help not only to the soul seeking guidance for its salvation and sanctification but also to the Nonconformist struggling with the doubts inevitably occasioned by the recurring confrontation with persecution, whether threatened or actual. In *The Pilgrim's Progress* Bunyan brilliantly links the needs of those addressed in what Patricia Demers calls the "literature of anxious gloom" with those of the suffering saints by addressing the underlying theme of tension, whether soteriologically or societally occasioned. The allegory struck a responsive chord, spawning a number of derivative texts that Susan Cook asks us to envision as partners with Bunyan's in a religious culture that valued shared narratives and expected to see repeatable patterns in conversion and the Christian life. The spiritual autobiographies examined by Demers constitute other expressions of this belief in recurring religious experiences. Bunyan, of course, was neither the inventor of the spiritual autobiography nor the creator of the pilgrimage allegory, but he was indisputably one of the greatest artists in each idiom, not least because of his keen sensitivity to the power of awakening words.

Bunyan obviously addressed these words to women as well as men. Quaker women suffered more than their nonconforming sisters at the hands of the Restoration regime, in part because magistrates, faced with the fact that the Friends had no ordained clergy who were easy targets to incarcerate, reacted by arresting entire groups of Quakers. Moreover, only the Friends among Restoration-era dissenters allowed their women to preach. But less radical dissenting women were sometimes imprisoned or fined, as were several members of the Bedford gathered church in 1670, including Mary Tilney, widow of a gentleman, who paid £20, and Mrs. George Winright, a tenant of the earl of Exeter, whose fine was £10 5s. Bunyan may have known Elizabeth Calvert, who went to prison for illegally publishing Nonconformist literature; her husband, Giles, was associated with Francis "Elephant" Smith, who published several of Bunyan's works, including the second edition of *The Holy City*. The printer of the first edition had been another woman, Joan Dover, who also issued Quaker works. Women were numerically preponderant in the Bedford church, outnumbering men two to one. Like any minister, Bunyan had to deal with gender relations, and his nonfictional works do so in a traditional manner, as Aileen Ross reminds us. He objected even to women's prayer meetings, accusing their defender, a Mr. K., of being *"Nunnish"* at a time when anti-Catholic feelings were still running strong among Nonconformists. Only "Extraordinary" women could preach or participate in the church's government, but he claimed to know of no such women (*MW*, 4: 306–7) and may have left open this possibility only because of the role of women such as Deborah in the Old Testament.

Affirming the traditional nature of Bunyan's view of women's role in church and society is not, however, the whole story. Nearly everything he asked of the faithful, he expected of women as well as men. The core of Nonconformist religious experience transcended gender, a point effectively made by Demers in recognizing the "many ideological and discursive positions" Bunyan shared with Sarah Wight, Elizabeth Major, and Rebecca Travers (141). This shared ground extended well beyond the inner spiritual life, embracing an ethic of suffering and responsibility no less applicable to women than to men. Viewed in this broader perspective, women were anything but passive. This recognition provides a more accurate historical context in which to understand the second part of *The Pilgrim's Progress*. Interpreting women as the prototype of the church in Bunyan's sequel, Melissa Aaron persuasively finds Bunyan giving them multifaceted roles as catechists, protesters, resisters, role models, and servants to the church. Mounting the pulpit and serving in the eldership were still out of the question, but they could teach in the home and help inculcate a communitarian ethic so powerful that it withstood the state's efforts to crush the dissenting movement. Christiana's company, as Aaron tellingly notes, "does not merely survive monsters, but utterly defeats and overwhelms them" (183). Women's potency in the Nonconformist community is thus reflected in a careful reading of the second part of *The Pilgrim's Progress*.

The master of multiple allegory, Bunyan was no less gifted in his ability to offer his readers several levels of meaning throughout his prose, primarily by the careful use of biblical examples and analogies. The essays in this volume demonstrate how much can be learned from a close reading of Bunyan, with especial sensitivity to his handling of scriptural themes and citations. Given his conscious use of words to awaken and sustain his readers, coupled with his deep grounding in the Bible, we cannot expect to grasp either his intended meaning or how his audience interpreted him if we fail to analyze his work with meticulous attention to its biblical guideposts, however subtly they may be presented, or his use of types and emblems. The skill he evinced in teasing meanings out of Scripture informed his writings and played a crucial role in articulating the kind of godly community he envisioned. At root, this was a suffering community, for which he, like many of his contemporaries, espoused a special ethic, but it was also a community that would ultimately triumph. Beyond the throes and threats of persecution lay assured victory for those who persevered in the godly cause. Born of hope, sustained by faith, and tempered in the fires of his own struggles, this was the conviction that formed the core of Bunyan's message.

Notes

1. George Whitehead et al., Petition to Charles II, [1683] (PRO SP 29/423/15).
2. Order of the Grand Jury of Devonshire, April 1682 (PRO SP 29/418/197).
3. John Maidwell to his daughter and son-in-law, from Leicester jail, 6 July 1685, Dr. Williams's Library, MS 12.63.(22).

Abbreviations

PP *John Bunyan, The Pilgrim's Progress*, ed. James Wharey, rev. Roger Sharrock (Oxford: Clarendon Press, 1960).

GA *Grace Abounding to the Chief of Sinners*, ed. Roger Sharrock (Oxford: Clarendon Press, 1962).

HW *The Holy War*, ed. Roger Sharrock and James F. Forrest (Oxford: Clarendon Press, 1980).

Badman *The Life and Death of Mr. Badman*, ed. James F. Forrest and Roger Sharrock (Oxford: Clarendon Press, 1988).

MW *The Miscellaneous Works of John Bunyan*, 13 volumes, general editor Roger Sharrock (Oxford: Clarendon Press, 1976–94).

Awakening Words

"Till one greater man / Restore us . . .": Restoration Images in Bunyan and Milton

N. H. KEEBLE

JOHN BUNYAN ALMOST CERTAINLY NEVER MET JOHN MILTON AND THERE is no firm evidence that either writer had read, or even heard of, the other. This is small wonder, for, separated by far more than the twenty years' difference in their ages, they inhabited culturally discrete worlds.[1] Milton's was one of intellectual and political privilege. In scholarship and poetry he was heir to Europe's Classical and Renaissance tradition while in prose his became the authorized voice of the state. Bunyan had no such standing. His education was negligible, his knowledge of languages nonexistent, his acquaintance with literature confined largely to the romances and chapbooks of his youth, his experience socially and geographically very limited. Milton's texts are freighted with echoes and allusions, but for Bunyan such intertextuality is a kind of hypocrisy:

> I never endeavoured to, nor durst make use of other men's lines, *Rom.* 15.18 . . . for I verily thought, and found by experience, that what was taught me by the Word and Spirit of Christ, could be spoken, maintained, and stood to, by the soundest and best established Conscience. (*GA*, §285; cf. §300)

"Brought up . . . in a very mean condition, among a company of poor Countrey-men," Bunyan is far from constrained or abashed by the fact that he "never went to School to *Aristotle* or *Plato*." On the contrary, his ignorance is vaunted as evidence of integrity and of divine inspiration. With 1 Corinthians 2 in mind, he asserts: "I have not writ at a venture, nor borrowed my Doctrine from Libraries. I depend upon the sayings of no man: I found it in the Scriptures of Truth."[2] Milton may have shared some of his notions with radical Puritans, and there may be affinities between his emphases and those of Bunyan (certainly the Christ of *Paradise Regained* has no more time for Aristotle or Plato than has Bunyan[3]), but he did not share either Bunyan's Calvinist theology or his cultural temper.

While Bunyan's insistently practical and pastoral inspiration found in Paul its literary and homiletic model,[4] it was Virgil to whom Milton turned for precedent in his poetry. Bunyan is a vulgar writer, in manner and matter, and he has in mind chiefly a vulgar readership. Milton, though he may have allowed the vulgar to escape from Samson's destruction,[5] allows them neither political nor cultural authority. There is no place for the "rude multitude" in the perpetual "general councel of ablest men" which in *The Readie & Easie Way* he proposes should govern the Commonwealth, nor do the vulgar form any part of that "fit audience" in whom he anticipates an informed sensitivity to literary decorum and to historical precedent.[6]

Something, however, the two men did share: by the late autumn of 1660 the consequences of the Restoration had brought them both to the same sorry pass. In November of that year Bunyan "was desired by some of the friends in the country to come to teach at *Samsell*, by *Harlington*, in *Bedfordshire*." Arriving at a friend's house shortly before the meeting, he found "there was a whispering that day I should be taken, for there was a warrant out to take me." His friend, "being somewhat timorous," wondered "whether it might not be better for me to depart" and for the meeting to be abandoned. Bunyan would have none of it: "By no means, I will not stir, neither will I have the meeting dismissed for this." Thinking to himself that "if I should now run, and make an escape, it will be of a very ill savour in the country" and that it would dismay "my weak and newly converted brethren" whom his cowardice would make "afraid to stand, when great words only should be spoken to them," he formed "a full resolution to keep the meeting, and not to go away." Consequently, "though I could have been gone about an hour before the officer apprehended me," he was arrested on 12 November 1660 (*GA*, §318, 105–6).

It was probably in that same November that, in London, Milton too was arrested. Without Bunyan's intense pastoral and evangelical commitment he had, following the Restoration in May, taken the prudent course of withdrawing into hiding while the Act of Oblivion was being debated and the restored regime was settling its accounts with those it had replaced. On 16 June the Commons ordered that Milton should be taken into custody, but, despite this interest in, and animus toward, him, his name was not amongst those excepted from the Act of Oblivion. By September he had emerged from hiding, only to have the resolution of June unexpectedly put into effect.[7]

Bunyan had begun what would prove to be a twelve-year term of imprisonment. Milton was released in December 1660,[8] but, though not in confinement, he continued to live for much of the 1660s, as his friends Andrew Marvell and the Quaker Thomas Ellwood both remarked, "a private and retired Life,"[9] a life in this respect not dissimilar to Bunyan's, and perhaps in other respects too, if reports of Milton's impoverishment and miserable circumstances are to be believed.[10] Bunyan feared, erroneously, that his life might have been in danger (*GA*, §§333–38); Milton's life certainly had been at risk, and he knew it.[11] Both were discredited men, marginalized and ostracized, sharing in that larger disappointment which afflicted all who had been committed to the Good Old Cause and to Puritanism.[12] This coincidence of experience effects a rhetorical bridge between the two men for, despite all their differences of temperament, cultural experience, theological commitment, and generic obligation, it leads to the construction of strikingly similar literary personae. Both men intrusively and autobiographically fashion textual selves who are situated in oppressed and adverse circumstances and who dissent from the prevailing ideology and sympathies of the Restoration. Their writing is consequently transgressive and subversive in its imaging of the contemporary world, which they set not in the context of recent providential history preferred by royalist and Episcopalian writing but in a biblical context whose emblematic and typological patterns offer a very different exegetical key.

Bunyan is characteristically straightforward and direct about the fact that a great many of his works are prison books. His texts locate themselves very precisely, and explicitly: in jail. Disregarding—or defying—the odium of confinement ("Men do say, we do disgrace / Our selves by lying here / Among the rogues" [*Prison Meditations*, *MW*, 6: 47]) they advertise themselves as the fruit of Bunyan's prison years. The title page of *Christian Behaviour* ([1663]) identifies its author as "a Prisoner of *Hope*," and the first edition was subscribed "*Farewel. From my place of Confinement in* Bedford, *this* 17th *of the* 4th *Month*, 1663" (*MW*, 3: 5).[13] Advertising that, *inter alia*, it will relate what its author "hath met with in Prison," the title page of *Grace Abounding* attests that the complete text "was written by his own hand *there*." For "preaching Grace and Faith," Bunyan writes in his *Prison Meditations* of 1665 (where the title itself situates both writer and text),

> Hands on me they laid,
> 'Twas *this* from which they pluck'd me out,
> And vilely to me said

> You Heretick, Deceiver, come
> To Prison you must go,
> You preach abroad, and keep not home,
> You are the Churches foe . . .
>
> Wherefore to Prison they me sent,
> Where to this day I lie . . .
>   (*GA*, xliv; *MW*, 6: 44; emphasis mine)

While "in prison," "where I lie waiting the good will of God, to do with me, as he pleaseth," "in Bonds," Bunyan is subject to the "rage" of "persecuting Men" (*MW*, 6: 43, 45, 50; *GA*, 113). This is one of the ways in which he associates himself with Paul. From the account in Acts 23–24 of the charges preferred against Paul before Felix, the Roman procurator of Judaea, Bunyan infers that "*an hypocritical people, will persecute the power of those truths in others, which themselves in words profess,*" and, tellingly, he adds (probably in 1665): "I am this day, and that for this very thing persecuted by them" (*Resurrection of the Dead*, *MW*, 3: 204). The "Denn" upon which the narrator happens as he "walks through the wilderness of this world" at the opening of *The Pilgrim's Progress* is marginally glossed "Gaol," and it is "from the *Lions Dens*," from the prison where "I stick between the Teeth of the Lions in the Wilderness" that Bunyan addresses his prefatory epistle to the reader of *Grace Abounding*. *Lions* signify here, as they do in *The Pilgrim's Progress*, the terrors and cruelties of persecution (*PP*, 8, 45–46, 218–19; *GA*, 2). Dens are inhabited by lurking lions in the wildernesses of biblical story (Ps. 10:9; Amos 3:4), and by cockatrices (Isa. 11:8) and dragons (Jer. 9:11, 10:22) too. They are fearful places, their floors strewn with torn carcasses (Nah. 2:12), the haunt of robbers (Jer. 7:11) and defeated Israelite refugees (Judg. 6:2). That single monosyllable hence tells a good deal about the plight of Nonconformists under the Great Persecution and of Bunyan's relationship to the Restoration authorities.[14]

Autobiography is essential to Bunyan's homiletic manner. In a fashion characteristically Puritan he took Paul as his model in declaring "what God has done for my soul" (Ps. 66:16) as the surest form of evangelism (*GA*, 2). This was not Milton's business nor his method, but, despite the very different generic obligations of epic, the narrator of *Paradise Lost* is pressed by circumstances very similar to Bunyan's. His is no disembodied bardic voice. On the contrary, he is situated in a very specific biographical context, and one curiously at odds with the generic pretensions of epic and the decorums of the high style. In the opening paragraph of *Paradise Lost* Milton is as convinced as any Renaissance scholar or writer that epic is, in Sir Philip Sidney's words, the "best and most accomplished kind of Poetry," through its "lofty image[s]" inculcating moral and political excellence.[15] This epic poet, however, is far removed from those cultural and political centers of power that might authorize him to speak on such matters. He has no official endorsement, no status, no patron (at least, no mortal patron). Like Bunyan's, his situation is marked by danger, humiliation, and isolation, and apparently by impotence. Milton sings

> . . . with mortal voice, unchanged
> To hoarse or mute, though fallen on evil days,
> On evil days though fallen, and evil tongues;
> In darkness, and with dangers compassed round,
> And solitude.
>
> (7: 24–28)[16]

These lines may derive from Milton's particularly dangerous situation immediately following the Restoration, when he was in hiding,[17] and it was in 1660 that Milton was most vociferously assailed by "evil tongues." During that year he was variously saluted in print as a "musty Pedant" whose pen was "dipt in the blackest and basest venome," a "base Scribe" and "*Billingsgate* Author," "wonderfully . . . stricken blind" for his seditious antimonarchism, a "blind Adder" spitting poison who proves that "Devils may indue Humane shapes."[18] For Milton to insist that in such "evil days" he sings "unchanged / To hoarse or mute" is, as Christopher Hill and Michael Wilding have remarked, to identify the epic poet with the John Milton of the 1640s and '50s whom the reader would know "as the defender of divorce, regicide and the republic."[19] It asserts a continuity between that earlier polemical voice and the imaginings of the inspired poet "touched with hallowed fire," and affirms, despite the "change of times" and his lamentable predicament, continuing commitment to the Good Old Cause.[20]

This affirmation is not confined to the autobiographical invocation to Book 7 of *Paradise Lost*. When Abdiel returns to Heaven having refused to join Satan's rebellion, he is thus commended by the Father:

> Servant of God, well done, well hast thou fought
> The better fight, who single hast maintained
> Against revolted multitudes the cause

> Of truth, in word mightier than they in arms;
> And for the testimony of truth hast borne
> Universal reproach, far worse to bear
> Than violence: for this was all thy care
> To stand approved in sight of God, though worlds
> Judged thee perverse.
>
> (6: 29–37)

The Father's commendation of Abdiel's stand is prudently couched in general terms, but there is something curious about his generalities. Abdiel has, indeed, resisted the appeal of "revolted multitudes," but it is hardly the case that he has "borne / Universal reproach" or been judged "perverse" by "worlds." Milton, however, had, and not only Milton. The Nonconformist heirs of the Puritans had witnessed the revolt of multitudes in 1660, and had subsequently borne all but universal reproach. That their cause was nothing but perversity was a commonplace of polemic, preferred repeatedly by such champions of the new order as Sir Roger L'Estrange. When Abdiel later confronts Satan on the field of Heaven, the identification of his cause with that of nonconformity becomes all but explicit in Abdiel's references to his "dissent" from Satan and to the loyal angels as "my sect":

> . . . there be who faith
> Prefer, and piety to God, though then
> To thee not visible, when I alone
> Seemed to thy world erroneous to dissent
> From all: my sect thou seest, now learn too late
> How few sometimes may know, when thousands err.
>
> (6: 143–48)

Following the Restoration, only one group of people was known as "dissenters" and "sectarians," few in number, and judged by the prevailing royalist and Episcopalian ideology both erroneous and perverse, enemies to the established church and to the state, and hence to God. Yet here these very terms denominate not rebelliousness and sedition, as in common usage, but opposition to Satanic rebellion. A lexical reversal has been effected: the thousands who err are no longer the dissenters but those who stand against the dissenters, that is, Episcopalians and royalists against Puritans. And the epic poet places himself in their dissenting camp: Abdiel cannot "change his constant mind"; Milton sings "unchanged" (*Paradise Lost,* 5: 902, 7: 23).[21] "I alone" may be judged by the contemporary Restoration world erroneous, but, like Abdiel, will be vindicated. The "servant of God" commended by the Father is a dissenter.

Imprisoned and subject to ridicule and vilification, Bunyan is similarly concerned to vindicate himself against the "revolted multitudes." His own accounts of his arrest, examination, and trial present him as the defender of liberty of conscience and of inner commitment against the ranged authorities of the state which would impose uniformity of belief and practice, in particular, subscription to the *Book of Common Prayer* (*GA*, 114–18).[22] In what may be the first piece he wrote following his arrest, the tract *I Will Pray with the Spirit* ([1662?]),[23] he develops the arguments put at his trial to contrast the sincerity of true spirituality with the formalism of liturgies and prescribed rites, opposing, as does Milton, "the upright heart and pure" to the "temples" preferred by the ecclesiastical policy of the restored regime as articulated in the Act of Uniformity (*Paradise Lost*, 1: 17–18). Prudently, Bunyan's name does not appear on the title page. In 1661 or 1662 to denounce "the ignorance, prophaness, and spirit of envy, that reigns in the hearts of those men that are so hot for the Forms, and not the Power of prayer" was perforce to denounce supporters of the *Book of Common Prayer*, that is, the fiercely Episcopalian members of the Cavalier Parliament and Church of England. They would be less than impressed to learn,

> Scarce one of forty among them, know what it is to be born again, to have communion with the Father through the Son; to feel the power of Grace sanctifying their hearts: but for all their prayers, they still live cursed, drunken, whorish, and abominable Lives, full of Malice, Envy Deceit, Persecuting of the dear Children of God. Oh what a dreadful after-clap is coming upon them! which all their hypocritical assembling themselves together, with all their prayers, shall never be able to help them against, or shelter them from. (*MW*, 2: 240)

The "wise men of our dayes," the "Doctors of our day" (and who are they but the bishops?), whose "cursed presumption" leads them to prescribe set forms of behavior and ritual and to prefer the hypocrisy of uniformity to the integrity of conscience, perform "a very juggle of the Devil" (*MW*, 2: 247–48, 283).

It is above all their "Persecuting of the dear Children of God" that situates these Episcopalians, and consequently the speaker, for it sets the former in the tradition of Edmund Bonner, "that blood-red Persecutor," and the speaker in the tradition of "God's People" who, "as it hath always been" (Ezra 4.12 to 16.), are vilified, maligned, and oppressed. He is to be counted among the Lord's "poor tempted and afflicted People," for he is in gaol, and if you

> look into the Goals in *England*, and in to the Alehouses of the same . . . I believe, you will find those that plead for the Spirit of Prayer in the Goal, and them that look after the Forms of mens Inventions only, in the Alehouse. (*MW*, 2: 253, 266, 284)

Bunyan's "alehouse," the haunt of the unregenerate oppressors of the faithful, is the demotic equivalent of the "barbarous dissonance / Of Bacchus and his revellers" whom, in their Cavalier riot, Milton distinguishes from his "fit audience" in *Paradise Lost* (7: 30–35). As in the former are to be found the royalist and Episcopalian "Persecutors of the dear Children of God" who conscientiously scruple the *Book of Common Prayer*, so in the riotous horde of Bacchus's train are to be found those who, Michael foresees, "Spiritual laws by carnal power shall force / On every conscience,"

> Whence heavy persecution shall arise
> On all who in the worship persevere
> Of spirit and truth; the rest, greater part
> Will deem in outward rites and specious forms
> Religion satisfied; truth shall retire
> Bestruck with slanderous darts, and works of faith
> Rarely be found.
>   (12: 521–22, 531–38)

As Milton retorts to the Restoration followers of Bacchus that he sings "unchanged," so Bunyan is equally unyielding in his retort to the denizens of the alehouse. In his *Prison Meditations* he replies in just the strains of Abdiel to the "carnal Men" who call him "Heretick, Deceiver," the "Churches foe," one of a company of "Fools," and, though in a very different poetic vein, with Miltonic confidence that

> The *Truth* and *I*, were both here cast
>   Together, and we do
> Lye Arm in Arm, and so hold fast
>   Each other; This is true.
>   (*MW*, 6: 49, 44, 45, 46)

He, too, is "unchanged" by the circumstances to which his commitment has brought him. There were, of course, those who did not "hold fast" and in 1660 changed sides:

> Here we can see who holds *that* ground
>   Which they in *Scripture* find;
> Here we see also who turns round
>   Like *Weathercocks* with' Wind.
>
> (*MW*, 6: 47)

By-ends, who "never strive[s] against Wind and Tide," is the most pointedly ironic portrait in *The Pilgrim's Progress* (99–102) and those who proved inconstant are repeatedly the target of Bunyan's scorn as "*seeming* Friends" and "*Hypocrites*":

> When we did walk at liberty.
>   We were deceiv'd by them,
> Who we from hence do clearly see
>   Are vile deceitful men.
> These Politicians that profest
>   For base and worldly ends,
> Do now appear to us at best
>   But Machivillian Friends.[24]

Though betrayed by such friends, Bunyan, like the Abdiel in whom the epic poet "fallen on evil days" finds an image of constancy and fidelity, yet enjoys divine fellowship, love, and approval:

> Though men keep my outward man
>   Within their Locks and Bars,
> Yet by the Faith of Christ I can
>   Mount higher than the Stars.
>
> (*MW*, 6: 43)

Going to prison, he "carried the peace of God along with me" and is met by "God sweetly in the prison"; God "can make a Gaol more beautiful than a palace; restraint, more sweet by far than liberty" (*GA*, 112, 113; *MW*, 10: 21).

For all their differences, then, each writer fashions himself as an embattled individual at odds with his age whose texts, whatever else they might be about, are concerned to defy prevailing opinion and to vindicate their writers. Milton's "evil days," however, are no more peculiarly his lot than is the imprisonment of the narrator of *The Pilgrim's Progress* his solitary misfortune. Both join their readers in a community of suffering. In *I Will Pray with the Spirit* it is the shared experience of persecution that binds writer and reader and that has become the defining quality of God's people. Luke 6:22 ("Blessed are they that are persecuted for righteousness' sake, for theirs is the Kingdom of Heaven") should encourage the saints not only to anticipate reward for the suffering and affliction their witness incurs on earth but also to embrace suffering as the condition of election, as an assurance of eternal bliss: not only is there "a reward for the afflicted, according to the measure of affliction" but "afflictions, and so every service of God, doth make the heart more deep, more experimentall, more knowing, and profound; and so more able to hold, contain, and bear more" (*Resurrection of the Dead, MW,* 3: 237, 238–39). It is in just these terms that Evangelist exhorts Christian and Faithful. They are warned that they "must through many tribulations enter into the Kingdom of Heaven" and that "in every City, bonds and afflictions abide in you; and therefore you cannot expect that you should go long on your Pilgrimage without them, in some sort or other." In the town of Vanity, "you will be hardly beset with enemies, who will strain hard but they will kill you." And, as the source texts in Ecclesiastes remind us, there is no way round Vanity and its Fair: they are ubiquitous (Eccles. 1:2, 14; 2:11; 3:19). This inescapable experience of repression and persecution is epitomized in the trial before Vanity's Lord Hate-good.[25] So little is he concerned with safeguarding the liberty of the subject that he is bent as cruelly upon its obliteration as was the future Chief-Justice of the King's Bench, Sir John Kelyng, at Bunyan's own trial (*GA,* 113–19). This personal experience that "good men suffer for God's way / And bad men at them rage" informs Bunyan's *Seasonable Counsel: or, Advice to Sufferers* of 1684. Directed to the *"many at this day . . . exposed to sufferings"* it seeks to persuade them that there are *"Acts of our graces, that cannot be put forth, or shew themselves in their splendor, but when we Christianly suffer"* and that *"it is for our own present and future good"* that believers are persecuted.[26] It was a well-worn theme. Nearly twenty years earlier, his *Prison-Meditations* of 1665 had been *Directed to the Heart of Suffering Saints and Reigning Sinners.* The adjectives are all but definitive.

Just such a vision of the sad predicament of suffering saints in the hands of reigning sinners recurs throughout Michael's preview of human history in Books 11 and 12 of *Paradise Lost* as "the world go[es] on, / To good malignant, to bad men benign." "Heavy persecution" is the lot of those who "in the worship persevere / Of spirit and truth" while, like Bunyan's *"seeming"* and "Machivillian Friends," those subdued by worldly might

> Shall with their freedom lost all virtue lose
> And fear of God, from whom their piety feigned

In sharp contest of battle found no aid
Against invaders; therefore cooled in zeal
Thenceforth shall practise how to live secure
Worldly or dissolute, on what their lords
Shall leave them to enjoy.
(11: 537–38, 798–804; 12: 531–33)

Milton's Samson—and, after the recent work of Blair Worden we can now be confident that this *is* a late text, postdating the Restoration[27]—is "fallen on evil days" (*Paradise Lost*, 7: 25), blind, confined, a "prisoner chained" scarce able to "draw / The air imprisoned also, close and damp, / Unwholesome draught," and in despair that he is apparently cast off "as never known" by God and left "helpless" in the power of his "cruel enemies" (*Samson Agonistes*, 7–9, 641–44). In this, "delivered to the Power of the Philistine Gentiles," Samson is a type of Christ, "delivered to the Power of the Roman Gentiles," and so of the experience of the true Christian, persecuted by the world.[28] Samson's representative plight prompts the Chorus to adduce examples of God's apparently arbitrary dealings with his elect that Bunyan's Evangelist would recognize: abandoned to the "heathen and profane," "captived" and brought before "unjust tribunals, under change of times / And condemnation of the ingrateful multitude" (*Samson Agonistes*, 693–96).

This, of course, is the world of the Restoration from the point of view of Nonconformist experience.[29] After the event, Bunyan claimed to have foreseen it: "Before I came to Prison, I saw what was a coming," and he accordingly prepared himself to endure imprisonment, and to face death (*GA*, §324).[30] It does appear that, following Cromwell's death, the Bedford congregation grew increasingly apprehensive. Its Church Book records a number of days of prayer in 1659 which were probably occasioned by anxiety about the turn in national affairs.[31] The minute for 29 January 1660, recording the decision "to set apart the 5th day of the next weeke to seeke the Lord," adds explicitly "especially upon the account of the distraction of the nation."[32] Milton had certainly known what was coming. In the revised second edition of *The Readie & Easie Way* (April 1660) his enlargements of what Austin Woolrych calls "those great set pieces that condemned monarchy" (*CPW*, 7: 207) were in no doubt what the consequences of the Restoration would be: a reactionary tyranny of decadent indulgence. "Triumphing enemies" will think "they wisely discernd and justly censur'd both us and all our actions as rash, rebellious, hypocritical and impious." "The old encroachments" would come on "by little and little upon our consciences," exacerbated by the anxiety of "kings to com, never forgetting their former ejection" "to fortifie and arm themselves sufficiently for the future against all such attempts hereafter from the people: who shall be then so narrowly watched and kept so low" that they can anticipate only a kind of ignoble slavery. In contrast to the equitable freedom of a commonwealth, "wherin they who are greatest . . . are not elevated above thir brethren; live soberly in thir families, walk the streets as other men, may be spoken to freely, familiarly, friendly, without adoration," there will be a culture of servile deference to a king who "must be ador'd like a Demigod, with a dissolute and haughtie court about him, of vast expence and luxurie, masks and revels, to the debaushing of our prime gentry both male and female," and who has "little els to do, but to bestow the eating and drinking of excessive dainties, to set a pompous face upon the superficial actings of State, to pageant himself up and down in progress among the perpetual bowings and cringings of an abject people, on either side deifying and adoring him for nothing don that can deserve it" (*CPW*, 7: 422, 423, 449, 425, 426). Milton would never again be able to express such impassioned republicanism so openly, but contempt for monarchy and for court culture continues to inform his depictions of evil. It is with the ascendancy of the tyrant Nimrod, "from heaven claiming second sovereignty" in good Stuart style, that the period of pastoral simplicity succeeding the Flood is brought to an end and human history enters another swift decline (*Paradise Lost*, 12: 13–62).[33] Satan is the devil who would be king, for whom it is "Better to reign in hell, than serve in heaven." The motor of the Fall is his "monarchical pride" and it is in a kind of nightmare presence chamber that the "great sultan" Satan, "High on a throne of a royal state," displays the tyrannical barbarism of regal rule (*Paradise Lost*, 1: 263, 428, 348; 2: 1–6). Courts in *Paradise Lost* are the locus of loveless, contrived, and exploitative amours (4: 765–70), the antithesis of prelapsarian sexual love, as they had been for Milton ever since, in his "stately palace," Comus had exhorted the Lady in the words of many a libertine Cavalier lyric to "be not coy, and be not cozened / With that same vaunted name virginity, / Beauty is Nature's coin, must not be hoarded, / But must be current" (*A Masque*, lines 736–39). The "tedious pomp that waits / On princes," with "their rich retinue long / Of horses led, and grooms besmeared with gold," can never recover the native dignity of Adam. It is their preoccupation with the pageantry and paraphernalia of courts that is one reason for

Milton's antipathy to chivalric epic and Renaissance romance (*Paradise Lost*, 5: 350–57, 9: 29–41).

There is no evidence that Bunyan shared Milton's republican views, rather the contrary. In prison in 1661 he protested that he had no intention "to disturb the peace of the nation," that he abhorred Fifth Monarchist insurrection, and

> I look upon it as my duty to behave myself under the King's government, both as becomes a man and christian; and if an occasion was offered me, I should willingly manifest my loyalty to my Prince, both by word and deed. (*GA*, 120)[34]

Twenty years later, he characterized himself as "one of the old-fashion Professors, that *covet to fear God, and honour the King*" (*Of Antichrist, MW,* 13: 489). He holds that "*it is amiable and pleasant to God, when* Christians *keep their Rank, Relation and Station, doing all as become their Quality and Calling*" and he admonishes his readers that they are "to give thanks to God for all men, *for Kings, and for all that are in authority*" and not to "mock at men in Place and Power" (*Christian Behaviour*, 1663, *MW*, 3:10; *Seasonable Counsel*, 1684, *MW*, 10: 35–39). And, as in Nonconformist literature generally at this time, there is a pronounced quietist and pacifist strain in his writing: "It becomes all godly men to study to be quiet." He distinguishes from the sufferings of true Christians the pains of those punished for seditious practices ("*I am no comforter of such*") and he writes directly against those "of an unquiet, and troublesome spirit" who seek redress and revenge: "*A Christian must be a harmless Man, and, to that end, must imbrace nothing but harmless Principles*," for, in the words of John 18:36, "*the Kingdom of God . . . is not of this World*" (*Seasonable Counsel, MW*, 10: 5, 75, 99–104).[35] Just so, the Christ of *Paradise Regained* refuses to adopt the "politic maxims, or that cumbersome / Luggage of war" (3: 400–401) recommended by Satan to establish the Messiah's kingdom, and in *Paradise Lost* Milton relegates political and military expedients to the frustrated fallen angels in Hell, reserving for his epic subject the "better fortitude / Of patience and heroic martyrdom" (9: 31–32), the victory not of retaliation but of "suffering for truth's sake" (12: 569)[36]

Such submissive protestations notwithstanding, clerics and courtiers receive scarcely more courtesy from Bunyan than from Milton. *I Will Pray with the Spirit* is an openly oppositional text, identifying the imposition of the *Book of Common Prayer* with Roman Catholic persecution and the juggling of the devil. The "after-clap" with which Bunyan threatens its proponents, though, like the "two-handed engine" with which Milton had threatened the Episcopal clergy, imprecise, might very well, like that engine, be taken to portend revolution as well as final judgment ("Lycidas," line 130). He was inclined, if only in general terms, to assume that it was kings and courts that were "drawn into [the] lewdness" of "the *Mother of Harlots*," becoming so "entangled with her Beauty, and with her Fornication, that they have been adulterated from God and their own Salvation," and so, no less than Milton, to associate them with the opulent decadence that Roman Catholicism and the baroque suggested to his Puritan sensibility (*Holy City*, MW, 3: 149). Like Milton, he can characterize Satan as a tyrannical king (*Seasonable Counsel*, MW, 10: 13-14). It is hence no wonder that "God sometimes visits Prisons more / Than lordly Palaces" (*Prison Meditations*, MW, 6: 46). And for Bunyan, no less than for Milton, Nimrod's exercise of power is uncomfortably reminiscent of the Stuarts'. Bunyan is "apt to think he was the first that in this *New World* [after the Flood] sought after Absolute Monarchy," who "could not be content, till *all* made Obeisance to him" and who sought "to enforce Idolatry and Superstition" on his subjects through persecution. So Bunyan takes Nimrod's hunting (Gen. 10:9) to signify persecution, and that he was a "mighty hunter" to show that "he went beyond others; he was more cruel and barbarous" (*Exposition on the Ten First Chapters of Genesis*, MW, 12: 267-68).[37] Vanity, with its arbitrary monarch and persecution of conscientious dissent, is in the line from Nimrod. At its Fair, "the Ware of *Rome* and her Merchandize is greatly promoted" and "*Mystical Babel*," "*Romish Babel*," "*Nimrod's* Invention," "could not be kept at *Rome*, but hath spread it self in many and might Kingdoms" (*PP*, 89), including, we may surmise, England, with its established Episcopal church, too Roman in its orders and polity, and a clergy who "pretended Religion: That they had their Orders from the *Apostolical Sea*: That they were the true sons of *Shem*, or Disciples of Christ" (MW, 12: 270). And if the social and legal systems of Vanity are uncomfortably like those not only of Babel but of Restoration England, and if Lord Hategood is disturbingly reminiscent of Sir John Kelyng, then whose in England is the role of Nimrod, of the Beelzebub who is the "chief Lord," "King" and "noble Prince" of Vanity and its Fair? On this "Prince of this Town, with all the Rablement his Attendants," Faithful's judgment is that they "are more fit for a being in Hell, then in this Town or Countrey" (*PP*, 89, 93, 94, 95).

Men and women impressed by this prince and the culture that

flows from his court do not fare well in Bunyan. Indeed, to delight in the Restoration *beau monde*, to ape noble and courtly superiors, to be preoccupied with forms of civility and etiquette, with status and hierarchy, with fashion, dress, and manners, is for Bunyan a definitive sign of moral turpitude, and especially of superficiality, mendacity, and avarice. By-ends is a figure of hypocrisy and time-serving, but the form of his hypocrisy is culturally specific: he is monied and mannered, socially accomplished, and his wife is of high breeding (*PP*, 98, 99). He is from "*Fair-speech*," "a *Wealthy place*," where *fair* suggests *polite* and *elegant*, as well as *pleasing* and *specious*.[38] The Latitudinarian moralism recommended to Christian by Worldly-Wiseman may be learned not only from that "very judicious man" Legality but also from that "*pretty young man*" his son, Civility, "*that can do it . . . as well as the old Gentleman himself*" (*PP*, 19). Mercy's suitor Mr. Brisk, a "man of some breeding" who "pretended to Religion" but who proves merely mercenary, is a kind of fop, an aspiring Restoration rake (*PP*, 226).[39] What Mr. Badman calls his "neatness, handsomness, comeliness, cleanliness . . . following of fashions" is construed, and condemned, by Mr. Wiseman as pride. To pride, Restoration female fashions add shamelessness and licentiousness. "Their Bulls-foretops, with their naked shoulders, and Paps hanging out like a Cows bag" outrage Mr. Wiseman as "the Attire of an Harlot" (Prov. 10:7), enticing to "the sin of uncleanness, by the spangling shew of fine cloaths" (*Badman*, 121–22, 125). A very similar aesthetic and moral sense finds in the nakedness of Adam and Eve, "Simplicity and spotless innocence" and has Adam meet Raphael "without more train / Accompanied than with his own complete / Perfections, in himself was all his state" (4: 318, V: 351–53). Dalila, we recall, was "so bedecked, ornate, and gay" that, "Like a stately ship," she approached Samson, "With all her bravery on, and tackle trim" (712–17), like, that is to say, "a fashionably dressed seventeenth-century lady . . . a courtly theatrical heroine."[40] These are the manners and dress of gentlefolk. Christopher Hill has observed that the gentles come out of Bunyan rather badly, that he "spoke for the poor against the rich,"[41] and so he does. Bunyan finds it readily understandable that in the parable of Dives and Lazarus "the ungodly [are] held forth under the notion of a rich man," for are they not "most ready to be puft up with pride, stoutness, care of this world, in which things they spend most of their time, in lusts, drunkenness, wantonness, idleness"? "Methinks to see how the great ones of the world will go strutting up and down the streets sometimes, it makes me wonder." By contrast, God's own "are most commonly of the poorer sort"; "the Saints of the Lord . . . are for the most part a poor, despised, contemptible people," "a despised, afflicted, tempted, persecuted people."[42] We are not, Bunyan insists, to be unduly impressed by social status, bearing, or class, and this at a time when the notion of *quality* as a social signifier, and the phrase *person of quality*, are gaining currency through the heightened social sensitivity consequent upon the comparative novelty of a royal court, and a Frenchified court, as the center of taste and patronage.[43] It is precisely their alert sense of their own quality, their snobbery and sensitivity to social slur and insult, that signals the moral standing of the natives of Vanity. Their hostility to Christian and Faithful reproduces that fundamental biblical opposition whose metaphorical vehicles structure *The Pilgrim's Progress*: it illustrates the enmity between the serpent's seed and the woman's (Gen. 3:15), the rejection of those who are strangers and pilgrims in the earth (Heb. 11:13), the plight of the children of light walking in darkness (1 Thess. 5:4–5). Bunyan's attention to social detail, however, transforms the inhabitants of Vanity from general types of unregenerate hostility to the saints into culturally specific "rulers of the darkness of this world" (Eph. 6:12). The case against Christian and Faithful (both poor men) is pressed by "the Gentry of our Town," allegedly "bespattered" by Faithful. The prosecution witnesses are "worthy Gentlemen" and gentlemen, of course, make up the jury (*PP*, 95, 96).

The "laudable doings" which these "gentlemen" would defend against the challenge of the pilgrims are represented in the "trade" at Vanity Fair, where "Houses, Lands, Trades, Places, Honours, Preferments, Titles, Countreys, Kingdoms, Lusts, Pleasures, and Delights of all sorts" are for sale (*PP*, 93, 88). "Places, honours, preferments" were in the gift of the court.[44] "Lusts, Pleasures, and Delights of all sorts" is a terse summary of one view of the court culture epitomized in, let us say, Rochester. Though he would not care to be named in the same sentence, Bunyan is as convinced as the William Penn of *No Cross, No Crown* that such a culture is a general pollutant.[45] Under the guise of *"Harmless-mirth"* Lord Lasciviousness, one of the chief Diabolonians in *The Holy War*, is able to infiltrate and to corrupt Mansoul (*HW*, 144, 168). It is no accident that he is a peer. *"Uncleanness,"* opines Mr. Wiseman, is "one of the most reigning sins in our day," practiced, agrees Attentive, by *"those that one would think had more wit, even among the great ones."* Through their example, it permeates society, for, as the marginal note admonishes, the "Sins of great men [are] dangerous":

usually Examples that are set by them that are great and chief, spread sooner, and more universally, then do the sins of other men; yea, and when such men are at the head in transgressing, sin walks with a boldface through the Land. As *Jeremiah* saith of the Prophets, so may it be said of such, *From them is profaneness gone forth into all the land*; that is, with bold and audacious face, *Jer.* 23.15. (*Badman*, 49)

Just such behavior (as Dalila has reminded us) is to be found among Milton's Philistines: the ungodliness of Restoration culture is epitomized in their idolatrous paganism ("The Philistines understand me not" observes Bunyan [*GA*, 1]), the temper of its nobility represented in the drunken, gluttonous and exulting Philistine lords, its treatment of Nonconformists in their humiliation of Samson. This is hardly the image the restored regime had of itself, nor, in this drama, can line 1660 any longer be claimed to signify divine approval of it. That number now marks not vindication and victory but nemesis and destruction, for it is at line 1660 that the Chorus begins its celebration of Samson's "dearly-bought revenge, yet glorious" upon the Philistine "Lords, ladies, captains, counsellors, or priests, / Their choice nobility and flower" in the midst of their revels and their triumph, "While their hearts were jocund and sublime, / Drunk with idolatry, drunk with wine" (lines 1653–54, 1660, 1669–70).[46]

For Milton and Bunyan, then, the Restoration and its culture epitomized the hostile wilderness of this world through which the saints pass and the temptations with which they are beset. It was for them part of a continuity, merely another revolution in the seventeenth-century sense of that word,[47] and not, as figured by the dominant ideology, a divine mercy, unique, unprecedented, inexplicable.[48] On the contrary, it was all too easily explicable. There was nothing remarkable about it save the clarity and telling particularity with which it represented the adverse circumstances the saints are to expect in all ages. For Nonconformists and the heirs of the Puritans, in contrast to the Latitudinarians and the increasingly prevalent deism of the Church of England,[49] true Christianity by its very nature was, and always had been, at odds with the world: "the people of God are a suffering people" Bunyan had succinctly stated in *Seasonable Counsel* (*MW*, 10: 95). "Who best / Can suffer, best can do" declares Milton's Christ (*Paradise Regained*, 3: 194–95). Matthew 5:11 ("when men shall revile you, and persecute you, and shall say all manner of evil against you falsely for my sake; rejoice, and be exceeding glad, for great is your reward in heaven; for so persecuted they the prophets which were before you") encouraged Bunyan to embrace suffering as a validation of his testimony: "it belongs to my Christian Profession, to be vilified, slandered, reproached and reviled" (*GA*, §§311–12). In a construction much indebted to Foxe, Nonconformist writing consequently seized upon persecution as a confirmation of witness which could invoke a tradition stretching back through "worthy *Wickliff, Hus, Luther, Melancton, Calvin*, and the blessed Martyrs in Q. *Maries* days," "the holy and goodly Martyrs and Saints . . . *Hus, Bilny, Ridly, Hooper, Cranmer*, with their Brethren," to the early church (*Holy City, MW*, 3: 134, 154).[50] For its part, the persecuting Restoration regime was set in an equally venerable tradition, that of Antichrist:

> Touching mens prosecuting their *Zeal* for their *Worship*, &c. that they do think right: How hot hath it been, though with no reason at all. *Nebuchadnezzar* will have his *Fiery-Furnace*, and *Darius* his *Lyons-Den* for *Nonconformists*, Dan. 3.6 & 6.7, &c.
>
> Again, they have persecuted men even to strange Cities; have laid traps and snares in every corner, to intrap and to entangle their words; and if they could at any time but kill the persons that dissented from them, they would think they did God *good service*, Acts 26.11. *Luke* 11.53, 54. *John* 16.1, 2. But what need we look so far from home, (were it not that I would seal my Sayings with Truth) we need look no further to affirm this position, than to the *Papists* and their *Companions*: How many have they in all Ages *hanged, burned, starved, drowned, wracked, dismembred*, and *murdered*, both openly and in secret? (*Christian Behaviour, MW*, 3: 18).

Bunyan's lexical choices in this passage are as pointed as Milton's in connection with Abdiel.[51] To denominate *Nonconformists* those whom Nebuchadnezzar and Darius persecute and *dissenters* those whom the Papists and their companions torture implicitly identifies them with those of Bunyan's contemporaries who suffer at the hands of the Restoration judicial system. To the royalist and Episcopalian authorities is allocated the role of Babylonish, Median, and Romish oppressors. Had not Bunyan set Episcopalians in the tradition of Bonner,[52] and are not Nebuchadnezzar and Darius cited approvingly by the judge at the trial of Christian of Faithful? (*PP*, 96).

The Restoration world is, then, Nimrod's world, Babel, it is Nebuchadnezzar's Babylon, the Fair of the Prince of Vanity, an idolatrous Philistia devoted to Dagon, the kingdom of Beelzebub, the domain of the Great Whore. These are types of tyranny, oppression, superstition, and Romanism, and consequently of the devil. We may therefore suppose in the fourth line of *Paradise Lost*—"Till one greater man restore us"—some slippage between being restored to divine favor from the machinations of Satan and being restored to liberty from the oppression of tyrants. Greater than whom? Not only Adam. At that date, the word *restore* would have had an inescapable topicality, for one greater man had recently been involved in a very notable restoration and one which, in the eyes of its beneficiaries, rendered superfluous any further work of restoration. Though *revolution* was the word occasionally used for the events of 1660, on the royalist side *restoration* (initially more usually in the form *restauration*) instantly became the usual term to denote what had occurred.[53] It is the word used in the *Journals of the House of Commons* under 30 May 1660; it is Clarendon's word at the end of his *History* (16: 214); it is Evelyn's (though not Pepys') in his *Diary* under 29 May 1660; it is Sir John Reresby's in his *Memoirs* under 25 April; it is Cowley's in his *Ode* and Dryden's in *Astraea Redux*.[54] Possibly in part for this reason, Milton never uses this substantival form, preferring *restorement*,[55] but his choice of verb at the opening of his epic recalls the commoner usage and, recalling it, dismisses the events of recent history as of no consequence to true (eternal) restoration. This, in their more sober moments, even its most adulatory supporters would have to allow, but there is also, in this diminution of so momentous an event, the implication of its temporal inadequacy and insufficiency. And that implication grows ever more insistent as, like Bunyan, Milton draws upon Restoration images to figure not the return to right order and harmony carousingly celebrated by "committed" royalist "linnets," but Satanic disorder, that perversion, indeed, inversion, of right order ironically saluted in the jaunty ballad stanza of his friend Marchamont Nedham:

> Then let us chear, this merry New-year;
> For *CHARLES* shall wear the crown:
> "Tis a *damn'd Cause*, that damns the Laws,
>   And turns all up-side down.[56]

Notes

1. Pointing to the grandeur of conception, machinery of devils, alternating scenes in heaven and hell, and the contrivances of Diabolus, William York Tindall, *John Bunyan, Mechanick Preacher* (New York: Columbia University Press, 1934), 200–202, claims that the influence of *Paradise Lost* upon *The Holy War* is demonstrable. However, the claim is reduced to a conjecture by his suggestion that the influence may have been only "at second hand" (with George Cockayne or John Owen as possible informants) and by his acknowledgment that these features

might have been learned from Benjamin Keach (who was culturally, religiously, and socially much closer to Bunyan).

2. *MW*, 2: 16, 7: 51. Cf. *GA*, §2, and see further the discussion of Bunyan as "a man with no inherited intellectual pedigree" who, "born to no authority within his own culture," had to define for himself an alternative empowering tradition, in Juliet Dusinberre, "Bunyan, and Virginia Woolf: A History and a Language of Their Own," *Bunyan Studies* 5 (1994): 15–46.

3. *Paradise Regained*, 4: 286–321, in *The Poems of John Milton*, ed. John Carey and Alastair Fowler, rev. ed. (London: Longman, 1980), 1151–52. All subsequent citations to Milton's poetry are to this edition. Milton is associated with radical Puritanism most tellingly in Christopher Hill, *Milton and the English Revolution* (1977; repr., London: Faber, 1979) and both Milton and Bunyan are discussed in radical terms in id., *The World Turned Upside Down* (1972; Harmondsworth: Penguin, 1975), 44–49, and id., *The English Bible and the Seventeenth-Century Revolution* (1993; Harmondsworth: Penguin, 1994), 371–91.

4. See Felicity Heal, "*Grace Abounding to the Chief of Sinners*: John Bunyan's Pauline Epistle," *Studies in English Literature* 21 (1981): 147–60; and Margaret Olofson Thickstun, "The Preface to Bunyan's *Grace Abounding* as Pauline Epistle," *Notes and Queries* 230 (1985): 180–82. The title of Bunyan's spiritual autobiography of course echoes Paul in I Timothy 1:14–15.

5. *Samson Agonistes*, l. 1659, in *Poems of John Milton*, 398. John Carey's note in *Poems of John Milton* points out that this detail is a Miltonic addition to the biblical account. Cf. Hill, *Milton*, 438–39.

6. *Paradise Lost*, 7: 31, in *Poems of John Milton*, 777; "The Readie & Easie Way to Establish a Free Commonwealth" (1660), in *Complete Prose Works of John Milton*, ed. Don M. Wolfe et al., 8 vols. (New Haven and London: Yale University Press, 1953–82), vol. 7, ed. Robert W. Ayers, rev. ed. (1980), 368–75, 432–46. All subsequent citations to Milton's prose works are to this edition (cited parenthetically in the text as *CPW*).

7. William Riley Parker, *Milton: A Biography*, 2 vols. (Oxford: Clarendon Press, 1968), 1: 567–76 (mentioning the simultaneous case of Bunyan on 575–76); J. Milton French, ed., *The Life Records of John Milton*, 5 vols. (1956; repr., New York: Gordian Press, 1966), 4: 322–23, 339–40; Austin Woolrych, "Historical Introduction," in *Complete Prose Works of John Milton*, 7: 220–23.

8. French, *Records*, 4: 349–50.

9. Andrew Marvell, *The Rehearsal Transpros'd*, ed. D. I. B. Smith (Oxford: Clarendon Press, 1971), 312; Thomas Ellwood, *The History of his Life* (1714), 131. Curiously, Marvell's comment that, since the Act of Oblivion, Milton has "expiated himself in a retired silence," is omitted from the passage as extracted in French, *Records*, 4: 352; but Ellwood's similar remark is included (4: 367).

10. French, *Records*, 4: 352–53, 390.

11. Parker, *Milton*, 1: 567–74. There is some evidence that, after the passing of the Act of Oblivion, Milton continued to fear that he might be assassinated (French, *Records*, 4: 358–59).

12. For two, rather different, accounts of this disappointment and its effect upon the Puritan temper, see Christopher Hill, *The Experience of Defeat: Milton and Some Contemporaries* (London: Faber and Faber, 1984), and N. H. Keeble, *The Literary Culture of Nonconformity in Later Seventeenth-Century England* (Leicester: University of Leicester Press, 1987).

13. In the third edition of 1672/3(?) the title page description has become "a Servant of Christ" and the subscription is dropped, presumably by Bunyan himself (*MW*, 3: 3, 5–6, 7).

14. This passage derives from Keeble, *Literary Culture*, 262.
15. Sir Philip Sidney, *An Apology for Poetry*, ed. Geoffrey Shepherd (Manchester: Manchester University Press, 1965), 119.
16. These lines are quoted in Anne Ferry, *Milton's Epic Voice: The Narrator in Paradise Lost* (Chicago and London: University of Chicago Press, 1983), 151, but, though she argues that the identity, manner, and point of view of the narrator are crucial to the design of *Paradise Lost*, she does not reflect on the significance of the circumstances in which he is here placed.
17. As Alastair Fowler's editorial note supposes (*Poems of John Milton*, 776).
18. *Seriatim* George Bate, Richard Perrinchief, Henry Foulis, John Taylor (?), Robert South, and Roger L'Estrange, as cited in French, *Records*, 4: 359, 365, 366, 379, 315.
19. Hill, *Milton*, 365 (cf. 238, 404–5); Michael Wilding, *Dragons Teeth: Literature in the English Revolution* (Oxford: Clarendon Press, 1987), 237. For a sustained and compelling analysis of Milton's relationship to the restored regime, see Laura L. Knoppers, *Historicizing Milton: Spectacle, Power and Poetry in Restoration England* (Athens: University of Georgia Press, 1994).
20. Milton, "On the Morning of Christ's Nativity," l. 28, and *Samson Agonistes*, l. 695.
21. Cf. Hill, *Milton*, 370–71, 391.
22. For the strategy and purposes of nonconformist accounts of trials, including Bunyan's, see Keeble, *Literary Culture*, 84–90.
23. No copy of the first edition is known to be extant; the second edition appeared in 1663. It was consequently written between 1661 and 1663; Richard L. Greaves favors 1662 (*MW*, 2: xl–xli). The reference to the "silencing of God's dear Ministers" (*MW*, 2: 284) may indicate a date of composition after St. Bartholomew's Day, 24 August 1662, when the Act of Uniformity came into force.
24. *MW*, 6: 43, quoted in Christopher Hill, *A Turbulent, Seditious and Factious People: John Bunyan and His Church* (Oxford: Clarendon Press, 1988), 119, citing the case of the Bedfordshire man John Child. Hill points out how frequent in Bunyan's work—and especially in *The Pilgrim's Progress*—are unsympathetic portraits of those who change their allegiance (131–34, 215–16, 244).
25. *PP*, 87 (alluding to Acts 14:22), 92–98. The rhetorical shaping of this episode is illuminatingly discussed in John R. Knott, *Discourses of Martyrdom in English Literature, 1563–1694* (Cambridge: Cambridge University Press, 1993), 201–5. See also Brean S. Hammond, "*The Pilgrim's Progress*: Satire and Social Comment," in *The Pilgrim's Progress: Critical and Historical Views*, ed. Vincent Newey (Liverpool: Liverpool University Press, 1980), 119–22.
26. *MW*, 6: 47, 10: 5, 6. *Seasonable Counsel* is discussed in Knott, *Discourses of Martyrdom*, 181–85. Cf. the argument of the posthumous *Paul's Departure and Crown*, in *MW*, 12: 357ff, esp. 361–64.
27. Blair Worden, "Milton, *Samson Agonistes* and the Restoration," in *Culture and Society in the Stuart Restoration*, ed. Gerald MacLean (Cambridge: Cambridge University Press, 1995), 111–36.
28. Edward Taylor, *Upon the Types of the Old Testament*, ed. Charles W. Mignon, 2 vols. (Lincoln: University of Nebraska Press, 1989), 1: 207.
29. For accounts of Puritan and Nonconformist experience during the Restoration period, see G. R. Cragg, *Puritanism in the Period of the Great Persecution, 1660–1688* (Cambridge: Cambridge University Press, 1957); Hill, *Experience of Defeat*; Keeble, *Literary Culture*; and M. R. Watts, *The Dissenters: From the Reformation to the French Revolution* (Oxford: Clarendon Press, 1978), 221–62.

30. It is not clear how far in advance Bunyan is claiming to have foreseen what was coming. It is just possible that (as implied by Hill, *Turbulent People*, 106, n. 10) Restoration and Episcopalian reaction are anticipated by the prayer with which the prefatory epistle to the reader of *A Few Sighs from Hell* concludes:

> pray for me, that my God would not forsake me, nor take his holy Spirit from me; and that God would fit me to do and suffer, what shall be from the world or devil inflicted upon me. I must tell thee, the world rages, they stamp and shake their heads, and fair they would be doing: the Lord help me to take all they shall do with patience. (*MW*, 1: 248)

The book's title page bears the year-date 1658. Its undated epistle could have been written during 1657, well in advance of publication, or in 1658, either shortly before publication or while the book was in press. Even so, if G. K. Fortescue is correct in suggesting September as the month of publication (*Catalogue of the Pamphlets . . . Collected by George Thomason*, 2 vols. [London: British Museum, 1908], 2: 216], it would have required great prescience in Bunyan to have foreseen at that stage that the death of Cromwell on 3 September would lead to the collapse of the Protectorate, to the return of episcopacy and to persecution. Probably no more than an unfocused desire to bear true witness in a hostile world is expressed in this passage.

31. So interpreted by Richard L. Greaves in *MW*, 3: xxxix.

32. H. G. Tibbutt, ed., *The Minutes of The First Independent Church (now Bunyan Meeting) at Bedford, 1656–1766* (Bedford: Bedfordshire Historical Record Society 55, 1976), 35.

33. Cf. Hill, *Milton*, 382. Nimrod was commonly taken to represent not merely oppressive monarchy but (by their opponents) Charles I and Charles II: see Hill, *Turbulent People*, 326–27; and Tindall, *John Bunyan, Mechanick Preacher*, 141–42.

34. Richard L. Greaves, "John Bunyan and the Fifth Monarchists," *Albion* 13 (1981): 83–95, argues that Bunyan at one time had held Fifth Monarchist views, but finds no evidence of revolutionary or seditious political involvement. Cf. Hill, *Turbulent People*, 106: "Bunyan was no plotter, no politician."

35. On pacifism and quietism in Nonconformist writing at this time, see Keeble, *Literary Culture*, 19–20, 23–24, 191–214, and for Bunyan in particular, see Richard L. Greaves, "Bunyan and the Ethic of Suffering," in *John Bunyan and His England 1628–88*, ed. Anne Laurence, W. R. Owens and Stuart Sim (London: Hambledon Press, 1990), 63–75.

36. For discussion of this strain in Bunyan and Milton, see Keeble, *Literary Culture*, esp. 191–204; Laura L. Knoppers, "*Paradise Regained* and the Politics of Martyrdom," *Modern Philology* 90 (1992): 200–219; Knott, *Discourses of Martyrdom*, esp. 168–78, 181–85; David Loewenstein, "The Kingdom Within: Radical Religious Culture and the Politics of *Paradise Regained*," *Literature & History*, 3rd ser., 3 (1994): 63–89; and works cited in these pieces. In *Deliver Us from Evil: The Radical Underground in Britain, 1660–1663* (New York: Oxford University Press, 1986) and *Enemies under His Feet: Radicals and Nonconformists in Britain, 1664–1667* (Stanford: Stanford University Press, 1990) Richard L. Greaves exhaustively documents plotting and suspected plotting, to argue that nonconformity was far more subversively active than has been appreciated.

37. Accordingly, in *The Holy War* Nimrod is the captain of "the *Tyrannical* and *Incroaching Bloodmen*; his *Standard*-bearer bare the Red-colors, and his *Scutcheon* was the *Great Bloodhound*" (*HW*, 229).

38. *OED*, sense 4: "Of language, diction: Elegant. Hence *fair speaker. Obs.*"

Although no example of the adjective is given later than 1477, adverbial usage ("to speak fair"), with the sense *civilly, courteously*, is illustrated into the nineteenth century, and some such sense is clearly required here.

39. Relevant senses recorded in *OED* are "smartly or finely dressed" and "a gallant, a fop."

40. Nicholas Jose, *Ideas of the Restoration in English Literature, 1660–71* (Cambridge: Harvard University Press, 1984), 162.

41. Hill, *Turbulent People*, 125–30, 212–15.

42. *A Few Sighs from Hell* (1658), in *MW*, 1: 252, 253–54, 255, 256. Bunyan is careful to add that the poor can be ungodly too.

43. In the sense of "Nobility, high birth or rank, good social position" the terms enter English in the late sixteenth century, but their vogue, and the sense of socially accomplished manners and of acquired or demonstrable status independent of birth, belong to the late seventeenth and eighteenth centuries (*OED*, sense 4; Jose, *Ideas of the Restoration*, 19).

44. As noted by Hill, *Turbulent People*, 224.

45. For discussion of this aspect of Penn, and of Nonconformist writing, see Keeble, *Literary Culture*, 215–29.

46. Jose, *Ideas of the Restoration*, 155, 160. For such a reading of *Samson Agonistes* see Jose's whole chapter (142–63); the essay by Blair Worden cited above, n. 27; and Hill, *Milton*, 428–48.

47. That is, of recurrence, repetition, return to a previous situation (*OED*, sense 2), but also "An instance of great change or alteration in affairs" (*OED*, sense 6b). Christopher Hill, "The Word 'Revolution,' " in his *A Nation of Change and Novelty* (1990; repr. London: Bookmarks, 1993), 100–120, assembles a great deal of linguistic evidence to suggest that, under the pressure of the events of midcentury, this second sense developed into the modern political meaning, denoting discontinuity, innovation, and a new beginning, long before 1688.

48. For numerous examples, see Jose, *Ideas of the Restoration*.

49. On these contrasting biases, see Isabel Rivers, "Grace, Holiness and the Pursuit of Happiness: Bunyan and Restoration Latitudinarianism," in *John Bunyan: Conventicle and Parnassus, Tercenterary Essays*, ed. N. H. Keeble (Oxford: Oxford University Press, 1988), 45–69, and, with much fuller contextualization, id., *Reason, Grace, and Sentiment: A Study of the Language of Religion and Ethics in England, 1660–1780* (Cambridge: Cambridge University Press, 1991), chaps. 2, 3, esp. 81–87.

50. A representative list of comparable citations from Foxe is given by J. Sears McGee in *MW*, 3: xxxv, n. 1. Knott, *Discourses of Martyrdom*, delineates this Foxean tradition, and, in relating Bunyan's writings to it, shows how he presented himself as "one of the spiritual heirs" of the Marian martyrs and construed the Restoration as "an episode in the long history of suffering for truth" (179–215). See also Keeble, *Literary Culture*, 187–91, and both Dusinberre, "Bunyan and Virginia Woolf," and Thomas S. Freeman, "A Library in Three Volumes: Foxe's *Book of Martyrs* in the Writings of John Bunyan," *Bunyan Studies* 5 (1994): 15–27, 47–57.

51. See above, 31–32.

52. See above, 33–34. Cf. J. Sears McGee in *MW*, 3: xxiv–xxv.

53. *Restauration*, *OED*, sense 1c; *restoration*, *OED*, senses 1a, 2a; *revolution*, *OED*, sense 8a.

54. Professor Annabel Patterson has pointed out to me that twenty years later, following the disarray of the Exclusion Crisis, Dryden sought to recover and to

reassert this positive sense of the word in the concluding lines of *Absalom and Achitophel*: "Henceforth a series of new time began, / The mighty years in long procession ran: / Once more the godlike David was restored, / And willing nations knew their lawful lord" (*John Dryden*, ed. Keith Walker [Oxford and New York: Oxford University Press, 1987], 204).

55. It is not recorded either in Laurence Sterne and Harold H. Kollmeier, eds., *A Concordance to the English Prose of John Milton* (Binghampton, N.Y.: Medieval & Renaissance Texts and Studies, 1985) or in William Ingram and Kathleen Swaim, eds., *A Concordance to Milton's English Poetry* (Oxford: Clarendon Press, 1972).

56. Marchamont Nedham, *A Short History of the English Rebellion* (London, 1661), 37, quoted in Jose, *Ideas of the Restoration*, 14–15, with an incorrect reference to [83]. The "linnets" are Lovelace's in "To Althea, from Prison." See *The Poems*, ed. C. H. Wilkinson (Oxford: Clarendon Press, 1953), 78–79.

Bunyan and the Cry of Blood

John R. Knott

My point of departure is an episode from the second part of *The Pilgrim's Progress* that I have always found disconcerting: Mercy's encounter with three men that she sees "hanged up in irons" by the side of the way. Great-heart responds to her questions by summarizing the case against the three (Simple, Sloth, and Presumption), explaining that they formerly turned pilgrims out of the way by mocking their enterprise and giving "an evil report of the Good Land" that is the object of their pilgrimage. We see none of these activities in the first part, where Simple, Sloth, and Presumption are memorable chiefly for the sleepy complacency with which they respond to Christian's efforts to rouse them. Christiana, accepting Great-heart's indictment, regards them as bad men justly punished (*"they have but what they deserve"*) and expresses approval of the display. When Great-heart invites the two to "go a little to the Wall" and inspect the engraved plate describing their crimes, Mercy responds with vehemence, "*No no, let them hang and their Names Rot, and their Crimes live for ever against them.*" Mercy recoils at the thought of moving closer, but she is quick to approve the punishment. Her response mingles repulsion, fear (she has just said it is fortunate that they were hanged, since "*who knows else what they might a done to such poor Women as we are*"), and vigorous moral judgment. Her subsequent song, directed to the three victims, affirms her moral superiority and transforms their bodies into a warning for pilgrims:

> Now then, you three, hang there and be a Sign
> To all that shall against the Truth combine:
> And let him that comes after, fear this end,
> If unto Pilgrims he is not a Friend.
>
> (PP, 214)

Mercy begins her journey as a shy, uncertain young woman and develops into the embodiment of mercy, busying herself with making clothes for the poor. When Mr. Cruelty says of Faithful at the conclusion of his trial in Vanity Fair, "*Hanging is too good for him*" (97), the comment at least seems in character. But Mercy's harshness ("*let them hang and their Names Rot*") seems startlingly out of character, here and a little later when she endorses the punishment of Mistrust and Timorous ("*burned thorough the Tongue with an hot Iron, for endeavouring to hinder Christian in his Journey*" [218]) by quoting Psalm 120: "*what shall be done unto thee thou false Tongue? sharp Arrows of the mighty, with Coals of Juniper.*" In the second instance, Bunyan authorizes the punishment and Mercy's acceptance of it by the fierceness of the biblical metaphor, but the shift from the metaphoric to the literal (a hot iron burning through the tongues of malefactors) jars, as does the image of rotting bodies in irons. Mercy may avoid speaking of bodies—she would have their *names* (reputations) rot and would fix their significance as a sign—but readers cannot avoid the presence of these bodies at the center of the scene.

Mercy's uncharitable sentiments seem surprising, even unintentionally ironic, to a modern reader, but they reflect an uncompromising attitude toward unregenerate sinners and temptations to sin that runs through *The Pilgrim's Progress*. Bunyan frequently shows the presumptuous and the unwary meeting violent ends, as exemplary in their way as the criminal justice administered by some mysterious agency to a Sloth or a Timorous. In the first part, for example, Formalist and Hypocrisy quickly find themselves on dangerous ground, with one taking the way to Destruction where he meets his death in the surreal "wide field full of dark Mountains" (*PP*, 42); Christian and Hopeful see the bodies of those who have fallen from the Hill of Error "dashed all to pieces" (120) at the bottom; Ignorance is snatched from the gate of Heaven and thrust into Hell, prompting critics to seek explanations for what has seemed to some a gratuitous severity. Bunyan enacts a form of judgment in such cases, offering a fictional analogue to the supposed judgments of actual sinners he reports in *The Life and Death of Mr. Badman*.[1] The "judgments" of sinners in *The Pilgrim's Progress*, like the conventional ones Bunyan invokes in *Mr. Badman*, reflect a need to see events as providentially ordered. They offer confirmation of a divine power to punish the erring, although without removing the sense of danger and uncertainty that hangs over the way. One can easily fall into a pit and be dashed to pieces, the unhappy fate of Vain-confidence.

One can find an explanation for the violence of such judgments, whether in the form of deliberate punishments or of unexpected deaths, in the severity of the Calvinist thought Bunyan absorbed, which allows no room for mercy for the reprobate and a considerable amount for the wrath of God. Thomas Luxon has argued recently that false pilgrims are personifications of the attachment of true pilgrims such as Christian and Faithful to "worldly things and worldly thinking"; he explains the violence, interestingly, by claiming that Christian and Faithful "violently 'out' their own carnal nature and attach it to others, who must be destroyed."[2] The Calvinist emphasis on relentless mortification of the flesh would support such a view, although some false pilgrims may seem more nearly projections of the weaknesses of Christian and friends than others. A problem with this view of the allegory is that it risks dissolving the social ground of Bunyan's frequently satiric vision. That is, it slights the sense in which these characters embody social types as well as tendencies to which would-be pilgrims may be subject. Bunyan's "judgments" should be seen, I think, as reflecting attitudes toward these types as well as recognition of tendencies to particular forms of sin. I would agree with Luxon in finding brutality in the treatment of Sloth, Simple, and Presumption and Mercy's reaction to it. He locates this ultimately in Bunyan's religion and suggests that "Allegorizing the world helps to make such brutality thinkable."[3] The question of why one finds this kind of brutality in Bunyan's imaginative writing, if brutality is indeed the right word, deserves further exploration.

Cultural violence offers another kind of explanation. Bunyan's writings reflect a culture in which the Quaker leader James Nayler could be punished for blasphemy, by act of Parliament, by having his tongue pierced with a hot iron (he also had his forehead branded with a "B" and was whipped through London and Bristol, the site of his alleged impersonation of Christ). Heads of those convicted of treason were still displayed as a warning. In January 1661, in a notorious incident that commemorated the execution of Charles I, those of Cromwell, Bradshaw, and Ireton were exhibited on poles on top of Westminster Hall after their bodies were exhumed.[4] One could find other manifestations of violence in the culture, but the interesting question, to which I will return, is why Bunyan incorporated the kinds of violence he did in his allegory. Bunyan was far from sympathetic with Nayler's views, but why would he inflict on false pilgrims (Mistrust and Timorous) a brutal punishment for blasphemy most likely to be used against Nonconformists?

I believe that the answer is to be found partly in the atmosphere of Bunyan's imaginative world, in which violence against the reprobate and the enemies of God cannot be separated readily from instances of violence that Bunyan uses to express the struggles of the soul and of the Christian community on the path to the New Jerusalem. The violent confrontations that effectively blend Bunyan's reading in chapbook romances with biblical imagery, from Christian's combat with Apollyon to Great-heart's victories over the giants of the second part, convey a sense of urgency that is fundamental to Bunyan's Christianity. All uses of the popular imagery of Christian warfare in the period suggest some degree of urgency, but Bunyan's, especially in the first part of *The Pilgrim's Progress*, create an atmosphere of virtually continuous crisis. Bunyan would have his readers believe that the journey is a matter of life and death, from the moment of Christian's flight from the City of Destruction, with danger and incipient violence never far away until one reaches the security and ease of Beulah, in the environs of the New Jerusalem. Even then the crossing of the river lies ahead, dangerous for those who forget the promises that sustain them, as Christian nearly does. In the world of *The Pilgrim's Progress* those who feel an insufficient sense of crisis, and are consequently neither anxious nor watchful, are frequently surprised by disaster. To claim a truth one does not in fact possess, or to impede others in the pursuit of truth, is to invite a violent end that suggests the damnation of the soul.

The hazards that Christian encounters reflect an anxiety about election that often takes the form of fears of destruction. I have commented elsewhere on Bunyan's habit of expressing psychic states through imagery of bodily abuse, including the spectacular physical torments inflicted upon the early Christian martyrs.[5] Bunyan's fascination with the most extreme form of bodily abuse, dismemberment, suggests a dread of losing the sense of identity as a member of the elect that he continually seeks to confirm. Images of dismemberment surface when Christian's grip on this identity, and even his sanity, seems most precarious. In the Valley of the Shadow of Death Christian imagines that he will be "torn in pieces" (63) by the fiends whose noises he hears; Giant Despair's ultimate threat to Christian and Hopeful, after beating them and urging suicide, is to tell them how he tore their predecessors in pieces and how "within ten days I will do [the same] to you" (117). Such threats of annihilation suggest a paralyzing dread that would undermine the faith necessary to sustain the journey.

Bunyan's imagination was haunted by images of lions, which he could have found in popular romances but knew primarily from Scripture, where lions frequently threaten destruction and in the New Testament come to be associated with Satanic power, notably in Peter's description of the devil as a "roaring lion" walking about and "seeking whom he may destroy" (1 Peter 5:8). Bunyan uses lions to suggest the external threat of persecution, as in the case of the lions that flank the way up Hill Difficulty, but they typically suggest a threat to psychic equilibrium as well. When Timorous and Mistrust tell Christian about the lions in the path, his imagination leaps to the thought of them ranging in the night for their prey: "how should I escape being by them torn in pieces?" (45). Christian manages to control this potentially disabling dread, barely, encouraged by Watchful's assurance that the lions are chained, and thus survives what Bunyan presents as a trial of faith. Bunyan's lions take on some of the resonance they have for the psalmist, who prays for deliverance from his persecutors, "lest he tear my soul like a lion, rending it to pieces" (Ps. 7:2). The threat to the body becomes a threat to the soul, and to Christian's sense of identity as a pilgrim. Apollyon the destroyer, with his lion's mouth, suggests both the pride Christian must master if he is to get through the Valley of Humiliation and a demonic power that challenges the truth and authority of God and threatens Christian's whole being. The superior power of the Scripture he remembers in the nick of time enables him to survive this particular trial of faith, of course, and Christian can emerge from his death struggle to give thanks "to him that hath delivered me out of mouth of the Lion" (60), in words that echo Paul's upon his (temporary) escape from Nero's persecution in Rome (2 Tim. 4:17).

I dwell on this fear of being devoured, or torn to pieces, because it seems to me related to the violence Bunyan shows visited upon sinners and, especially, upon persecutors of the godly.[6] In reading Bunyan's imaginative works one gets the sense of entering a world in which violent forces are in play, representing divine as well as demonic power. The violence of these forces, which Christian must somehow understand and survive, has the effect of establishing the intensity of his spiritual life and the urgency of the crises in which he finds himself. His initial flight is precipitated by a vision of collective destruction ("*This our City will be burned with fire from Heaven*" [8]), and he quickly finds himself personally threatened by the terrors of the law in the form of a lowering hill flashing fire. The wrath of God hovers over *The Pilgrim's Progress*, although once Christian has passed through the wicket gate and committed himself to the way he finds himself dealing with other kinds of forces in the threats presented by Apollyon and the Valley of the Shadow of Death and by the hostility of society toward pilgrims in Vanity Fair. Confronting and mastering the terrors such experiences arouse, by drawing strength from the sustaining power of God's Word, becomes a necessary part of the process of establishing his identity as a member of the elect. The violence or threatened violence that he must contend with in these trials of faith confirms him in his role of Christian soldier. Bunyan would have seen this process as analogous to that by which the violence directed at the early martyrs ("thrown to the *wild Beasts*, burned at the *Stakes* . . . and a thousand other fearful Torments" [*MW*, 5: 167]) strengthened their faith and enabled them to triumph spiritually over their persecutors. If Christian is a soldier who stumbles in the first part of *The Pilgrim's Progress*, he becomes more clearly heroic when seen from the distancing perspective of the second part. Greatheart tells the story of Christian and Faithful standing "undaunted" before the judge of Vanity Fair, "a couple of Lyon-like Men" who "set their Faces like Flint" (272).

To call Christian "Lyon-like" is to invest him with a boldness and power that derive from faith and from the confidence in divine support that faith engenders. Those not so bold or persevering as Christian and his godly companions are more obviously exposed to the wrath of God. One way to see the fate of such characters as Sloth and Timorous is as a manifestation of this wrath, although in these cases judgment takes the form of punishment that would have been recognizable to Bunyan's contemporary audience. It was important to establish the force of this wrath, to show it as the dominant power in the imaginative world of *The Pilgrim's Progress* and to see it as vindicating the perseverance of the faithful. The satisfaction that Bunyan's pilgrims often take in the judgments of those who lack their vision or who actively oppose them suggests a need to see the evidence of this power displacing that of the state in a world in which they can believe.

Bunyan gave divine wrath a more explicit and powerful role in *The Holy War*, written at a time of intensified pressure on Nonconformists.[7] In their initial conquest of the lapsed Mansoul the captains of Shaddai display a remarkable ferocity. Judgment speaks in the language of Isaiah (66:15) in an effort to arouse terror in the besieged inhabitants: "*He hath prepared his Throne for Judgment; for he will come with fire, and with his Chariots like a whirl-wind, to render his anger with fury, and his rebukes with flames of fire*" (*HW*, 46). Execution, following him, invokes a homelier and more immediately threatening New Testament metaphor from Matthew (3:10): "*Behold the Ax is laid to the root of the Trees, every Tree therefore that bringeth not forth good fruit, is hewen down and cast into the fire*" (46). When Boanerges and Conviction take possession of Mansoul in the name of Emanuel, after a slaughter that Bunyan represents in graphic terms (Conviction splits Secure's head open with a two-handed sword), we are told that "their faces were the faces of Lions, and their words like the roaring of the Sea" (93). Bunyan draws here upon Old Testament passages representing God as a lion in his wrath[8] to heighten the ferocity of the captains and to suggest that they embody a power superior to that of Diabolus, described earlier as roaring upon Mansoul "as a Lyon upon the prey" (11).

In the posture of these captains, and in the insistence of the victorious Emanuel upon complete submission by the inhabitants of Mansoul, Bunyan offers an allegorical version of the process of salvation that places heavy stress upon the wrath and threatened judgment of God and the impotence of the sinner before God. I would agree with Stuart Sim that these scenes embody a severity and intolerance that reflects Bunyan's Calvinism, and a suggestion of revenge in Emanuel's treatment of the conquered Diabolus, chained to the wheels of the chariot in which Emanuel rides in triumph through Mansoul.[9] Bunyan conveys a mood of "terrour and dread," in the words of his captains, using images of violence and impending violence to suggest the scope of the wrath of God directed against the resisting sinner. Yet one should distinguish between the majority of the inhabitants of Mansoul, granted mercy when they finally do submit, and the unrepentant and unpardoned Diabolus and his followers.

Diabolus, represented as a tyrant in his governance of Mansoul, constitutes one version of a figure that assumes a large importance in Bunyan's writings, the persecutor or enemy of the godly. Persecutors in Bunyan's work, as in the tradition of Christian martyrdom that he absorbed from the Bible and from John Foxe's *Acts and Monuments*, typically rage against the godly out of an apparent hatred of their claims to truth and goodness and the potential for subversion of custom and established authority that these claims represent. We see an instance of this rage in the attitudes of judge and jury in the trial of Christian and Faithful in Vanity Fair and the ferocity of the punishments inflicted upon the body of Faithful. Christian escapes, we are informed, because "he that over-rules all things, having the power of their rage in his own hand, so wrought it" (*PP*, 97), but we get no promise or foreshadowing of God's punishment of persecutors here, only an affirmation of Faithful's spiritual triumph in his translation to heaven and in Christian's memorializing song. The thrust of the episode is to show that Christians must be prepared to suffer persecution, and to resist even "unto blood" as Evangelist warns they should be. The balance of power appears to shift in the second part, in Great-heart's decisive victories over the giants, whose prominent role reflects the renewed persecution of Nonconformists and elevated fears of Catholicism at the time Bunyan wrote. As critics have noted, Great-heart's heroism is a measure of Bunyan's increased sense of the importance and effectiveness of the Nonconformist pastor, especially in offering spiritual guidance to the weaker members of the church, but it also suggests a need to represent the vengeance of God against the enemies of the church.

Great-heart's interventions, against a series of enemies who threaten or impede pilgrims (Grim with his lions, Maul, Slay-good, the monster in the woods outside Vanity Fair), can be read allegorically as a deliverance from fear, chiefly of persecution, whether this is local persecution under the penal laws used against Nonconformists or the broader persecution represented by the history of the Catholic Church as this was understood by Protestants. These deliverances reinforce the emphasis on assurance that characterizes the second part. Yet the violence and bloodiness of the victories also suggest a delight in the prospect of vengeance for the oppression of the true church. Great-heart is a vehicle for the wrath of God, which Bunyan believed would overwhelm the rage of persecutors so prominent in the history of the true church. When Great-heart tells Slay-good that he has come "to revenge the Blood of Pilgrims" (209) and then displays his head as a "Terror" to those tempted to imitate him, he enacts a kind of decisive justice that Bunyan could not reasonably expect to see in this life. By rendering it allegorically, he could indulge in a form of prophecy, or perhaps wish fulfillment, that would have been assuring to his readers. Such readers could exult in these bloody victories over evil in God's name, as they presumably did in reading about the violent conquests of St. George and other heroes of faith in *The Seven Champions of Christendom*.

Most critics would agree that Bunyan preferred what he called "patient enduring" to any kind of action against the state ("Keep company with holy, and quiet, and peaceable men" [*MW*, 10: 78, 79]) and distanced himself from those who advocated violent resistance. In his unfinished *Exposition on the Ten First Chapters of Genesis* he views persecutors as the "brood of Cain" and predicts that they will be punished, but, as W. R. Owens has noted, insists that vengeance be left to God (*MW*, 12: xlv–xlvii). In *Seasonable Counsel* in particular Bunyan argues that Christians should bear suffering with patience and understand that it is sent for the trial and strengthening of their faith, developing what Richard Greaves has characterized as an ethic of suffering.[10] I have argued elsewhere for the pervasiveness of Bunyan's use of the language and the attitudes associated with Protestant martyrdom as a way of dramatizing the ideal of Christian suffering. I want to argue here, however, for more attention to what could be regarded as the other side of Bunyan's advocacy of suffering: a confidence, even exultation, in a divine justice that will ensure that those who inflict the suffering will be punished.

Bunyan could urge his readers to "suffer with *Abel*, until your Righteous Blood be spilt," patiently enduring the violence of "wicked and blood-thirsty Men," because he was confident that "our Blood will cry from the ground against them" (*MW*, 12: 173, 172). He tended to associate various kinds of suffering with martyrdom, as a means of dramatizing and giving greater significance to this suffering, and would have seen the powerful cry of Abel's innocent blood as anticipating that of Christian martyrs "slain for the word of God," shown in Revelation 6:9–10 as crying with a "loud voice" from under the altar: "How long, O Lord, holy and true, dost thou not judge and avenge our blood on them that dwell on the earth?" In his commentary on Genesis Bunyan offers repeated assurances that the cry of blood will be answered:

> O the Cries of Blood are strong cries . . . that never cease to make a noise, untill they have procured Vengeance from the hands of the *Lord of Sabbath*. (166)

> The Voice of Blood is a very *killing voice,* and will one day speak with such Thunder and terror in the Consciences of all the brood of *Cain*, that their pain and burthen will be for ever unsupportable. (167)

The notion of a "killing voice" speaking with thunder invests the persecuted with a sense of agency, as if this voice not only calls forth the vengeance but itself embodies the power of divine wrath to terrify and punish.[11] At the same time that Bunyan counsels suffering patiently, and leaving acts of vengeance to God, he takes satisfaction in the prospect that the violence historically inflicted upon the followers of the true church will be redirected against persecutors. If he needed to imagine violence against himself to establish the urgency and intensity of his spiritual struggle, he also needed to believe that violence would be returned upon the heads of persecutors, in a validation of God's authority and power.

In his commentary on Genesis Bunyan displaces the violence to be suffered by persecutors to an indefinite future, "one day," and he typically expresses it by invoking the apocalyptic imagery of Scripture, notably in the posthumous *Of Antichrist, and His Ruine*. Like so many Protestants, he found in Old Testament prophecies of "the day of the Lord's vengeance" and in Revelation the destruction of Rome and of all persecutors of the true church, although unlike some he avoided fixing dates for the return of Christ or working out scriptural keys to historical events.[12] By counseling obedience to kings and representing them as the agents of the destruction of Antichrist, Bunyan made it clear that Christians should trust to God and not seek their own means of deliverance from affliction. Yet it is significant that Bunyan could counsel political moderation, and dwell on the necessary trials of the suffering church, while enthusiastically embracing biblical language showing the wrath of God unleashed against Antichrist. Thus he can anticipate the destruction of the ordinances of Antichrist, including civil laws under which Nonconformists suffer in England, by "the *Spirit of his Mouth*, and the *Brightness of his Coming*," drawing upon the resonant language of 2 Thessalonians (7–8). Or invoke Old Testament representations of divine wrath to suggest the character of God's revenge: "I will make mine arrows drunk with blood, and my sword shall devour flesh" (Deut. 32:42; *MW*, 13: 43, 453). *Of Antichrist*, in particular, reveals Bunyan's strong attraction to this scriptural rhetoric of violence.

Bunyan was not unique, certainly, in his ability to reconcile a Pauline theology of suffering with prophecies of divine vengeance. The New Testament provided a model, and various kinds of Protestant writing, from Foxe's martyrology to commentaries on Revelation, offered more immediate examples. What seems more remarkable is the way Bunyan incorporates violence against evil in his imaginative works while embracing the ideal of patient suffering. One should recognize that such suffering does not have to be passive or wholly submissive. Faithful can accept the role of martyr and yet give aggressive testimony of God's truth before an abusive judge, defying the authority that empowers him. Even less obviously combative stances such as the one Bunyan reports adopting in *A Relation of My Imprisonment* embody a form of aggression. In declaring his willingness to "lie down and to suffer what they shall do unto me" (*GA*, 125), Bunyan chose to give his testimony by remaining in prison, thereby challenging the civil authority under which he was held and providing an example of resistance to those who might be tempted to conform. By adopting a posture of readiness to suffer for a superior truth, that the Pauline injunction to go forth and preach the gospel should take precedence over a law restricting preaching, he was boldly claiming the spiritual high ground. One can see a more subtle kind of defiance in William Penn's parting remarks to the court after being sentenced to Newgate for speaking at an illegal gathering: "I scorn that Religion that is not worth Suffering for. . . . Thy Religion persecutes, and mine forgives: and I desire my God to forgive all you that are concerned with my commitment, and I leave you all in perfect Charity, wishing your everlasting salvation."[13] One could call this aggressive forgiveness. Penn opposes the stance of Christ, which he imitates here, to that of a judge determined to stamp out conventicles, as a way of asserting that God's truth cannot be defeated by secular power. Faithful, the Bunyan of *A Relation*, and Penn all practice a kind of bold speaking, authorized by the example of the apostles before their accusers, that has the effect of opposing one kind of power to another, an assumed spiritual power to the visible authority of law and the courts.

Such examples illustrate the inherent tension between an ideal of testifying to the truth before a hostile audience and an ethic of suffering that enjoins one to "take thy affliction with meekness and patience," as Bunyan urges in *Seasonable Counsel* (*MW*, 10: 97). This tension is particularly apparent in the case of Faithful, whose last reported words are a denunciation of the ruling class of Vanity Fair as "more fit for a being in Hell, then in this Town and Countrey" (95). It is much less apparent in a work of practical divinity such as *Seasonable Counsel*, in which Bunyan was concerned to advise his readers how to suffer in a period of intensified persecution and to assure them that they could endure. The "holy boldness" he advocates there is a boldness in facing suffering and trusting God. The way "to imbolden thy face against the faces of thine enemies," he advises, is to be willing to accept any amount of suffering; one can thus assure a "quiet conscience" and provoke God to "appear for thy rescue, or to revenge thy blood when thou art gone" (*MW*, 10: 98). One of Bunyan's emphases in *Seasonable Counsel* is on the need to avoid a desire for revenge. Revenge is "of the flesh"; it proceeds from the "*gross* motions of an angry mind" (*MW*, 10: 100, 101). The implication here, as in Bunyan's commentary on Genesis, is that vengeance should be left to God.

Yet in the imaginative works Bunyan often seems to appropriate vengeance to himself, as narrator, acting on behalf of a justice we are encouraged to read as divine. In the cases of Sloth and Timorous, to which Mercy reacts so vigorously, we see the punishments but not the agency by which they are administered. And, interestingly, such justice as Sloth and Timorous and their companions receive takes the form of punishments that mimic those of a judicial system whose victims were frequently Nonconformists in the period in which Bunyan wrote. It is as though Bunyan appropriated the machinery of a system he would have seen as repressive in many of its workings to show, not without irony, how it would be replaced by the superior justice of God. I want to conclude by examining another episode that resembles the one with which I began, in the sense that it offers an instance of violence being turned against the wicked, in this case against those who could be considered persecutors or enemies of God on one allegorical level. This is the trial, actually two trials, of the Diabolonians in *The Holy War*.

In the trial scenes of *The Holy War*, as in the trial of Christian and Faithful in Vanity Fair, Bunyan showed himself a master of the kind of allegorical trial popularized by such writers as Richard Bernard (in *The Isle of Man*) and Richard Overton (in *The Araignement of Mr. Persecution*).[14] Something interesting happens, however, when we move from the trial in Vanity Fair, in which Bunyan exposes the ruthlessness with which the machinery of justice was used against Restoration Nonconformists and associates this with the callousness of the ruling class (Lord Hategood the judge, and such jurors as Lord Lechery and Sir Having-Greedy), to the trials of the ungodly in *The Holy War*. While there are crucial differences (False-peace tries to deny his identity while Faithful frankly declares his and defies the court), the judge and jury in Mansoul are similarly relentless, now in the name of truth and righteousness. The outcome, execution, is similarly foreordained and in *The Holy War* takes the shocking form of crucifixion. The editors of the excellent Oxford edition of *The Holy War*, James Forrest and Roger Sharrock, call this a flaw and see Bunyan as betrayed by his trust in the language of the Bible, in this case the Pauline metaphor of crucifying the flesh.[15] Perhaps Bunyan did miscalculate the effect of literalizing the biblical metaphor, yet the mood of *The Holy War*, not only in the trial scenes but in others in which the Diabolonians suffer violence, suggests that this effect is not wholly accidental. Bunyan shows an unmistakable gusto, even rough humor, in rendering the punishments and setbacks of the Diabolonians. When he describes the mutiny against the rule of Diabolus led by Understanding and Conscience, which leads to what amounts to a street brawl, he relishes the damage inflicted by the rebels: "Nor did the other side wholly escape, for there was one Mr. *Rashhead*, a *Diabolonian*, that had his brains beat out by Mr. *Mind*, the Lord *Willbewills* servant; and it made me laugh to see how old Mr. *Preju-*

dice was kickt and tumbled about in the dirt" (*HW*, 61). Mr. Prejudice escapes this time with "his crown soundly crackt," but later we see him "cut down to the ground" by Captain Execution in what Bunyan describes as the "very great slaughter" that accompanies the conquest of Mansoul by Diabolus (89).

The most furious and malignant of the Diabolonians are the Bloodmen ("They must have blood, the blood of *Mansoul*, else they die" [230]), led by captains whose names suggest the history of persecution (they include Cain, Nimrod, and Pope). By showing captains Credence and Patience put in charge of the defense against the Bloodmen, Bunyan suggests that the best resistance to persecution is to practice the faith and patient endurance associated with martyrdom. One might expect that Bunyan would show the destroyers destroyed, in the spirit of representing divine vengeance, but Emanuel stops the killing by commanding that they be taken alive and the worst of them bound over for the day of Judgment, "the great and general Assizes" (234). The implication is that the only sufficient punishment is the ultimate one, eternal torment in hell. Overton had reserved a similar punishment for Mr. Persecution and his defenders, sentenced to be held in dungeons for the "great Assises" where they will be arraigned before the King of Kings. The spirit of vengeance that informs Overton's allegorical trial, in his case directed against the Presbyterians, resembles what one finds in *The Holy War*. In Overton's tract Persecution is charged with guilt for almost "*all the blood of the whole earth from the blood of righteous* Abell *unto the blood of these present times.*" The judge tells his advocate, Sir Symon Synod, that "here's no place of mercy for thee, the Vengeance of God cannot be dispensed with, thou art not in the *High Commission*, nor before the *Assembly*."[16] Foxe's Marian martyrs had responded to condemnation by predicting that their examiners would someday stand before a greater judge. Overton, and Bunyan four decades later, claimed the writer's privilege of trying their enemies in print, with an obvious delight in showing them stripped of power and subjected to an inexorable process of judgment.

In *The Holy War* the jurors of the liberated Mansoul recall those of Vanity Fair in their vehemence, although these pronounce their verdicts in the name of truth. At the end of the first trial Zeal for God declares "*Cut them off, they have been the plague, and have sought the destruction of Mansoul*" (132). The same jurors condemn the Doubters (Election-doubter, Vocation-doubter, and the rest) in the second trial, like the first presented as a trial for treason that culminates in crucifixion for the accused. The vindictive spirit of the trials extends to the hunting down and hanging of Diabolonians still lurking in the town. Clip-promise, "a notorious villain," is made a public example by being "arraigned and judged to be first set in the Pillory, then to be whipt by all the children and servants in *Mansoul*, and then to be hanged till he was dead" (243). The narrative voice interrupts, in an unusual intrusion, to acknowledge that "Some may wonder at the severity of this mans punishment" and then to insist that because of the great abuse Clip-promise is capable of "all those of his name and life should be served even as he" (243). The felt need to justify such harshness suggests that Bunyan was aware of its apparent excess. He makes a similar gesture of recognizing and dismissing potential criticism in a scene that follows, in which Self-love is taken from custody and "brained" by soldiers of Self-denial. Bunyan tells us that there was some muttering over this action, which amounts to what we would call a lynching, but that Emanuel makes Self-denial "a Lord in *Mansoul*" for his brave act (*HW*, 244). Bunyan seems to defy norms of conventional justice here, as though to demonstrate that God's justice overrides them.

One early critic defended Bunyan by insisting that he was "portraying only the struggles of an elect soul against religious errors and fleshly lusts" in the trial scenes of *The Holy War*,[17] but if this is the most obvious dimension of the allegory it is not the only one. The accused function in the narrative as enemies of God and of the godly community of the elect (in Bunyan's England and in the history of the true church) as well as participants in a psychodrama. The links that Bunyan established between these trials and that of Christian and Faithful reinforce their status as social drama. In *The Holy War* he delighted in showing the tables turned, with persecutors forced to experience a version of their own justice.[18] Now the Diabolonians are described as "outlandish men," as Christian and Faithful were in Vanity Fair. The aristocracy and gentry become the accused rather than the accusers. The hapless attempt of Mr. Lustings to pull rank in the dock, "I am a man of high birth, and have been used to pleasures and pastimes of greatness" (121), suggests the irony of the reversal. By introducing an informer (Diligence) telling how he spied upon a "Diabolonian Conventicle," Bunyan uses his satiric gifts to turn a favorite tactic against the oppressors.[19] Election-doubter's surprising declaration, "If I must die for my Religion . . . I shall die a Martyr" (240), shows him attempting to claim a spiritual victory in the manner of Faithful, but Bunyan presents his stand as a travesty of Faithful's. Election-doubter is a false martyr, condemned by the judge for overthrowing "a great Doctrine of the Gospel" and thus belying the Word.

Christopher Hill, clearly troubled by the violence unleashed in the name of God in *The Holy War* (he observes that Emanuel and Diabolus adopt the same policies, including purges and terror), wonders whether the trial scenes imply that Bunyan endorsed the use of espionage and death sentences against unbelievers in the godly society.[20] I think it more likely that he was indulging a fantasy of a world turned upside down, in which Nonconformists would no longer seem "outlandish" and in which the godly would sit in the place of a Judge Jeffreys or a Justice Kelyng and enact a justice consistent with their understanding of the Word. The trial scenes, along with others representing the punishment of the Diabolonians, show Bunyan's knack for exploiting the ironies of such a reversal. Yet his willingness to invoke violence in the name of God, in scenes that because of their lively realism have a capacity to shock that Bernard's woodenly allegorical ones do not, suggests a desire for a more immediate kind of vengeance than that promised Christian and Hopeful by the Shining Ones: "when he shall sit upon the Throne of Judgment. . . . you shall also have a voice in that Judgment, because they were his and your enemies" (160). Perhaps Bunyan could embody a desire for vengeance in *The Holy War* because he knew there was no chance of seeing it realized.

In focusing on some of Bunyan's more violent imaginings I do not mean to suggest that he was bloodthirsty, or hypocritical in advocating patient suffering and quiet obedience, rather that one should recognize the aspects of his temperament and his religion that give rise to them. Violent assaults of anxiety, or doubt, or temptation prompt violent reactions, expressed allegorically in "judgments" of characters associated with particular threats to spiritual equilibrium. The very violence of the reactions suggests the difficulty of mastering doubt and a tendency to sin. Yet Bunyan was also preoccupied with violence directed against those who suffer for truth's sake, violence seen as the external expression of demonic power, and he often blurs the line between psychological and social orders of being. Whether represented by a heresy trial (as in Vanity Fair) or by giants or by the armies of Diabolus, such external violence calls forth representations of divine vengeance against the enemies of the godly and the demonic force they are seen as embodying. While Bunyan was not as fierce in his expectations of vengeance as some (George Fox, for example, and early Quaker writers who saw themselves as caught up in the Lamb's War which they expected would transform England), he could look back with genuine yearning to the heroic period of the Marian persecution as a time when, as he put it, "Coals of burning Fire still dropped here and there upon the Heads of those that hated God" (*MW*, 13: 427). In his imaginative works he found a variety of ways of anticipating God's response to the "Voice of Blood," which I believe he would have understood as the voice of suffering Christians generally and not just that of those who literally died for their faith. Perhaps his symbolic punishments of those he saw as hating God and persecuting true Christians (Lord Hategood, Giant Grim, Mr. Pityless, and the rest) should be seen as an effort to take divine justice out of the realm of apocalyptic prophecy and make it seem more immediate and credible to an audience unusually vulnerable to a sense of powerlessness; at the same time, he addresses the uncertainties that gnawed at faith by creating an imaginative world where coals of fire still fell from heaven.

NOTES

1. *A Mirrour or Looking Glass for both Saints and Sinners* (1671). See *Badman*, xix–xxvi, for a discussion of the popular tradition of judgment stories.

2. Thomas H. Luxon, *Literal Figures: Puritan Allegory and the Reformation Crisis in Representation* (Chicago: University of Chicago Press, 1995), 171, 181, 176–78.

3. Luxon, *Literal Figures*, 200.

4. Michael Lieb discusses this episode and also the mutilation and execution of the regicides. See *Milton and the Culture of Violence* (Ithaca: Cornell University Press, 1994), 76–79.

5. See John R. Knott, *Discourses of Martyrdom in English Literature, 1563–1694* (Cambridge: Cambridge University Press, 1993), chap. 6. An article by Sid Sondergard that appeared at about the same time focuses on Bunyan's use of imagery of violence to express suffering, particularly that of prison experience, and to authenticate his own spiritual authority as well as demonstrate the need for Christian fortitude. See " 'This Giant Has Wounded Me as Well as Thee': Reading Bunyan's Violence and/as Authority," in *The Witness of Time*, ed. Katherine Z. Keller and Gerald J. Schiffhorst (Pittsburgh: Duquesne University Press, 1993), 218–37.

6. I am indebted to Michael Lieb's discussion of Milton's images of *sparagmos* (e.g., the dismemberment of Orpheus), which he reads as embodying Milton's fears about his poetic identity. See *Milton and the Culture of Violence*, passim. Bunyan's fears have to do primarily with his identity as one of the elect.

7. James Forrest and Roger Sharrock discuss the government campaign to impose new charters upon towns, which generated a sense of crisis, in the introduction to their edition. See *HW*, xx–xxv.

8. See, for example, Lam. 3:10; Hos. 5:14, 13:7–8; Amos 3:8.

9. See Stuart Sim, *Negotiations with Paradox: Narrative Practice and Narrative Form in Bunyan and Defoe* (London: Harvester Wheatsheaf, 1990), 100–101. Sim's general emphasis is on the consequences of predestination and, in his read-

ing of *The Holy War*, on the way Bunyan avoids resolution by leaving Diabolus and some of his followers at large.

10. Richard Greaves, *John Bunyan and English Nonconformity* (London: Hambledon Press, 1993), chap. 10.

11. Cf. Bunyan on the victims of persecution in "Prison Meditations": "They conquer when they thus do fall, / They kill when they do dye" (*MW*, 6: 50).

12. See W. R. Owens, introduction to *MW*, 13: xxvi–xxvii. See also Aileen M. Ross, "*Paradise Regained*: The Development of John Bunyan's Millenarianism," *Bunyan in England and Abroad: Papers Delivered at the John Bunyan Tercentenary Symposium* (Amsterdam, 1988), ed. M. van Os and G. J. Schutte (Amsterdam: Vrije University Press, 1990), 73–89.

13. *A Collection of the Sufferings of the People Called Quakers*, ed. Joseph Besse, 2 vols. (London, 1753), 1: 435.

14. Roger Sharrock relates Bunyan's trial scenes to the personification of virtues and vices in sermons and moralities and compares his use of false naming to instances in Bernard and Overton. See "The Trial of Vices in Puritan Fiction," *Baptist Quarterly* 14 (1951): 3–12.

15. *HW*, xxxvii. The editors cite Gal. 5:24: "And they that are Christ's have crucified the flesh with the affections and lusts." See also Rom. 6:6, Gal. 6:14. Bunyan had a precedent of sorts in the sentence of Old-man in Bernard's *The Isle of Man*, condemned to be taken to the place of execution and there "*be cast off with all thy deeds, and all thy members daily mortified and crucified with all thy lusts*," although Bernard's allegory is so insistent that it is difficult to imagine a literal crucifixion. *The Isle of Man*, 14th ed. (London, 1668), 95.

16. Richard Overton, *The Araignement of Mr. Persecution* (London, 1645), 6, 40.

17. Clarence Eugene Dugdale, "Bunyan's Court Scenes," [Texas] *Studies in English* 5 (1941): 64–78.

18. Dugdale claims that only the Bloodmen, associated with the history of persecution, can be identified with human enemies (the Doubters are for him "abstract enemies of the soul") and notes that Emanuel's captains are charged to capture and not kill them. "Bunyan's Court Scenes," 77.

19. Christopher Hill sees the speech of Diligence as a witty parody of the manner of informers in testifying against Nonconformists. See *A Tinker and a Poor Man: John Bunyan and His Church 1628–1688* (New York: Knopf, 1989), 248.

20. Hill, *A Tinker and a Poor Man*, 249.

Honey from the Lion's Carcass: Bunyan, Allegory, and the Samsonian Moment

Sharon Achinstein

Although John Bunyan broke statutory law by addressing a conventicle in November 1660, critics generally agree he did not advocate active resistance or revolution against the restored Stuart monarchy. Despite the harsh treatment of Nonconformists in Bedford, Bunyan refrained from participating in movements for the overthrow of the state.[1] He disavowed the actions of Thomas Venner and the Fifth Monarchists; moreover, against the Restoration Tory Anglican persecuting regime, he preached patience, endurance, and, as Richard Greaves puts it, an "ethic of suffering."[2] In his long prose tract *Seasonable Counsel: or, Advice to sufferers* (1684) Bunyan commends an ethos of submission in the face of persecution after the model of Jesus, Paul, Daniel, and Jeremiah.

Current consensus holds that though Bunyan's prison works affirm passive resistance to the Uniformity Act, the author, though often radically millenarian, was not a revolutionary or a supporter of uprisings: "Rather than exhorting his readers to overthrow monarchy," Professor Greaves avers, "Bunyan tried to teach them that sovereigns would ultimately embrace Christ, even if they were the last ones to do so.... Bunyan perceived the struggle solely in spiritual terms."[3] Other scholars fill in the chorus; while Bunyan's writings—especially *The Holy War*—touch upon political contexts, the author's attitude toward active political rebellion always subordinates secular to spiritual concerns.[4] In the wake of various political plots against the crown and Church, his words to his congregation were those of consolation under suffering rather than calls for rebellion. Richard Greaves has called our attention to Bunyan's tract *Seasonable Counsel*, in which the author pursued a path of passive disobedience rather than insurrection. Writing in the aftermath of the Popish Plot, and, more particularly, following the exposure of the Rye House conspiracy, Bunyan insisted upon loyalty to earthly powers.[5] Scholars may have retreated from the suggestion of his nineteenth-century editor, George Offor, that Bunyan was a true loyalist and an active supporter of the Stuart regime; but neither was he, according to current consensus, a fire-breathing revolutionary.[6]

Since the scholarship of Christopher Hill and Annabel Patterson, who show how oblique or allegorical writing often served political and not just aesthetic needs, writing under persecution needs more careful reading.[7] Many Nonconformist writers in the Restoration adopted oblique modes of writing in order to evade persecution, as N. H. Keeble has demonstrated. To explain this proliferation of "coded" writing, Keeble offers that, for Nonconformist writers, "Fictional worlds were perhaps safer" than the real one.[8] Restoration England was a persecuting culture, and understanding the political content of its literature, if it is subversive, is very difficult for writing under persecution, especially since religious dissent was the main domestic sore spot of Restoration governments.[9] It is true that political content, and radical political content at that, is often not far from the surface of Bunyan's work; in *The Holy War*, for example, the citizens of Mansoul are repeatedly assaulted by Diabolus and his agents in an allegory about which even the editors admit "it cannot be denied that the struggle for man's soul is seen as emphatically a political transaction." In their magnificent editorial project, the editors supply the local political and historical contexts that Bunyan draws upon in imagining this spiritual fight, so that modern readers might be able to "read between the lines."[10]

Finding local political contexts for Bunyan's writing has been the task of much recent promising scholarship in Bunyan studies; and yet the relationship between fictional writing itself and the political world has been established by reading Bunyan's fictional writings as *romans à clef*: finding that in *The Holy War*, for example, the "Bloodmen" incidents represent the persecution of Nonconformists after the Restoration, or that the shuffling of the government of Mansoul reflects the reforms of Bunyan's local Bedford municipality, the editors pursue a critical presumption that allegorical writing may be matched in a one-to-one correspondence to historical contexts.[11] Likewise, incidents such as the imprisonment, torture, and execution of Faithful in *The Pilgrim's Progress* undoubtedly reflect the current persecution of Nonconformists by the Anglican regime. Seeming to refute Stanley Fish's critique of authorial intention as a guide for interpreting allegory, these kinds of readings presume that Bunyan's allegories provide stable sets of meanings, meanings that are visible once the "key" has unlocked their mystery.[12]

Yet understanding the relation between fictional worlds and the real one is a tricky business, not only because elliptical writing displays a willed resistance to clear univocal interpretations—it would not be safe for the author otherwise—but also because a writer like Bunyan deliberately plays upon his own literariness, seeming to delight in his ironical glosses, his directions to the reader, his biblical allusions, and the layers of allegory and fable that are folded within his texts. In this essay I seek to understand the political meanings of Bunyan's fiction, not by locating precise topical allusions, but by seeking to understand the use of allegory itself as a practice that performs political work. I wish to take Fish's critique of authorial intention seriously, and to ask not only what is "in" the allegory but, more specifically, what does allegory "do"? The argument I pursue here is that fictional writing and reading fictions serve as kinds of resistance.

ALLEGORY AND RESISTANCE

Bunyan loves allegories. They are integral to his spiritual project, and they are central to his mission of educating his readers. So much is nothing new. Stanley Fish has powerfully cast doubt on the whole project of meaning-making in the allegory *Pilgrim's Progress* by focusing on lapses in understanding, those gaps between sign and signifier in which God's mystery is hidden.[13] My own reading, however, places in these gaps the powerful, and multivalent, figure of Samson.

In the opening pages of the preface to *Grace Abounding to the Chief of Sinners*, Bunyan explains that duty compelled him to write a book as a substitute to the preaching that is barred to him by his current situation in prison. In this explanation, Bunyan importantly alludes to the biblical story of Samson: "I have sent you here enclosed a drop of that honey, that I have taken out of the Carcase of a Lyon (Judg. 14. 5, 6, 7, 8). I have eaten thereof my self also, and am much refreshed thereby" (*GA*, 1). The story from Judges teaches that Samson, in an act of heroic strength and bravery, killed a lion in whose carcass he later found a nest of bees making honey. In this allusion, Bunyan's own text *is* the "drop of honey," that holy writing that is a gift from God. And in some sense, Bunyan *is* Samson, who ate and who shared with his family the honey he found in the lion he killed. Both the sweetness and the sharing are the unwitting consequences of his violent act of destruction. In the first meaning, the gift of honey comes unasked for, as a result of heroic struggle. When, however, Bunyan explains what he means here, he includes a parenthetical addition: "(Temptations when we meet them at first, are as the Lyon that roared upon Sampson; but if we overcome them, the next time we see them, we shall find a Nest of Honey within them)" (GA, 1). Now a moral teaching, the story of honey out of the lion's carcass is a lesson in patience, fortitude, and endurance: a story of overcoming an enemy is the story of overcoming temptation.

Living under persecution offers many temptations for the suffering saint. As Bunyan advised in *A Seasonable Counsel*, "They that suffer have other kind of temptations upon this account than other Christians have. The liberty of others while they are in bonds, is a temptation to them. . . . And this temptation, were it not that we have to do with a God that is faithful, would assuredly be a great snare unto them. *But God is faithful, and will not suffer you to be tempted*, as to this, *above what you are able* (1 Cor. 10.13)" (MW, 10: 89). In advising his readers to consider the story of Samson as a story of overcoming temptation, Bunyan writes that there is a reward to come, a "drop of honey." Like the drop of honey, his own writing serves as a taste of such reward. The Samson story thus holds out several possibilities for the Restoration writer, and several points of identification between biblical type and the living writer. Deliverance is possible after suffering and overcoming temptation. The honey is a sign of this grace.

But, significantly, Bunyan adds a third thought on the subject of this "drop" of honey: "The Philistines understand me not" (GA, 1). In the biblical source, the Philistines were unable to solve the riddle of the sweetness: and Samson's strength against them held until he betrayed his secret to his wife, the woman of Timnah, who in turn betrayed the secret to her people. Bunyan's use of the "riddle" of Samson, however, stops the story before the secret is betrayed. Frozen at that point in the narrative, Samson's secret is safe, and the Philistines are not only without knowledge, but also without power over him. The riddle, then, divides Samson from those who do not understand: in the larger allegory, the riddle divides the chosen nation, Israel, from the outsider Philistine nation. Significantly, the Philistines' lack of understanding takes place in the present tense: "The Philistines understand me not." Bunyan is writing allegory here concerning his own potentially hostile Restoration readers. As a model of reading, then, Samson's riddle offers a second meaning, a moment of exclusion of outsiders. Further, the text asks readers not to break their seal of silence, and to act with a resistance in a manner the loose-lipped Samson had not. Interpretation is only possible for those in the know, those chosen by God for the privilege of inclusion in understanding, and those who commit to shared practices of reading.

What are we to make of this Samsonian moment, this recurrent motif in Bunyan's writing, this pointed use of the figure of Samson as a practitioner of allegory? To preview, I suggest that this "moment" signals a moment of interpretive choice, and in that moment, a number of actions occur: readers enact their inclusion in a community of readers; readers momentarily partake in God's Word; and perhaps readers perform a kind of activism, broadly conceived as interpretive power. Reading Bunyan becomes a form of action, a collective identification through shared myths. These aspects of Samsonian writing are present in *The Holy War*, the long prose narrative concerning the fate of the town of Mansoul as it is repeatedly engaged in war with Diabolus and his agents. In a prefatory poem to the reader, Bunyan ends his introduction by taking on the Samson persona:

> Nor do thou go to work without my key
> (In mysteries men soon do lose their way);
> And also turn it right, if thou wouldst know
> My riddle, and wouldst with my heifer plough.
>
> (HW, 5)

The Bible story tells that Samson condemns the Philistine men for encroaching on his own rights as a husband, on discovering that his wife has revealed his secret: "if ye had not ploughed with my heifer, ye had not found out my riddle." Rather than this breaking or betraying, however, Bunyan offers his readers help to understand his own riddle: the assistance of the marginal gloss.

Riddles recur throughout the *Holy War*. Emanuel (the figure for Christ) holds a banquet after which riddles feature as the after-dinner entertainment. "Oh how they were lightned! they saw what they never saw, they could not have thought that such rarities could have been couched in so few and such ordinary words . . . as they were opened, the people did evidently see. . . . Oh they were transported with joy, they were drowned with wonderment, while they saw and understood" (116). But Emanuel also uses riddles to convey his battle tactics to the warriors of Mansoul; they have a difficult job of interpreting his commands. As the gloss puts it, "Captain *Credence* receives that from his Prince which he understandeth not" (217); in *Pilgrim's Progress*, part of the education of Christian in the Interpreter's House is in reading and interpreting riddles as well. Bunyan's final anagram at the end of *Holy War* forces the reader to practice "reading between the lines" to discover the author's name:

> Witness my name, if Anagram'd to thee,
> The Letters make, *Nu hony in a B*.
>
> (251)

This anagram contains Samson's riddle in its act of identifying Bunyan's authorship. Bunyan could not be clearer about his own personal Samsonian commitment.

Bunyan, through allegories, appealed to a community of dissenting readers, seeking to draw them toward spiritual enlightenment. The sign for Bunyan of this method was often Samson and his riddles. Bunyan's hornbook, *A Book for Boys and Girls* (1686), explains the educational mission that undergirds his practice of parabolic writing. Bunyan's prefatory note to the reader, in the model of Paul, admits, however, that the work is addressed not only to children but also to adults, those fools who "by their playthings I would them entice, / To mount their thoughts from what are childish toys" (*MW*, 6: 191, lines 48–49). Bunyan ends this preface defending his double-writing with a Samsonian utterance:

> May I by them [the poems] bring some good thing to pass
> As Sampson, with the Jaw-bone of an Ass
>
> . . . .
>
> I have my end, tho I myself expose
> To scorn; God will have Glory in the close.
>
> (*MW*, 6: 191, lines 93–94, 97–98)

In these lines, Bunyan couples the violence of the deliverer, Samson, with the practice of writing riddles. The Samsonian moment thus accomplishes several tasks. In this moment, Bunyan takes on the mantle of Samson himself by creating riddles that others do not understand, and thus divides those in the know from those who are outsiders. However many gaps there were between representation and reality, Bunyan *believed* these could be bridged by the partnership of humans and God in the effort of readers to understand and become enlightened. In his use of allegory, Bunyan aimed to educate Christians in proper habits of reading so that they could practice proper habits of living.[14] Bunyan's readers were to become active and engaged, bonded to each other and to the writer through these practices. Though Bunyan eschewed active political resistance to civil authorities, he was aware that he offered textual resistance in the form of his literariness.

Samson and Political Resistance

Can we gain insight into Bunyan's political teaching on resistance by attending to his knowledge of the evasiveness of his literary method? Is there such a bright line between interpretive resistance and political resistance, as Bunyan scholarship has drawn? The locus of Bunyan's antiresistance teachings, according to Greaves, is *Seasonable Counsel*. Written in the darkest period for Nonconformists, in the time of the "ultra-Tory" Anglican backlash against the Whig and Nonconformist bid for the exclusion of James from the throne, *Seasonable Counsel* offers that those who wish to remain loyal to God should do so with patience and submit to the suffering brought upon them by secular authority.[15] Active resistance is condemned in the strongest terms: "The Devil, who is the great enemy of the Christians, can send forth such Spirits into the World as shall not only disturb Men, but Nations, Kings, and Kingdoms, in raising divisions, distractions and rebellions" (*MW*, 10: 32). Among the examples against resistance cited here is Absalom, a common allusion in the Restoration period, most recently figured by John Dryden in his brilliant satire against the Earl of Shaftesbury, *Absalom and Achitophel* (1681), which, like *Seasonable Counsel*, was written in the context of the Exclusion crisis. Such an example, along with the figure of Abishai in 1 Samuel 26:7–8, was meant to warn Bunyan's readers that civil response to political oppression was not acceptable; only God would punish evil kings. Bunyan's use of the figure of Absalom, moreover, seems to provide clear evidence that he shared even the Tory Dryden's condemnation of the politics of active resistance. Nonconformists, however, did not all agree upon this point. Dissenters played a major role in plotting against the Stuart regimes, both in the Rye House plot and in support of Monmouth. Bunyan's printer, Francis Smith, was frequently associated with resistance plots, and was a member of the Baptist and Republican Salutation Tavern group, heavily tied to activist London radicalism.[16] Yet Greaves, after sifting evidence of Bunyan's association with radicals, including several Rye House plotters, concludes that "no evidence connects Bunyan with active resistance to the Stuart regime."[17]

In a closer look at the text, we can see that Bunyan's treatment of biblical civil insurrection did not take the form of simple condemnation. In citing Abishai's plans to commit regicide, Bunyan reflects, "Abishai, tho' a good man, would have kill'd the King, and that of conscience to God, and love to his Master. 1 Sam. 26. 7, 8. And had David delivered him up to Saul for his attempt, he had in all likelihood died as a Traitor" (*MW*, 10: 32). David, however, did *not* bring Abishai forward to the king as a traitor; he let the plotter be. A second case is brought forward, that of Peter: "Peter drew his Sword, and would have fought therewith, a thing for which he was blamed of his Master, and bid with a threatening, to put it up again. Mat. 26.52. Besides, Oppression makes a wise man mad; and when a man is mad what evils will he not do?" (*MW*, 10: 32). With these two scenes from the Bible, Bunyan expresses sympathy toward those who are driven to take up arms against persecutors or tyrants. In the first case, Abishai sought to relieve David of Saul's persecution since Saul had repeatedly broken David's trust. And yet David forbids Abishai from killing Saul, thus showing the good of resisting the temptation of violent action. David refused to let Abishai commit the murder when the occasion arose: "Destroy him not: for who can stretch forth his hand against the LORD'S anointed, and be guiltless?" (1 Sam. 26:9). The lesson against killing kings is clear; and yet in his redaction Bunyan seizes not only on this lesson, but also on David's ensuing compassion toward Abishai. Bunyan emphasizes that David did not deliver Abishai up to Saul for the attempt on his life; rather, David continued to rely upon Abishai to help him. David lets the would-be regicide live and flourish. In the second story, Peter is the would-be political activist; this time it is Jesus who prevents him from acting; Peter's impulse is made understandable in Bunyan's interpretation: "oppression makes a wise man mad." There is sympathy here for those who wish to take revenge on their persecutors. Revenge becomes an understandable, if misguided, response to persecution. Bunyan allows that impulses to violent revenge are permissible, although action is not. There might also be a message to the dissenting community concerning the compassionate treatment of rebels.

According to Bunyan, violent action against persecutors was a temptation to be avoided. "Doth not God, oft-times, even take occasions by the hardest of things that come upon us, to visit our Souls with the comforts of his Spirit, to lead us into the glory of his word, and to cause us to savour that love that he has had for us, even from before the world began, till now" (*MW*, 10: 35). Bunyan ends this consoling passage with an italicized allusion, and this time he unites the mysteries of God's grace with the violence that wrought such a conclusion: "*A Nest of Bees and honey did Sampson find, even in the belly of that Lion that roared upon him*"(*MW*, 10: 35). The figure of Samson stands as a figure for the solitary sufferer, the lone believer to whom God will return and for whom God will provide. Bunyan continues in his consolation, "it follows that we do with quietness submit our selves under what God shall do to us by them. . . . I speak now of the men that hurt me as was hinted afore . . . we must pass by those injuries that other men would revenge" (*MW*, 10: 35–36).

Samson is a curious figure to praise for resisting temptation: other figures in the Bible might serve as better models for patient suffering. Samson is one specially chosen by God as an instrument through which deliverance will come, and he figures later in the tract again as an example of God's promise not to depart from the suffering Israel (*MW*, 10: 92). However, seventeenth-century readers could not forget that Samson was a bloody warrior, the figure through whom God worked violent revenge upon the enemies of Israel. What are we to make of these other resonances heard in the figure of Samson?

THE RESTORATION SAMSON

For radical Protestants from the beginning to the end of the seventeenth century, Samson served as a token of God's providential workings, and also, more powerfully, as a symbol of physical strength. During the Interregnum, the figure of Samson was adopted as a symbol for the Good Old Cause; even one of Cromwell's warships was named *Samson*, unfortunately sunk by the Dutch in 1653. Samson was an emblem for the New Model Army. In its prayerbook he is touted as the exemplary soldier doing the Lord's battles. Samson was frequently alluded to in Cromwell's circle, and was used by radicals such as Lilburne as a model to imitate.[18] Milton's *Areopagitica* likens the reforming nation of England to the figure of Samson, as Milton imagines "a noble and puissant Nation rousing herself like a strong man after sleep, and shaking her invincible locks."[19] Defending violent resistance in *Killing Noe Murder*, Edward Sexby asked, "Now that which was lawful for *Samson* to do against many Oppressours, why is it unlawful for us to do against one? Are our Injuries less?"[20] Samson was a figure in Revolutionary England who raised the question of violence, specifically the question of political resistance to secular authority.

In the Restoration, the figure of the iconoclastic Samson took on a powerful resonance, both as a frightening specter of the violence of the civil war years, and as a threat to stable political order. Andrew Marvell glossed the 1674 edition of Milton's *Paradise Lost* with an introductory poem, acknowledging the fear that Milton might still be attached to the works of violence he had defended in his regicidal years. Marvell likened Milton to Samson, "So *Sampson* grop'd the Temple's Posts in spite." Milton's poem *Samson Agonistes* has been read as a brutally revolutionary fantasy.[21] Bunyan himself imagined Samson along these lines. Evoking the power and violence of Samson in his *Holy War*, the "true lovers of the town of Mansoul" rise up against the plotting Diabolonians in their midst, "like so many *Sampsons*, they shake themselves, and come together to consult and contrive how to defeat those bold and hellish contrivances" (*HW*, 82).

Bunyan's apocalyptic tract *Of Antichrist, and His Ruine* offers a Samsonian moment that helps us see how the figure of Samson is a fault-line on which we can see the interworkings of the literal and the figurative realms of being. In this account, Bunyan holds that the reign of the Antichrist is nearing an end, a fact that can be "read" by observing signs in the world. But rather than the typical "Annus Mirabilis" signs, where bad weather, road accidents, and the like are seen as auguries of God's wrath, Bunyan holds that the world needs to be read backwards.[22] In the case cited below, the apparent victory of the forces of evil is a sign of their spiritual emptiness, and of their imminent ruin. Drawing upon Revelation 11:10, Bunyan reads that joy and merriment are those signs that Antichrist's ruin is to come very soon:

> When the Philistines had, as they thought, for ever overcome Samson, that Nazarite of God, how joyful were they of the victory! . . . Poor Samson! While thou haddest thy Locks, thy Liberty, and thine Eyes, thou didst shake the Pillar that did bear up their Kingdom! But now they have conquered thee, how great is their Joy! How Great is their Joy, and how Near their Downfall! This therefore is a joy that is like that we have like under Consideration, to wit, the Joy of them that dwell on the Earth; for that the Witnesses that did bear up the Name of God in the world, were overcome and killed! (*MW*, 13: 479)

By these words, Bunyan reverses the standard meaning of joy, and the logic of reversal holds that Samson, once free, and now in chains, will yet be free again.[23] The way of reading joy is to invert the conventional providential interpretation that victory is a sign of God's favor. Samson here stands for all those witnesses who suffered under the reign of Antichrist; his liberation is to be a reversal of literal for spiritual truth. Only by "reading between the lines," by reversing the typical one-to-one correspondence between literal and figural, can one grasp the true picture. Samson, read in a Samsonic manner, is a figure of liberation, not one of degradation.

Samson the biblical avenger also appears in Bunyan's mild treatise *A Seasonable Counsel*, not in the list of biblical sufferers to be imitated, but toward the end of the writing as a consoling hope of God's deliverance: "For as surely as ever the spirit of God moved *Sampson* at times in the Camp of *Dan*, when he lay against the *Philistines*; so will the spirit of God move in, and upon thee to comfort and to strengthen thee, whilst thou sufferest for his name in the World" (*MW*, 10: 92). This is the Samson, not impotent in Gaza, but empowered as God's chosen warrior and the Danite leader of the Israelite nation.

We have two Samsons, then: the "riddling" Samson, and the promised violent deliverer. Did Bunyan counsel patience because he really believed in patience, or did he counsel patience because his hands were tied by censorship and persecution? The Samsonian moments open up a third alternative. Perhaps learning to read Samson's riddles was to give readers an experience of active resistance through reading, to signal their commitment, not to the literal, physical world filled with persecution and suffering, but to the world of the spirit. Through reading allegorically, readers signal their commitment to a collective, and to God's work in the meantime by their actions of reading and interpreting. As Bunyan wrote in *Seasonable Counsel*, in the passage examined above that cited the experience of Samson, "Doth not God, oft-times, even take occasions by the hardest of things that come upon us, to visit our Souls with the comforts of his Spirit, to lead us into the glory of his word, and to cause us to savour that love that he has had for us, even from before the world began, till now" (*MW*, 10: 35). With that "now," we see that perhaps grace is a local possibility, perhaps through violence, as reading perhaps turns out to be a weapon of warfare. The Restoration may have led to a turning inward of violent hopes, but the figure of Bunyan's double, Samson, heralds both the deliverer *and* the interpreter. By coupling interpretation and deliverance Bunyan offers a community of readers a mode of action, perhaps itself an allegory for revelation mirroring the arrival of God's deliverance through violence.

Notes

This paper was first presented at the Inaugural Conference of the International Bunyan Society, held in Banff, Alberta, in 1995. I wish to thank the organizers of this conference for including this paper, and the participants for their helpful suggestions.

1. The sufferings of the Bedford congregation, and the ethic of suffering, are

presented in *A True and Impartial narrative of some illegal and arbitrary proceedings* (1670).

2. Richard L. Greaves, *John Bunyan and English Nonconformity* (London: Hambleton Press, 1992), 177–83; and on Bunyan's commitment to liberty of conscience, see id., " 'Let Truth be Free': John Bunyan and the Restoration Crisis of 1667–1673," *Albion* 28, 4 (1996): 587–605.

3. Richard L. Greaves, "Conscience, Liberty, and the Spirit: Bunyan and Nonconformity," in *John Bunyan: Conventicle and Parnassus Tercentenary Essays*, ed. N. H. Keeble (Oxford: Clarendon Press, 1988), 29. See also id., *Bunyan and Nonconformity*, chap. 10.

4. Roger Sharrock and James F. Forrest see Bunyan's own sufferings as typical of Nonconformists at this time, and *The Holy War* as an allegory for that great period of persecution. See *HW*, ix–xxxix. For the political contexts of Bunyan's writing, see B. R. White, "John Bunyan and the Context of Persecution," in *John Bunyan and His England, 1628–88*, ed. Anne Laurence, W. R. Owens, and Stuart Sim (London: Hambledon Press, 1990), 51–62.

5. Greaves, *Bunyan and Nonconformity*, 115–17; 170–83.

6. See Greaves, *Bunyan and Nonconformity*, 103, 102–26, for a discussion of this topic. Christopher Hill suggests that armed resistance is implicit in Bunyan's millenarian writing: "He did not say that this government must be overthrown, but the conclusion was inescapable." See *Tinker and Poor Man*, 153.

7. Christopher Hill, "Censorship and English Literature," in *Writing and Revolution in 17th Century England* (Amherst: University of Massachusetts, 1985), 32–72. Annabel Patterson, *Censorship and Interpretation: The Conditions of Writing and Reading in Early Modern England* (Madison: University of Wisconsin Press, 1990), 24–48; and id., *Reading between the Lines* (Madison: University of Wisconsin Press, 1993), 7.

8. See N. H. Keeble, *The Literary Culture of Nonconformity in Late Seventeenth-Century England* (Athens: University of Georgia Press, 1987), 119, 110–20, for Nonconformist responses to censorship.

9. See Nicholas Tyacke, "The 'Rise of Puritanism' and the Legalizing of Dissent, 1571–1719," in *From Persecution to Toleration: The Glorious Revolution and Religion in England* ed. Ole Peter Grell, Jonathan I. Israel, and Nicholas Tyacke (Oxford: Clarendon Press, 1991), 17–49; Gordon Schochet, "From 'Persecution' to 'Toleration,' " in *Liberty Secured? Britain before and after 1688*, ed. J. R. Jones (Stanford: Stanford University Press, 1992), 122–57; John Spurr, *The Restoration Church of England, 1646–1689* (New Haven: Yale University Press, 1991); Tim Harris, "Introduction: Revising the Restoration," in *The Politics of Religion in Restoration England*, ed. Tim Harris, Paul Seaward, and Mark Goldie (Oxford: Basil Blackwell, 1990), 10; Richard L. Greaves, *Deliver Us from Evil: The Radical Underground in Britain, 1660–1663* (New York: Oxford University Press, 1986); and id., *Enemies under his Feet: Radicals and Nonconformists in Britain, 1664–1677* (Stanford: Stanford University Press, 1990).

10. *The Holy War*, xx.

11. *HW*, xxxiii–xxxiv; E. P. Thompson, *The Making of the English Working Class* (New York: Vintage, 1966), 34–36.

12. Stanley E. Fish, "Progress in *The Pilgrim's Progress*," in *Self-Consuming Artifacts: The Experience of Seventeenth-Century Literature* (Berkeley, Los Angeles, and London: University of California Press, 1972).

13. Thomas H. Luxon, in *Literal Figures: Puritan Allegory and the Reformation Crisis in Representation* (Chicago: University of Chicago Press, 1995), 143,

149, brilliantly explores the ways that Bunyan's allegory works to enact the mystery of the soul's contact with God's word. The shuttling between the literal and the figural is the key for Paul Salzman, *English Prose Fiction, 1558–1700* (Oxford: Clarendon Press, 1985), 246, who links Bunyan with earlier literary traditions.

14. Vincent Newey has seen the progress of *Grace Abounding* as a progress specifically in reading, in " 'With the eyes of my understanding': Bunyan, Experience, and Acts of Interpretation," in *John Bunyan: Conventicle and Parnassus Tercentenary Essays*, ed. N. H. Keeble (Oxford: Clarendon Press, 1985), 189–216.

15. Spurr, *The Restoration Church*, 85–87; Keeble, *Literary Culture*, 61; and Gary S. De Krey, "London Radicals and Revolutionary Politics, 1675–1683," in *The Politics of Religion in Restoration England*, ed. Tim Harris, Paul Seaward, and Mark Goldie (Oxford: Basil Blackwell, 1990), 133–62.

16. De Krey, "London Radicals," 142.

17. Greaves, *Enemies under His Feet*, chap. 6; and id., *John Bunyan* (Abingdon, Berkshire: Sutton Courtenay Press, 1969), 17, 117, 167. Bunyan certainly traveled in resisting company; also associating with Owen and Griffith, accused of complicity in the Monmouth rebellion.

18. John Lilburne, *The Resolved Man's Resolution* (London, 1647); see Joseph Wittreich, *Interpreting Samson Agonistes* (Princeton: Princeton University Press, 1986), 193–238.

19. *Areopagitica*, in *Complete Prose Works of John Milton*, vol. 2, ed. Ernest Sirluck (New Haven: Yale University Press, 1959), 558; for another identification between England and Samson, see id., vol. 1, ed. D. M. Wolfe 858–59.

20. Edward Sexby, *Killing Noe Murder* (1659), 9, cited in Wittreich, *Interpreting Samson Agonistes*, 213.

21. Jackie DiSalvo, " 'The Lord's Battels': *Samson Agonistes* and the Puritan Revolution," *Milton Studies* 4 (1972): 39–62; see also my "*Samson Agonistes* and the Drama of Dissent," *Milton Studies* 33 (1996).

22. For this genre of Nonconformist writing, see, for example, *Mirabilis Annus, or the year of Prodigies* (1661), where the anonymous authors note that "accidents of this kind do portend the futurition or manifestation of some things as yet not existent or not known, which usualy carry in them some kind of agreement and assiumulation to the Prodigies themselves" (A3).

23. Laura L. Knoppers, *Historicizing Milton: Spectacle, Power and Poetry in Restoration England* (Athens: University of Georgia Press, 1994), 67–78, on the royalist politics of "joy" in Restoration England.

John Bunyan and English Millenarianism

W. R. OWENS

IN A SERMON PREACHED IN THE EARLY 1640S, JUST AS CIVIL WAR WAS breaking out in England, the Independent divine Thomas Goodwin revealed to his audience that he had been a millenarian for the past twenty years. His belief in a literal earthly millennium when the true church would triumph over its enemies and reign in glory with Christ for a thousand years had developed, he said, under the influence of Tempest Wood, a Lincolnshire vicar and close student of the Book of Revelation, whom Goodwin described as the first English millenarian.[1]

We shall hardly be likely to agree with Goodwin that Tempest Wood actually was the first English millenarian, for the origins of millenarianism go back to the early church fathers, and it had flourished in various forms right through the Middle Ages.[2] Goodwin was no doubt thinking of *Protestant* millenarianism, which is what I shall be concentrating on in this essay, and what is striking is his sense that this was a recent and rather unorthodox belief in early seventeenth-century England. Thanks to a number of valuable studies published in the past thirty years or so, we now know a great deal about the emergence and development of millenarianism in English Protestant thought.[3] It is clear, for example, that it was not until the seventeenth century that millenarianism in the sense of a belief in a *future* millennium emerged. Although there was an intensely apocalyptic strain in the sixteenth-century Protestant outlook, this did not include millenarianism. The early reformers believed they were living in the last days during which the long struggle between the true church and its great enemy, the Roman Antichrist, was approaching its climax. Antichrist would be overthrown, Christ would return for the Last Judgment, and the world would be dissolved. There was no expectation here of a spectacular overthrow of the existing social and political order which would usher in a thousand years of peace and glory for the church on earth before the second coming and the end of the world. On the contrary, the early English reformers agreed with their European counterparts in condemning millenarianism as a dangerous heresy which could easily be used as justification for moral anarchism and social revolution. In fact, rejection of the doctrine of a literal future millennium had been the official policy of the Christian Church ever since Augustine had denounced it in his *City of God*.[4] If evidence was needed to demonstrate the threat posed by millenarianism, the anarchistic fervor unleashed in the Anabaptist uprising in Munster in 1534 provided it.[5]

The story of how such an alarming doctrine nevertheless took hold, and even became respectable in seventeenth-century England, is familiar enough to students of the period. According to one scholar, the extent of acceptance of millenarianism by the middle of the century may be gauged by the fact that over 70 percent of all clergymen who published three or more works between 1640 and 1653 can be identified as millenarians.[6] Among the key figures in bringing about this change in English Protestant eschatology were the Puritan clergyman Thomas Brightman (1562–1607), whose most important work, *A Revelation of the Revelation*, was first published in English in 1615; the German Calvinist scholar and encyclopedist Johann Heinrich Alsted (1588–1638), whose exposition of the twentieth chapter of Revelation was first published in 1627 and translated into English in 1643 as *The Beloved City*; and, most influential of all in England, the distinguished Cambridge biblical scholar Joseph Mede (1586–1638), whose celebrated work *Clavis Apocalyptica* was first published in Latin in 1627, and then in a second, revised edition in 1632, before finally being translated into English in 1643 and published as *The Key of the Revelation*.

The labors of exegetes such as these three served to persuade many—perhaps even a majority of—English Protestants in the mid-seventeenth century that, despite the opposition of St. Augustine and the lack of enthusiasm of the early reformers, the account in Revelation 20 of a thousand-year period when the saints would reign with Christ on earth and Satan would be bound in the bottomless pit must be taken literally. This happy period was certain to come about in the future, perhaps even in the near future. Events both within England and on the Continent seemed to chime unmistakably with apocalyptic prophecies. Joseph Mede, for example, took the account of the pouring out of the seven vials of wrath in Revelation 16 to refer to the gradual stages of the destruction of the Roman Antichrist, after which the millennium would commence. According to this interpretation, the pouring out of the first three vials had already taken place. The first was when the Waldensians and Hussites began to renounce the authority of the Pope; the second when the preaching of reformers like Luther led to "whole Provinces, Dioceses, Kingdoms, Nations, and Cities" breaking away from Rome; the third was the enactment, particularly in England under Elizabeth, of laws against Roman Catholicism. The fourth vial, Mede believed, was being poured out at the time he was writing: he predicted that the Protestant champion Gustavus Adolphus would shortly seize the German Empire and so remove it from the domination of Rome. The fifth vial would be the destruction of Rome itself; the sixth the conversion of the Jews; and the seventh would be the final overthrow of Satan, which would clear the way for the millennium.[7] Mede was quite aware that in placing the fall of Antichrist and the commencement of the millennium in the near future he was making a radical break with earlier Protestant thought.

With the collapse of censorship at the beginning of the civil war, the ideas of Brightman, Alsted, Mede, and other commentators began to circulate freely in England. Millenarian themes became a favorite with Puritan preachers and such ideas spread quickly among parliamentarian supporters in all sections of society. Henry Wilkinson, preaching before the House of Commons in 1643, informed the House that it was "general talk . . . among the domesticks . . . that Christ their king is comming to take possession of his Throne."[8] The events of the 1640s, culminating in the execution of Charles I, intensified millenarian excitement. When the royalist clergyman Edward Symmons questioned a group of parliamentarian prisoners, they told him that they had taken up arms "against Antichrist and Popery," because, they said, " 'tis prophesied in the Revelation, that the Whore of Babylon shall be destroyed with fire and sword, and what doe you know, but this is the time of her ruine, and that we are the men that must help to pull her down." Symmons tried to persuade them that Antichrist was "at Rome, and not here in England," but they remained convinced that "all the true godly Divines in England . . . were of their opinion."[9] A paper published by soldiers and junior officers of the parliamentary army sent to Scotland in 1650 explained to the Scots that Charles's death was essential because it was clear that he was "one of the ten horns of the Beast" spoken of in Revelation.[10]

The 1640s and early 1650s, however, became the high-water mark of the wave of millenarianism in England. Many socially conservative commentators began to warn that millenarian hopes, if taken too literally, could have dangerous political consequences.[11] Their warnings seemed to many to be borne out by the activities of a group of extreme millenarians known to contemporaries as the Fifth Monarchy Men. The concept of the Fifth Monarchy was widely discussed well before the seventeenth century. The vision in Daniel 7 of the rise and fall of four great kingdoms which would be succeeded by a fifth and everlasting one was generally interpreted as referring to the empires of Babylon, Assyria, Greece, and Rome, and in the seventeenth century the last was also taken to include the Holy Roman Empire and the Papacy. As Bernard Capp has shown in his study of the group, Fifth Monarchists differed from other millenarians in seventeenth-century England chiefly in the willingness of some (though not all) of their leaders to contemplate the use of physical violence in preparing the way for the millennial Fifth Monarchy under King Jesus, and in their greater readiness to depict in some detail the political, social, and economic structure of society during the millennium. In 1657, exasperated by lack of progress in this direction, a small group of Fifth Monarchists attempted an armed coup against Cromwell who in their eyes had succeeded Charles as the Beast.[12]

Mention of the Fifth Monarchists brings us to Bunyan and his place within English millenarianism. Bunyan had become an active preacher and writer during the 1650s when the influence of the Fifth Monarchy movement was at its height. Many of Bunyan's acquaintances were Fifth Monarchist supporters or sympathizers.[13] In an important article, Richard Greaves offers convincing evidence confirming what earlier scholars such as William York Tindall had suggested, namely, that Bunyan himself was at one time drawn to the ideas of the Fifth Monarchy Men. Greaves quotes from Bunyan's *The Advocateship of Jesus Christ*, a work published just before his death in 1688, in which Bunyan admitted that "I did use to be much taken with one Sect of Christians, for that it was usually their way, when they made mention of the Name of *Jesus*, to call him, *The blessed King of Glory*." As Greaves notes, this can only refer to the Fifth Monarchists.[14]

The fact is of considerable significance. Greaves carefully explores other evidence suggesting that Bunyan's involvement with Fifth Monarchism may have been deeper and longer lasting than his comment in 1688 may suggest. Nevertheless it is difficult to draw very firm conclusions. There was in fact, as Bernard Capp has demonstrated in compelling detail, a wide spectrum of different opinions among Fifth Monarchists about the timing and nature of the coming millennium, and whether or when it was justified to resort to physical force to bring it about. Capp further argues that during the 1670s the movement split between a majority who adopted a "quietist" millenarianism, and a minority who became ever more deeply involved in plotting and violence.[15] Whatever the full extent of his involvement with the "Sect" may have been, Bunyan consistently refused to be drawn into attempts to calculate the dates when apocalyptic events would occur, and repudiated the use of carnal weapons in establishing Christ's kingdom.

An important statement of his position on the use of physical force came in the wake of a significant uprising of Fifth Monarchists which took place in January 1661, when Thomas Venner led a doomed attempt to overthrow the restored Charles II and make way for the return of King Jesus.[16] Bunyan was in Bedford gaol when the revolt occurred, and like most other dissenters, particularly Baptist leaders, he condemned Venner's resort to arms. This did not mean, however, that he renounced his own millenarian hopes. On the contrary, in 1665, while he was still in prison, Bunyan composed and published one of his most important millenarian works, *The Holy City*. This took the form of a lengthy and detailed exposition of the description of the New Jerusalem in Revelation 21. Bunyan's imagination was stirred as he contemplated the glory of the coming millennium and the impending relief of the persecuted saints:

> Never was fair weather after foul, nor warm weather after cold, nor a sweet and beautiful Spring after a heavy and niping and terrible Winter, so comfortable, sweet, desirable and welcome to the poor Birds and Beasts of the field, as this day will be to the Church of God. . . . Now also will all the pretty *Robins*, and little Birds in the Lords Field, most sweetly send forth their pleasant Notes, and all the Flowers and Herbs of his Garden spring. . . . You know how pleasant this is . . . not onely to Birds and Beasts, but men; especially it is pleasant to such men that have for several years been held in the Chains of affliction: it must needs therefore be most pleasant and desirable to the afflicted Church of Christ, who hath lain now in the Dungeon of Antichrist for above a thousand years: But Lord, how will this Lady, when she gets her liberty, and when she is returned to her own City, how will she then take pleasure in the warm and spangling Beams of thy shining Grace! . . . Blessed is he whose lot it will be to see this holy City descending and lighting upon the place that shall be prepared for her situation and rest! Then will be a Golden World; Wickedness shall then be ashamed, especially that which persecutes the Church: Holiness, Goodness, and Truth, shall then with great boldness, countenance, and reverence, walk upon the face of *all the Earth*. . . . 'Twil be then alwayes Summer, alwayes Sunshine, alwayes pleasant, green, fruitfull, and beautiful to the Sons of God.[17]

This glowing and evocative description of life during the millennium strongly recalls Bunyan's depiction of the Delectable Mountains in *The Pilgrim's Progress*:

> behold at a great distance he [Christian] saw a most pleasant Mountainous Country, beautified with Woods, Vinyards, Fruits of all sorts; Flowers also, with springs and Fountains, very delectable to behold. Then he asked the name of the Countrey, they said it was *Immanuels Land*: and it is as common, said they, as this *Hill* is to, and for all the Pilgrims. And when thou comest there, from thence, thou maist see to the Gate of the Cælestial City, as the Shepherds that live there will make appear. (*PP*, 55)

Although not primarily a millenarian work, it is likely that Bunyan meant the reader of his allegory to interpret the Delectable Mountains as representing the millennium. It is significant that the mountains are referred to as "Immanuel's Land," Emmanuel being a favorite Fifth Monarchist name for Christ. A further, intriguing link with Fifth Monarchist thinking is that Bunyan here envisages the millennium as bringing about a radical transformation of the existing social and political order, with land being held in common, for the use and enjoyment of all the pilgrims. It was frequently alleged by their opponents that Fifth Monarchists advocated the common ownership of land and property, and although, as Bernard Capp shows, they may not have gone quite this far, it is certainly true that many did put forward radical plans for the redistribution of land and wealth.[18] Bunyan was surely aware of the resonances of such a description of the millennium for contemporary readers.

Bunyan's vision in *The Holy City* of a life of bliss during the millennium has much in common with other millenarian works produced in the seventeenth century, but the specific characteristics of his thought are worth noting. For instance, he is explicitly post-millennialist since he sees Christ's return in judgment as an event which would follow after the millennium.[19] The alternative, pre-millennialist position, in which Christ returns in person to set up his millennial kingdom and either rules with the saints for the entire thousand years or returns to heaven until the thousand years were past, was held by some, but by no means all, Fifth Monarchists.[20] Bunyan, in contrast, envisages the establishment of the New Jerusalem, not as a dramatic, supernatural intervention, but as a result of the efforts of the saints themselves. The process is a gradual one, and has indeed been ongoing since the start of the

Reformation. Each generation of builders is better equipped than the last:

> What Light, and with what clearness do the Saints in this day see the things pertaining to the Kingdom of God, beyond what the holy and goodly Martyrs and Saints did in the days that were before us, *Hus, Bilny, Ridly, Hooper, Cranmer*, with their Brethren, if they were now in the world, would cry out & say, *Our light and knowledge of the Word of the Testament of Christ, was much inferior to the Light that at this day is broken forth, and that will yet daily, in despite of Men and Devils, display its Rayes and Beams amongst the sons of men!* (MW, 3: 154)

When the New Jerusalem is finally built, all disputes among the saints will cease; labels such as Quaker, Presbyterian, Independent, and Anabaptist will disappear; all matters of doctrine and church government will be resolved by reference to the Bible alone (*MW*, 3: 115, 120). There will be a progressive enlargement of spiritual understanding, though complete perfection will not be achieved until after Christ's return (*MW*, 3: 154, 161). Multitudes of Jews and Gentiles will be converted and brought into the church during the millennium (*MW*, 3: 163–65). All persecution will cease: the beauty, power, and glory of the church will be such that the kings and rulers of the earth will either freely join with or be subjected to her (*MW*, 3: 166–69). The glory and honor of the church will, however, be spiritual, not carnal; Bunyan is severe with those, among them many Fifth Monarchists, who look for material benefits in the millennium, dismissing such rewards as "a little outward *trumpery*" (*MW*, 3: 173).

It is no coincidence that *The Holy City* was published by Bunyan in 1665. The following year, 1666, with its association with the mysterious number of the Beast in Revelation 13:18, had long been regarded as the momentous year that would see the destruction of Antichrist and the beginning of the millennium.[21] Bunyan, unlike many millenarians, avoided setting specific dates, but the whole tone of *The Holy City* suggests that the events he is describing were imminent: "the time of the return of the Saints to build the ruinous City is near, yea, very near" (*MW*, 3: 92).

The millennium, of course, did not begin in 1666, and I want to turn now to consider some of the ways in which millenarian thinking developed during the remainder of the seventeenth century, and Bunyan's place within that development. After the Restoration many jeered at disappointed believers in a millennium.[22] There was also much hostility to the kind of political activism associated with

Fifth Monarchism. Merely to be described as a Fifth Monarchist could bring serious consequences. To cite just one case: authorship of a book for children which contained some mildly millenarian sentiments was enough to have the Baptist minister Benjamin Keach condemned by the Lord Chief Justice Sir Robert Hyde as a dangerous Fifth Monarchist, put twice in the pillory, fined twenty pounds, imprisoned until sureties for good behavior could be found, and all copies of his book burned by the public hangman.[23]

Some historians have argued that, for these and a variety of other reasons, there was a sharp decline in millenarian thinking after the Restoration,[24] but in fact—and this is partly the point of my argument—this seems not to have been the case. Nor, indeed, was millenarianism in this period confined to a few persecuted dissenters like Bunyan. On the contrary, millenarian beliefs were deeply significant in the thinking of some of the most prominent intellectual figures of the latter half of the seventeenth century, including Robert Boyle, Thomas Burnet, Henry More, Sir Isaac Newton, John Evelyn, and a number of Latitudinarian bishops.[25] We may take Thomas Burnet as an example. In her studies of his writings, Margaret Jacob has shown how Burnet, in his celebrated work *A Sacred Theory of the Earth*, brought together scientific analysis and millenarian exegesis. Significantly, however, the more explicitly millenarian sentiments are to be found in the Latin edition of 1689. When an English translation was published the following year, after the Glorious Revolution, Burnet toned down or omitted altogether some of the more markedly millenarian passages.[26] These changes in Burnet's text remind us that, in the seventeenth century, millenarianism was not simply theological: it was inescapably political. Millenarianism was not dying out in the latter half of the century; instead, efforts were being made to divest it of its seditious flavor and to rehabilitate it in the eyes of a restored Anglican church and monarchy. This motivation is clear in the writings of Anglicans like Richard Hayter and Henry More. Hayter produced a lengthy study of the Book of Revelation in 1675, in order, he said, to dispel the gross misinterpretations of Scripture that abounded and that had led to such fatal consequences in the recent past: "a great in-let to our late Civil Wars, hath been the misinterpretation of the Revelation."[27]

The Cambridge Platonist Henry More likewise believed that it was essential for reasonable and intelligent men to work out an agreed interpretation of the apocalyptic Scriptures. The task was all the more urgent, More considered, because of what he regarded as the "wild Applications Enthusiasts make of the Ten-horned

Beast, and the Whore of Babylon, phansying in their mad mistaken zeal every legitimate Magistrate that Beast, and every well-ordered Church that Whore."[28] More defended the work of earlier millenarian scholars, especially Joseph Mede, and compiled an elaborate "Alphabet of Prophetick Iconisms" to help him determine with certainty

> whether those Comminations that threaten destruction to the Fourth Beast and the Whore . . . do primarily signify any bloudy or boisterous destruction, (such as the keen Fifth-Monarchy-men or any other Enthusiasts are over-forward to imagine;) or whether the Mystery of God may not rather be accomplished in such an orderly Reformation as was made by the Sovereign Power of England in King Edward and Queen Elizabeth's time.[29]

More looked forward to the destruction of Antichrist and the commencement of the millennium as confidently as any sectary, but his conservative Anglican millenarianism assigned to the established English church a central role in the unification of European Protestantism. Such a political unification would fulfill the work begun at the Reformation by bringing about the ultimate defeat of the Roman Antichrist and the Catholic powers in Europe, thus opening the way for the return of Christ and the inauguration of the millennium.

As more research is done on this subject it is becoming clear that in the Restoration period, millenarianism had lost little of its attraction as a way of interpreting events and imagining the future.[30] It is, of course, easy to poke fun at some of the more eccentric exponents of the doctrine. Two of these were John Mason and Thomas Beverley. Mason, who had a history of mental illness, had a vision in 1694 in which Christ revealed that the New Jerusalem was to be set up in Mason's own parish at Water Stratford in Buckinghamshire. Hundreds of enthusiastic believers gathered in the village as a result, to the alarm and fury of local landowners.[31] Beverley was one of the most prolific millenarians of the century. In a series of works published in the 1680s and 1690s, he predicted that the resurrection of the two witnesses spoken of in Revelation 11 would be completed in August 1697. Following this, preparations would be made for the return of Christ and the commencement of the millennium in 1772.[32] Beverley's confidence and persistence earned him a crushing rebuke from Richard Baxter, who thought Beverley's exposition to be "a meer mistake from the Beginning almost to the End . . . and how you will be able to bear it when providence and experience have confuted you in 1697 I know not."[33] Needless to say, Beverley found a way to bear it when August 1697 failed to confirm the accuracy of his forecasts. He admitted to "great disappointment," but after re-checking his figures, and with the aid of a message direct from God one night while he was staying at the home of "an Elect Lady, near Salisbury," Beverley discovered that, though his original calculations were quite correct, "there is by a curious Artifice of Prophecy, a Reserve of 3 Years and a half, reaching to 1700."[34]

Mason and Beverley are easily caricatured as types of the eccentric millenarian, but we should not see them as representative, or as evidence that millenarianism had completely lost intellectual credibility in the late seventeenth century. Many sober and intelligent people remained convinced that, interpreted rightly, the Bible did provide an account of human history that included the promise of a millennium on earth. The political excitement surrounding the Popish Plot and the Exclusion Crisis in the early 1680s, and the subsequent removal of James II and enthronement of William and Mary, together with the increasing persecution of Huguenots in France during the same period, all served to intensify millenarian speculation. John Evelyn recorded in his diary a conversation between William Lloyd, Bishop of St. Asaph, and Archbishop Sancroft, in which they discussed the merits of Joseph Mede's system of interpretation, and agreed that events on the Continent were evidence of the imminent destruction of Antichrist.[35] Similarly, many Dissenters held fast to their millenarian convictions. Hanserd Knollys, Edward Bagshaw, William Sherwin, Henry Danvers, Christopher Ness, and Benjamin Keach, to name just a few, all continued to write and publish fervently millenarian works.[36] Bunyan, then, was by no means unusual or alone in returning to the theme in the 1680s, though his most explicitly and sustainedly millenarian work of this period, entitled *Of Antichrist, and His Ruine*, was not published until 1692, four years after his death.[37]

Of Antichrist, and His Ruine makes an instructive contrast with Bunyan's earlier millenarian treatise, *The Holy City*. There, as we have seen, Bunyan presented an inspiring vision of the glory of the church during the shortly to be expected millennium. The later work, though betraying no doubt but that Antichrist would be destroyed to make way for the promised millennium, is one of Bunyan's most somber in tone, and bears many marks of having been written during a period of intense persecution. There is little here by way of description of life during the millennium: instead, much of the emphasis is on the signs by which the saints can tell that the destruction of Antichrist is under way. Bunyan rehearses the familiar Protestant arguments identifying Rome as the Antichrist, pointing to such features as Rome's blasphemy against the Holy Ghost in setting up a church structure contrary to that laid down in the Scriptures; attempts to deceive the faithful by false miracles and lying, wicked priests; cruel persecution of the saints as evidenced by the massacres in France, Ireland, and Piedmont; interference in political affairs, setting kings against the saints just as the Jewish synagogue used Pilate to condemn Christ; covetousness and pursuit of material wealth; and obstruction of the establishment of Christ's kingdom on earth (*MW*, 13: 489–99).

Although Bunyan, as I have said, is in no doubt that Antichrist will be brought down, he significantly places much less emphasis now on the role of the saints in bringing this about. Now it seems that God will employ *kings* to accomplish his judgment on the Great Whore.[38] In the meantime, the saints may have to undergo a period of even more intense persecution than anything seen heretofore. According to Bunyan's interpretation, the slaying of the witnesses has yet to take place; and he regards this as a metaphorical representation of an even more ferocious persecution than the saints have yet had to face, one during which the true church will be almost entirely extinguished from the face of the earth. This final, terrible period of tribulation would only last for a short time, however, and after it the saints would have their reward (*MW*, 13: 456–84).

The change of tone in *Of Antichrist, and His Ruine* is significant and is echoed in many of Bunyan's later works. His theme in these is one of endurance, of holding on in the face of what must have seemed like endless and intensifying persecution.[39] This is particularly evident in one of his most ambitious and complex allegorical works, *The Holy War*, published in 1682. The holy war of the title refers to battles between the armies of Diabolus (Satan) and those of King Shaddai, under the command of his son Emanuel, for possession of the town of Mansoul. Bunyan weaves together an allegorical scheme which takes in the entire sweep of human history since the Fall; the experience of conversion of the individual believer; recent political events in England; and the prospect of a coming millennium. The town is first of all taken by Diabolus, thus representing the fall of man, but is recaptured by Emanuel, who then returns to heaven; presumably this refers to Christ's death and resurrection. Diabolus returns to occupy the town a second time, possibly representing the rise of the Roman Antichrist, but a handful of inhabitants are besieged within a citadel and refuse to submit;

this might be the true church which, according to Bunyan and most English Protestants, had always existed. Their pleas are eventually answered when Emanuel returns with another army to drive Diabolus out. At one level this could refer to the introduction of Protestantism at the Reformation, or perhaps to the freedom of worship which existed for the first time in England under Cromwell. But at another level it may represent the inauguration of the millennium: significantly, Diabolus is bound in chains, the townspeople of Mansoul celebrate with much feasting and merriment, they put on trial and crucify their enemies, and they are given a charter by Emanuel granting them power over the world. Never was Mansoul, or the true church, in a more glorious state: "nothing was to be found but harmony, quietness, joy and health" (*HW*, 150). This period of tranquillity does not last, however: there is a backsliding, and Emanuel leaves the town. Diabolus emerges from hell and invades Mansoul once again, but Emanuel returns for a second time to defeat his vast army of Doubters and Bloodmen. If we take this to be happening at the end of the millennium, Bunyan may here be depicting the final great battle with Gog and Magog which would precede the Last Judgment.[40] Alternatively, or additionally, he may be predicting the eventual defeat of contemporary Bloodmen, those persecutors of the saints in the Restoration period. The book ends with a long speech by Emanuel in which he reviews the course of human history and holds out to the citizens of Mansoul an evocative vision of future bliss.

The Holy War is an exceedingly complex narrative, and scholars have long debated to what degree millenarianism is a significant strand in the allegory, and indeed how the work might be interpreted in millenarian terms.[41] Not all would agree with the scheme I have tentatively outlined. It seems certain, though, that however we interpret the details, Bunyan was including in his allegory an imaginative depiction of the apocalyptic prophecies of the time of tribulation which would precede the final liberation of the true church and the commencement of the promised millennium. Richard Greaves has said that "more than any other work of Bunyan's, *The Holy War* evokes a spirit akin to that in the Fifth Monarchist writings of the 1650s."[42] However true this may be, it is important, finally, to stress that for Bunyan the millennium will not be a period of utopian perfection on earth. Convinced though he is that it will come about, he believes that the saints will still have to exercise eternal vigilance. Diabolonians will still be lurking; self-conceit and carnal security may lead to backsliding and sin. Emanuel's final speech makes it clear that full spiritual understanding will only be possible in the world which is to come. Only then will the saints enjoy a permanent conquest over their enemies; only then will they be free for ever from the threat of Diabolonian persecution; only then will they enjoy everlasting felicity.

For yet a little while, O my Mansoul, *... I will ... take down this famous Town of* Mansoul, *stick and stone, to the ground. And will carry the stones thereof, and the timber thereof, and the walls thereof, and the dust thereof, and the inhabitants thereof, into mine own Country, even into the Kingdom of my Father; and will there set it up in such strength and glory, as it never did see in the Kingdom where now it is placed. ... There shall the Natives of* Mansoul *see all that of which they have seen nothing here; there shall they be equal to those unto whom they have been inferiour here. And there shalt thou, O my* Mansoul, *have such communion with me, with my Father, and with your Lord Secretary, as is not possible here to be enjoyed. Nor ever could be, shouldest thou live in* Universe *the space of a thousand years.* (HW, 247)

Notes

1. For Goodwin and Wood, see B. S. Capp, *The Fifth Monarchy Men: A Study in Seventeenth-Century Millenarianism* (London: Faber, 1972), 30.

2. See Wilhelm Bousset, *The Antichrist Legend: A Chapter in Christian and Jewish Folklore*, trans. A. H. Keane (London: Hutchinson and Co., 1896); Norman Cohn, *The Pursuit of the Millennium: Revolutionary Millenarians and the Mystical Anarchists of the Middle Ages*, rev. ed. (London: Paladin, 1970); Bernard McGinn, *Visions of the End: Apocalyptic Traditions in the Middle Ages* (New York: Columbia University Press, 1979); Richard Kenneth Emmerson, *Antichrist in the Middle Ages* (Manchester: Manchester University Press, 1981).

3. See William Lamont, *Godly Rule: Politics and Religion, 1603–1660* (London: Macmillan, 1969); *Puritans, The Millennium and the Future of Israel: Puritan Eschatology, 1600–1660*, ed. Peter Toon (Cambridge: James Clarke, 1970); Christopher Hill, *Antichrist in Seventeenth-Century England* (Oxford: Oxford University Press, 1971); Bryan W. Ball, *A Great Expectation: Eschatological Thought in English Protestantism to 1660* (Leiden: Brill, 1975); Richard Bauckham, *Tudor Apocalypse* (Abingdon, Berkshire: Sutton Courtenay Press, 1978); Paul Christianson, *Reformers and Babylon: English Apocalyptic Visions from the Reformation to the Eve of the Civil War* (Toronto: University of Toronto Press, 1978); Katherine R. Firth, *The Apocalyptic Tradition in Reformation Britain, 1530–1645* (Oxford: Oxford University Press, 1979).

4. See the twentieth book of *The City of God*, trans. John Healey, rev. R. V. G. Tasker, 2 vols. (London: J. M. Dent, 1945), 2: 276–308, where Augustine explains that the thousand-year period described in Rev. 20 represents either the period from the time of Christ to the year 1000, or, more likely, the period of time during which the Church would bear witness in the world before the Last Judgment.

5. For a vivid account, see Cohn, *The Pursuit of the Millennium*, 252–80.

6. Capp, *The Fifth Monarchy Men*, 38–49.

7. Joseph Mede, *The Key of the Revelation*, trans. Richard More (2d edn., London, 1650), Part 2 (separately paginated), 112–21.

8. Henry Wilkinson, *Babylons Ruine, Jerusalems Rising* (London, 1643), 21.

9. Edward Symmons, *Scripture Vindicated, from the Misapprehensions Misinterpretations and Misapplications of Mr. Stephen Marshall* (Oxford, 1644), sig. A3r&v. This revealing episode is cited and discussed by both Lamont, *Godly Rule*, 97, and Hill, *Antichrist*, 79–80.

10. *A Declaration of the English Army now in Scotland* (1650), extracts reprinted in *Puritanism and Liberty*, ed. A. S. P. Woodhouse (2d ed., London: J. M. Dent, 1974), 477.

11. See Hill, *Antichrist*, 90–93, 135–37.

12. See Capp, *The Fifth Monarchy Men*, 116–18; Hill, *Antichrist*, 120–23.

13. For a discussion of millenarianism in Bunyan's early writings, see my " 'Antichrist must be Pulled Down': Bunyan and the Millennium," in *John Bunyan and his England*, ed. Anne Laurence, W. R. Owens, and Stuart Sim (London and Ronceverte: Hambledon Press, 1990), 77–94. See also Aileen M. Ross, "*Paradise Regained*: The Development of John Bunyan's Millenarianism," in *Bunyan in England and Abroad: Papers Delivered at the John Bunyan Tercentenary Symposium, Vrije Universiteit, Amsterdam, 1988*, ed. M. van Os and G. J. Schutte (Amsterdam: VU University Press, 1990), 73–89.

14. Richard L. Greaves, "John Bunyan and the Fifth Monarchists," *Albion* 13 (1981): 83–95; repr. in id., *John Bunyan and English Nonconformity* (London: Hambledon Press, 1992), 141–53. See also *MW*, 11: xxxvii–xli, and, for other discussions of Bunyan's links with Fifth Monarchists, see William York Tindall, *John Bunyan, Mechanick Preacher* (1934; repr. New York, 1964), chap. 4; and Christopher Hill, *A Turbulent, Seditious and Factious People: John Bunyan and His Church* (Oxford: Clarendon Press, 1988), 94–99.

15. See Capp, *The Fifth Monarchy Men*, 216.

16. Capp, *The Fifth Monarchy Men*, 199–201. For Bunyan's condemnation of Venner, see *A Relation of my Imprisonment*, in *Grace Abounding to the Chief of Sinners*, ed. Roger Sharrouk (Oxford: Clarendon Press, 1962), 120.

17. *The Holy City*, in *MW*, 3: 95, 196, ed. J. Sears McGee; cf. Capp, *The Fifth Monarchy Men*, 155–56.

18. See Capp, *The Fifth Monarchy Men*, 146–50.

19. See *The Holy City*, *MW*, 3: 157. A similar view was held by the Fifth Monarchist leader, Henry Danvers; see his *Theopolis, or the City of God, New Jerusalem, in Opposition to the City of the Nations, Great Babylon* (London, 1672), 228.

20. See Capp, *The Fifth Monarchy Men*, 137; cf. Ball, *A Great Expectation*, 164.

21. See Capp, *The Fifth Monarchy Men*, 190–93, 213–14.

22. See Capp, *The Fifth Monarchy Men*, 193; and id., *Astrology and the Popular Press* (London: Faber, 1979), 174–75. See also Michael McKeon, *Politics and Poetry in Restoration England: The Case of Dryden's Annus Mirabilis* (Cambridge and London: Harvard University Press, 1975), 202–203.

23. See N. H. Keeble, *The Literary Culture of Nonconformists in Later Seventeenth-Century England* (Athens: University of Georgia Press, 1987), 100.

24. See H. R. Trevor-Roper, *Religion, the Reformation and Social Change* (2d ed., London: Macmillan, 1972), 292–93; Christopher Hill, "John Mason and the End of the World," in his *Puritanism and Revolution* (London: Secker and Warburg, 1958), 323–36, though the views there expressed are somewhat qualified in his *Antichrist*, chap. 4; Lamont, *Godly Rule*, 158, 172–73, but see also his more recent study, *Richard Baxter and the Millennium* (London: Croom Helm, 1979), for an important revision of his earlier views.

25. See M. C. Jacob, *The Newtonians and the English Revolution* (Hassocks, England: Harvester Press, 1976), passim.

26. Jacob, *The Newtonians*, 108–9, 113–19.

27. Richard Hayter, *The Meaning of the Revelation* (London, 1675), "To the Reader," sig. A3v.

28. Henry More, *A Modest Enquiry into the Mystery of Iniquity* (London, 1664), 185–87.

29. More, *A Modest Enquiry*, 194.

30. For a useful overview, see Paul J. Korshin, "Queuing and Waiting: The Apocalypse in England, 1660–1750," in *The Apocalypse in English Renaissance Thought and Culture*, ed. C. A. Patrides and Joseph Wittreich (Manchester: Manchester University Press, 1984), 240–65.

31. The fullest account is in Hill, *Puritanism and Revolution*, 323–36.

32. Among Beverley's numerous writings, see, for example, *A Sermon Upon Revel. 11. 11. &c. Summoning the Expectation of the Witnesses Rising: And of the Great Concurrent Works Daily Shewing Forth Themselves, and to be Compleat by 1697* (London, 1692).

33. Richard Baxter, *The Glorious Kingdom of Christ, Described and Clearly Vindicated* (London, 1691), 45.

34. Thomas Beverley, *The Good Hope Through Grace* (London, 1700), the Preface; cf. 33–43.

35. *The Diary of John Evelyn*, ed. E. S. de Beer, 6 vols. (Oxford: Clarendon Press, 1955), 4: 636; cf. 5: 25–26, 321–22. See also A. Tindal Hart, *William Lloyd 1627–1717* (London: S.P.C.K., 1952), 235–39, 245–46.

36. See Hanserd Knollys, *Apocalyptical Mysteries* (1667), *The Parable of the Kingdom of Heaven Expounded* (London, 1674), *An Exposition of the Eleventh Chapter of the Revelation* (London, 1679), *Mystical Babylon Unvailed* (London, 1679), *The World that Now Is; and the World that is to Come* (London, 1681), and *An Exposition of the Whole Book of the Revelation* (London, 1689); Edward Bagshaw, *The Doctrine of the Kingdom and Personal Reign of Christ Asserted and Explained* (London, 1669); William Sherwin, *A Brief Representation of the Doctrine of Christs Kingdom of Power to Come upon Earth* (London, [?1671]), *A Plain and Evident Discovery of the Two Personal Comings of Christ* (London, [?1671]), and *The True News of the Good New World (Shortly) to Come* (London, [?1675]); Henry Danvers, *Theopolis;* Christopher Ness, *A Distinct Discourse and Discovery of the Person and Period of Antichrist* (London, 1679), *The Signs of the Times* (London, 1681), and *A Compleat and Compendious Church-History* (London, 1681); Benjamin Keach, *Antichrist Stormed* (London, 1689), and *Distressed Sion Relieved* (London, 1689).

37. For an extended account of this work, see my Introduction to *MW*, 13: xxiv–xxxiv.

38. On this very significant development in Bunyan's millenarian thinking, see *MW*, 13: xxxi–xxxiv.

39. For discussions of Bunyan's response to state persecution, see Richard L. Greaves, "The Spirit and the Sword: Bunyan and the Stuart State," and "Amid the *Holy War*: Bunyan and the Ethic of Suffering," in his *Bunyan and Nonconformity*, 101–26, 169–83; Owen C. Watkins, Introduction to *MW*, 10: xiii–xxvii; Hill, *Turbulent People*, 310–34.

40. For an account of the final battle with Gog and Magog, see *The Holy City*, *MW*, 3: 170–71.

41. Important recent discussions of *The Holy War* include Sharrock and For-

rest's Introduction, *HW*, xx–xxxix; Michael A. Mullett, " 'Deprived of our Former Place': The Internal Politics of Bedford, 1660–1688," *Bedfordshire Historical Record Society*, 59 (1980): 1–42; Hill, *Turbulent People*, 240–59; Donald Mackenzie, "Rhetoric *versus* Apocalypse: The Oratory of *The Holy War*," *Bunyan Studies*, 2, 1 (1990): 33–45; Richard L. Greaves, *"The Holy War* and London Nonconformity," in his *Bunyan and Nonconformity*, 55–67; Stuart Sim, *Negotiations with Paradox: Narrative Practice and Narrative Form in Bunyan and Defoe* (London: Harvester Wheatsheaf, 1990), 90–107.

42. Greaves, "John Bunyan and the Fifth Monarchists," 148.

Bunyan's Exceeding Maze: *Grace Abounding* and the Labyrinth of Predestination

MICHAEL DAVIES

> But the same day, as I was in the midst of a game at Cat, and having struck it one blow from the hole; just as I was about to strike it a second time, a voice did suddenly dart from Heaven into my Soul, which said, *Wilt thou leave thy sins, and go to Heaven? or have thy sins, and go to Hell?* At this I was put into an exceeding maze; wherefore, leaving my Cat upon the ground, I looked up to Heaven, and was as if I had with the eyes of my understanding, seen the Lord Jesus looking down upon me, as being very hotly displeased with me.
>
> (*GA*, 10)

THE GAME-AT-CAT EPISODE IS ONE OF THE MOST REMARKABLE PASSAGES in *Grace Abounding* and one which has duly received substantial critical attention. While Vera Brittain views the episode instinctively as Bunyan's moment of conversion, Vincent Newey remarks upon the paradoxical effect a divine visitation has upon the young Bunyan: because Bunyan at this point mistakes his experience as confirmation of his damnation rather than salvation, the whole episode is self-negating, and so the visitation "occasions a misreading which defers, indeed challenges, the ends it theoretically promotes."[1] Newey views the whole of *Grace Abounding* as concerned with the "mistakings of the convert," of being blind and "of learning to 'see' correctly," but the game-at-cat episode reveals not only the problems of interpretation facing this convert-to-be but also the interpretative difficulties facing the reader of Bunyan's text. After all, Bunyan's descriptive techniques in his account of this and other experiences are particularly "a-mazing" for the reader. What is actually happening at this point? Do we understand that Bunyan physically hears a voice from heaven? Is this an example of the audibility and physicality of Bunyan's experiences that has characterized so much critical response to *Grace Abounding*?

Clearly the issue is not simple. Bunyan does not "hear" a voice from Heaven as such. Rather, he suggests that "a voice did suddenly dart from Heaven into my Soul." But what does this really mean? Is it an audible experience or not? Furthermore, the vision of Christ "looking down" upon the playing Bunyan operates in the same way. One may ask, is he actually seeing this or not? The matter is confused further by Bunyan's oft-used construction "and was as if." So, it was only *as if* he had seen the Lord looking down from heaven hotly displeased with him, then? For the reader an odd thing is happening in such passages. As much as we can appreciate that Bunyan is relating this experience to us metaphorically, the presentation of audibility and visibility in this episode is, nevertheless, strong enough to convey the sense that they are not metaphorical but literal and actual. The problem that faces the reader here is one of *hesitation*. Bunyan's experience is difficult to fathom as he both hears the voice and sees his vision and yet simultaneously—he does not. Facing this hesitation, the reader is placed in somewhat of an interpretative maze: which way does one turn?

Grace Abounding continues in this mode, applying such strategies of hesitation throughout, so that even by the end of the text the reader may not be totally convinced that Bunyan has "progressed" spiritually all that much, wondering, perhaps, where and when exactly "grace abounds" for Bunyan? When the narrative does "end," Bunyan is left in prison relating to us his temptations to blaspheme in the pulpit and his natural fears about being hanged. Despite the innately human aspect of this ending, Bunyan appears to be both better and no-better than when he started out on his soteriological journey. The text's various endings may also provoke a certain amount of narrative dissatisfaction, a textual dis-closure. Whilst commentators have been keen to take an author-based approach in offering doctrinal and psychological reasons to explain away the text's structural diffuseness and its complex ending, the pressure of interpretation is unavoidably and consistently being exerted upon the *reader* throughout *Grace Abounding*. Indeed, the figure of an "exceeding maze" is incisively appropriate in relation to Bunyan's text as a whole. Not only is the narrative's protagonist repeatedly placed in a state of a-mazement, but the reader's actual experience of reading *Grace Abounding* is distinctly a-mazing too. As Newey again notes,

> reading *Grace Abounding* is like travelling in a mighty maze whose plan is far from clear, and where at every turn we meet some new and puzzling psychodrama suggesting not so much providential design as solitary struggle in a spectacular universe of the mind's own making.[2]

But how useful is it to view *Grace Abounding* as a labyrinthine narrative? The figure of the labyrinth has traditionally served "as a metaphor for painful, even dangerous, but necessary or unavoidable experience," and as "a quest form, a mode of examination or exploration" seems inherently relevant to Bunyan's own experiential questing as a convert-to-be.³ Equally, there is considerable scope to relate Bunyan's texts and narrative strategies to other narratives that exploit labyrinthine forms. An obvious crossover point here would be, say, to call upon Bunyan's relation to postmodernist fiction and the work of writers such as Borges who self-consciously develop labyrinthine narratives and textual strategies within the compass of, for example, John Barth's notion of a "Literature of Exhaustion."⁴ If Thomas Luxon can assert that Bunyan is to be considered "as some kind of Ur-poststructuralist," no matter how uncomfortable or skeptical commentators may feel about it, then presumably the interface between the textual strategies of postmodernist writing and *Grace Abounding* could conceivably be both quite useful and literarily exciting.⁵ Inquiring into the significance of the labyrinth for postmodernist writing can offer some insight into how the labyrinth of *Grace Abounding* operates textually. As one scholar has recently suggested, the "labyrinth, web, or maze has become a dominant image of space in postmodern narrative," the labyrinthine form being "a step [beyond] the circular narrative. While a labyrinth contains circular movements, it simultaneously accounts for infinite regression. This paradox of circularity and regression is the core of the labyrinth."⁶ Furthermore,

> If one focuses on the very structure of labyrinths, another side of the paradox is revealed. The variety of paths in a labyrinth justifies the simultaneous possibility of being lost or saved. There is no apparent difference between these paths and people are not able to find their way by the usual rational . . . apparatus they [have] used to manipulate through centuries to find "truth." The only rule which governs a labyrinth is randomness.⁷

This is certainly one way to view how *Grace Abounding* is structured: as a labyrinth of the apparent randomness of spiritual experience which the constantly mistaking Bunyan attempts to rationalize and fails. His early endeavour, for instance, to prove "whether I had any Faith or no" (18) by logical and rational means merely sends Bunyan down other forking lines of inquiry after a long period of agonizing and humiliating doubt:

> Neither as yet could I attain to any comfortable perswasion that I had Faith in Christ, but instead of having satisfaction, here I began to find

> my Soul to be assaulted with fresh doubts about my future happiness, especially with such as these, Whether I was elected; but how if the day of grace should now be past and gone? (20)

Bunyan's rational approach to the spiritual matter of faith is worse than useless: it actually remains an unanswered issue and as such breeds, hydra-like, further questions of doubt and anxiety.

Though it would be interesting to relate postmodern textual strategies to Bunyan further, it is not in the scope of this essay to do so. What I am primarily investigating are the doctrinal implications of viewing *Grace Abounding* as a labyrinthine text. Unsurprisingly, the very notion of a labyrinth itself is heavily embedded with biblical/religious resonances: one can be either "lost" or "saved" in a labyrinth, for instance, whilst alternatively J. Hillis Miller views the labyrinth as a kind of paradoxical wilderness, "at once an enclosure and a place of endless wandering," indeed, "a desert turned inside out."[8] More specifically, what this essay aims to show is how investigating the implications of the labyrinthine form of *Grace Abounding* can establish an alternative critical perspective as to how this text functions as a doctrinally edifying and didactic work for Bunyan's congregation, whilst also taking to task any appraisal of it merely as a lasting example of the supposedly conventionalized generic form of spiritual autobiography.

Seventeenth-century spiritual autobiography has been thoroughly documented by commentators such as Paul Delany, Joan Webber, and Dean Ebner.[9] Furthermore, spiritual autobiography is now often seen as embodying what Roger Pooley and Stuart Sim, among others, call a "new sense of self." This new self-awareness marks the emergence of individuality into modern society, on the one hand, and an extremism of subjectivity on the other.[10] The source of this growth in introspection is often located in the paradoxes of Calvinist theology: if good works count for nothing, and if even the reprobate can experience some kind of faith or calling, then, and here comes the Calvinist clarion, how does one know if one is saved? Anxiety naturally abounds in such circumstances. Hence, Stuart Sim suggests that one "has only to look at *Grace Abounding* to see the degree of psychological confusion belief in election and predestination could create within a sensitive individual."[11]

Naturally, commentators link this anxiety with the rise of spiritual autobiography in seventeenth-century England and America. According to Delany, Calvinist theology forces the believer to internalize experience, to embrace "the struggle of conflicting mental forces," while procuring an "obsession with the enemy within":

Convinced that he was possessed by evil, the Calvinist naturally clutched at some kind of reassurance within himself, since no external observances—such as good works or sacraments—could avail a whit towards his salvation. His normal reaction was to embark on a complicated, even devious process of rationalization which always seemed to culminate in a semi-mystical assurance that *he*, at least, was enrolled among the elect.[12]

But there are a number of problems in approaching spiritual autobiography and Calvinism in this way. For instance, there is the contentious issue between Calvin and Calvinism, as expounded by R. T. Kendall. According to Kendall, the paradoxes and problems inherent in English Calvinism in the seventeenth century derive not from Calvin and his doctrines particularly but from those of his successors and followers, such as Theodore Beza who introduces the precarious notion of limited atonement into the Calvinist soteriological equation and whose doctrines later English Divines, such as William Perkins, wrongly accept as indistinct from Calvin's original teachings. Whilst many commentators quite happily cite Calvin as encouraging a new sense of self (particularly in his exhortation to self-knowledge in the opening pages of *Institutes of Christian Religion*), Kendall asserts that Calvin abhorred and actively warned against the notion of introspection as to one's soteriological status: "For even if the reprobate experience, 'almost the same feelings as the elect,'" writes Kendall, "Calvin warns against looking to one's feelings in any case. Indeed, the one thing above all else which Calvin emphasizes is that we must never look to ourselves for assurance."[13]

For Calvin, faith alone was assurance enough of salvation. According to him, Christ died for all men leaving faith as the distinguishing mark between the elect and reprobate. Calvin, as Kendall summarizes, describes faith as knowledge, particularly knowledge in the form of a "given, intellectual, passive" assurance.[14] Self-knowledge for Calvin is only useful as a first step in the soteriological process: it is a means to knowing our own carnal and corrupt nature through which Christ's role as savior can be truly understood. This self-knowledge involves no introspection per se for Calvin, leaving it necessary to revise our understanding of his position in relation to spiritual autobiography and Puritan self-analysis as a whole. While we may not be able to account for "Calvinism" in the same way, nevertheless what Calvin says about introspection and asking the famous question, "How do I know I am saved?" is intriguing. For Calvin, a person is incapable of reasoning with spiritual matters using the usual epistemological apparatus: what is demanded is the implicit, reassuring knowledge of faith above all else. Attempting to assess one's spiritual standing in rational terms is not merely folly for Calvin but preeminently dangerous for the self:

> The election of God is itself hidden and secret, and the Lord manifests it when he bestows it upon us by calling. They are madmen who seek their own salvation or that of others in the labyrinth of predestination, not keeping the way of faith which is exhibited to them.[15]

Significantly, Calvin's fear for those who seek knowledge of election and predestination reveals itself in the metaphor of the labyrinth or maze, the "pictorial figure . . . frequently employed [by Calvin] as a symbol of human frustration and confusion."[16] Fully aware of the power of the mind in religious matters, Calvin realizes that "when consciences once ensnare themselves, they enter a long and inextricable maze, not easy to get out of" (839). This ensnaring can occur, he asserts, in the contemplation of what some may call "vain frivolities," such as "the unrestricted eating of meat, use of holidays and vestments," all of which can cast man "into a pit of confusion" (839). Though generally keen to warn of how speculating on such "superfluous" issues as the divinity of God, the Trinity, and the nature of heaven can lead "men's minds, when they indulge their curiosity, [to] enter into a labyrinth," Calvin, aware of the doctrine's potential for anxiety, is particularly concerned with the concept of predestination.

"Human curiosity," he writes, "renders the discussion of predestination, already difficult of itself, very confusing and even dangerous" (922). It is, moreover, the duty of believers to restrain this anxiety:

> let them remember that when they inquire into predestination they are penetrating the sacred precincts of divine wisdom. If anyone with carefree assurance breaks into this place, he will not succeed in satisfying his curiosity and he will enter a labyrinth from which he can find no exit. For it is not right for man unrestrainedly to search out things that the Lord has willed to be hid in himself. (73)

What is to be understood of the secrets of God's will, Calvin suggests, is set down in the Word. The Word "is the sole light to illumine our vision of all that we should see" of the Lord and his will, and as such it "will readily keep and restrain us from all rashness" (923). Calvin describes the Word as the straight path necessary to follow "if we seriously aspire to the pure contemplation of God"

(73). The "splendor of the divine countenance, which even the apostle calls 'unapproachable' (I Tim. 6:16), is for us like an inexplicable labyrinth unless we are conducted into it by the thread of the Word" (73). Beyond the pathway of the Word "we must repeatedly wander, slip, and stumble":

> to seek any other knowledge of predestination than what the Word of God discloses is not less insane than if one should purpose to walk in a pathless waste.... And let us not be ashamed to be ignorant of something in this matter, wherein there is a certain learned ignorance. Rather, let us willingly refrain from inquiring into a kind of knowledge, the ardent desire for which is both foolish and dangerous, nay, even deadly. (923)

The relevance of Calvin's teachings, indeed of the very tropes he adopts, cannot be underestimated in terms of how we can approach *Grace Abounding*. What Bunyan's text arguably represents is the account of a man who has entered Calvin's labyrinth doctrinally, rhetorically, and textually. If *Grace Abounding* operates in any kind of a didactic or edifying way, perhaps it teaches the reader precisely not to ask the question, "How do I know I am saved?" In this sense, Bunyan's text is not so much a guidebook for the soul as a map of misreadings. What Bunyan urges in the preface to *Grace Abounding* is, after all, not self-introspection in terms of election or reprobation but, more simply, a remembering of God's mercies and grace. With this in mind, Delany's assertion that spiritual autobiography, as a genre of introspection, embraces the "complicated, even devious process of rationalization," culminating in a "semi-mystical assurance," could not be more inappropriate when applied to Bunyan's *Grace Abounding*, a text which reveals any sense of rationalizing the spiritual to be dangerously mistaken. Not only are we denied any lasting sense of assurance in *Grace Abounding*, semi-mystical or not, but Bunyan's narrative shows how devious reasonings lead him dangerously into a nightmare of doubts and epistemologically determined forking paths.[17] As such, the lesson that *Grace Abounding* is intent upon teaching its reader is precisely that,

> Though election is, in order, before calling, as to God, yet the knowledge of Calling must go before the belief of my Election, as to my self. Wherefore souls that doubt of the truth of their Effectual Calling, do but plunge themselves into a deeper labyrinth of confusion that concern themselves with their election; I mean, while they labour to know it before they prove their Calling. (*MW*, 11: 88)

In this way, *Grace Abounding* is clearly Bunyan's response by personal testimony to the pastoral issue of the sinner who doubts whether he or she is "elect, or chosen to salvation": "lay the thoughts of thy Election by, and ask thyself these question; Do I see my lost condition? Do I see salvation is no where but in Christ? Would I share in this salvation by Faith of him? . . . Do I love Christ, his Father, his Saints, his Word and Ways? This," Bunyan affirms unequivocally, "is the way to prove we are Elect." This is the way to avoid such a "labyrinth of confusion."[18]

Grace Abounding also represents the conversion experience in terms of learning to follow the thread of the Word through a labyrinth of misunderstandings. This is particularly important for Bunyan who not only knows experimentally of the necessity of wrestling with the Word but can also warn, with Calvin, of "prying too far" in spiritual matters; "take heed," he writes in *The Saints Privilege and Profit*, "for in Mysteries Men soon lose their way" (*MW*, 13: 225), a caution memorably reiterated in *The Holy War*'s verse address to the reader. In *The Saints Privilege and Profit*, however, Bunyan asserts that the "*breadths*, and *lengths*, and *depths*, and *heighths*" of Christ's love as set down in the Word are the kinds of mysteries rarely understood "save by those that are very well skilled in those mysterious methods of God." As "they are very mysterious in their workings," Bunyan writes, "For they work *by, upon,* and *against* oppositions," the role of the preacher-pastor becomes instrumental in the spiritual well-being of his congregation. Difficult but ultimately comforting scriptural sentences "are easily played with by a preacher, when in the pulpit," writes Bunyan, "specially if he has a little of the notion of things, but of the *difficulty,* and *strait,* that those are brought into . . . by reason of the force of the Labyrinths they are fallen into: of *those* [comforts] they experience nothing, wherefore to those they are utterly strangers" (*MW*, 13: 356–57). Bunyan's labyrinths here may not only be those of the world and sin and an entangled conscience. Bunyan implies that the Word itself may need mediating for the sinner by one skilled in the mysteries of God, and that the enigmatic Word itself may lock the sinner out of the comforts offered should there not be a hand proffering assurance and guidance.

The implications of Calvin's labyrinth of predestination are far-reaching. Calvin relates that through his conversion experience "God subdued my heart to teachableness." He thus stresses in the *Institutes* that believers should apply themselves to spiritual questions more "with teachableness than with subtlety."[19] *Grace Abounding* operates with this edifying intention also: the reader who reads *Grace Abounding* "aright" must learn to be teachable. In order to achieve this didactic aim, Bunyan presents a narrative which, in its mazelike structure of continuous spiritual progression and negation, and in its ultimately unresolved resolution, becomes impossible to read simply as a story. *Grace Abounding* thus becomes unapproachable as autobiography or a life-story, denying the most basic of narrative conventions, that of plot or fable, in order to foreground the ongoing struggles of the convert and the nature of grace. The labyrinth Bunyan enters in *Grace Abounding* teaches its reader experientially about both reading in doctrine and the doctrine in reading.

Naturally, such conclusions hold significant implications for approaching *The Pilgrim's Progress*. While *The Pilgrim's Progress* presents a more teleologically driven narrative than *Grace Abounding* (we do, after all, witness Christian entering the Celestial City), it nevertheless shares many of the conversion narrative's labyrinthine traits: Christian often loses his way, doubles back on himself, and enters mystical, mazelike (and impossible) spaces, such as the Interpreter's House. But in *The Pilgrim's Progress*, the didactic intent in presenting a labyrinthine narrative is far more conspicuous from the opening "Author's Apology for his Book" onwards. Bunyan's allegory promises not only to sound of *"honest Gospel Strains"* but also to place the reader in a whole new mode of perception. In this mode one can be *"in a Dream, and yet not sleep,"* can simultaneously *"Laugh and Weep."* The maze of the text is something to *"loose thy self"* in without harm, requiring no romance-device or fictive *"charm"* to recover oneself from (*PP*, 7). This could serve as a prefatory verse to *Grace Abounding*, stressing as it does Bunyan's emphasis upon the reading of his text and the ontological newness that his doctrine promises. But the Apology also warns of the dangers of overinterpretation and points to the text itself as providing the only commentary necessary in understanding its substance: one must read the *"Riddles"* along with *"their Explanation"* or *"else be drownded in thy Contemplation"* (7). As in *Grace Abounding*, and as Christian and Hopeful are to discover, too much speculation on a riddle can lead to being overwhelmed by the floods of doubt and mistaking.

Rational contemplation of one's elect status is particularly warned against throughout *The Pilgrim's Progress* (despite the perhaps misleading apologetic assertion that in reading the lines of this text the reader can *"know whether thou art blest or not"*). Indeed, it seems significant that Christian's initial cry is *"What shall I do to be saved?"* and not, "How do I *know* I am saved?" Just as in

Grace Abounding, the spiritual business of "knowing" is a crucial issue in Bunyan's allegory, particularly in relation to how its characters and protagonists often confuse the term's meaning (and not without some a-mazing effects either). While there is much that can be learned from Faithful's dialogue with Talkative about there being *"knowledge, and knowledge. Knowledge that resteth in the bare speculation of things, and knowledge that is accompanied with the grace of faith and love"* (82), Christian himself often fails to sustain his teachableness in such matters. His early entrapment by Worldly-Wiseman can be excused in terms of the young convert-to-be's doctrinal naiveté when faced with the seductive sophistry of Worldy-Wiseman's "civil" discourse (and it is seductive precisely because its moralism so authoritatively apes Calvin's discourse in warning of how *"weak men, who meddling with things too high for them, do suddenly fall into . . . distractions"* (18). But Christian's later lapses serve to re-instruct him (and the reader) about the nature of *"knowledge, and knowledge"* in spiritual matters.

Such re-edification is clearest in Christian's and Hopeful's encounter with the Shepherds of the Delectable Mountains. The initial exchange between Christian and the Shepherds is particularly a-mazing in both style and content for reader and pilgrim alike:

> *Chr. Is this the way to the Celestial City?*
>
> *Shep. You are just in your way.*
>
> *Chr. How far is it thither?*
>
> *Shep. Too far for any, but those that shall get thither indeed.*
>
> *Chr. Is the way safe, or dangerous?*
>
> *Shep. Safe for those for whom it is to be safe, but transgressors shall fall therein.*
>
> (119)

While one observer likens the Shepherds' responses to "the equivocations of a Buddhist master," such riddling is clearly consistent with the puzzling prevarications of Bunyan's initial *Apology* and of Faithful's discourse with Talkative.[20] What is significant about this episode, however, is not only the evasiveness of the Shepherds' answers but the apparent harshness of them too. As such, commentators traditionally cite the Shepherds' responses in stressing the severity of Bunyan's Calvinist doctrine. Stuart Sim suggests that "there is an entire theological position encapsulated in that line 'safe for those for whom it is to be safe,' one unmistakably based on the Calvinist doctrines of election and justification by faith, that is central to Bunyan's narrative practice."[21] John Stachniewski takes this approach further by proposing that the sights shown to the pilgrims by the Shepherds are actually engineered to induce further anxiety over one's elect status: "The terror of the inauthenticity of elect experience is what impels the pilgrims forward. It is to secure this effect," Stachniewski asserts, "that the euphemistic 'wonders' were put on show." Here, the "familiar system of mind control, playing on fears of hypocrisy and rejection, is being practised," he writes, "on the contemporary reader as well as the characters."[22]

But is it really the intention of the Shepherds (and of Bunyan) to induce anxiety over one's soteriological status? Hasn't *Grace Abounding* already taught us that interrogating the self in terms of damnation and salvation inevitably leads to a torturous and tortuous reasoning, a sliding into the labyrinth of predestination? Yet, if this is so, how *do* we equate the harsh implications of the Shepherds' answers with this didactic cautioning? One solution is to follow John Knott's suggestion that this episode merely reflects and reinforces "the subjectivity of the individual way of faith": "To give definite answers to the pilgrims' questions would be to ignore the uncertainty with which faith must live." Thus,

> The response of the shepherds to Christian's inquiries has the ... effect of turning the questions back on the questioner, though they can offer no assurances that Christian will get anywhere at all, because they are talking about a metaphorical way that depends upon a faith that may collapse at any moment.[23]

Such a response, however, seems to imply merely a milder admission of the Calvinist will-to-uncertainty. Moreover, the issue at stake is far greater than that of a metaphorical understanding of the Way. Christian is indeed in danger of soteriological a-maze-ment not because the Shepherds' responses are baffling but because his questions demand such equivocations. Christian's interrogations here are, more than anything, epistemologically governed. He is asking the type of questions that Calvin warns against asking and attempts to rationalize the Way not in spiritual but in carnal terms. Christian's overriding need is to *know* if he is geographically and situationally secure ("*Is this the way?*" and "*How far is it thither?*") before, and without getting the hint, he boldly asks whether the Way is "*safe, or dangerous*" (119). The responses are geared not to induce anxiety over one's elect status (although to a rationalizing pilgrim this could quite conceivably be the result) but to thwart such epistemologically and carnally determined reasonings. Significantly, this tactic appears to work: Christian and Hopeful query the Shepherds no further about the Way.

But learning to avoid the labyrinth of predestination is often a painful process for Christian. What his education by the Shepherds of the Delectable Mountains seems to emphasize is that it is not one's status as elect or reprobate one should be anxious about but rather one's complacencies in other areas of one's spiritual journeying—particularly that of hermeneutics. As one commentator has recently observed, because human "understanding cannot comprehend the pure reality of God . . . any claim to absolute knowledge must be indicative of hermeneutic delusion." In *The Pilgrim's Progress*, only "reprobates are confident of their own capacities to read and to understand." In this way, Protestant allegory can be said to valorize "uncertainty in interpretation" but not necessarily the uncertainty of one's election.[24] The pilgrims' experiences in the Delectable Mountains thus provide a particular form of much needed re-instruction. Indeed, the "wonders" shown are not dissimilar to the spiritually edifying visions revealed in Interpreter's House and the episode as a whole acts to humble the pilgrims in terms of any interpretative complacencies they may have: Christian's questions now take the simple form of "*What means this?*" (121) and, before leaving the Mountains, the pilgrims praise the Shepherds in song as being supreme hermeneutic instructors—"*Thus by the* Shepherds, *Secrets are reveal'd . . . / Things deep, things hid, and that mysterious be*" (123).

That Christian needs such lessons in interpretation is evinced not only by his initial questions about the Way but, more seriously, by the a-mazing consequences of an earlier episode at the monument to Lot's wife. There are, in fact, aspects of this episode that should alarm the reader into reconsidering what would appear to be a benevolent and otherwise unexceptional (if a little self-congratulatory) discourse between Christian and Hopeful. The first warning sign for the wary reader is that the memorial for Lot's wife is described by the narrator as a "sudden and *amazing* sight" (109, emphasis mine) from which arises the "discourse" following. Yet it seems that Lot's wife causes the pilgrims (and the reader) little amazement at all: the monument is easily and conclusively discoursed upon before the Way rewardingly brings them to a "pleasant River" for rest and spiritual nourishment. Yet it is in the very method of this discoursing that the pilgrims' fault lies. In fact, the reader should be doubly alarmed at Christian's final words on the matter of Lot's wife:

And it is most *rationally* to be concluded, that such, even such as these are, that shall sin in the sight, yea, and that too in despite of such examples that are set continually before them, to caution them to the contrary, must be partakers of the severest Judgements. (110)

The emphasis here, as throughout the discourse, is not only upon "severest Judgements" but upon rational conclusions; as we have seen, moreover, reason can often lead men into the mazes of their own spiritual considerations. The accent in this episode is upon just such a use of reason: Christian's summing-up, with all its complex clauses and subclauses, smacks of pompous legal sophistry. What attracts the pilgrims to the monument initially is "the strangeness of the form thereof": they are "concerned" by it. Their inspection of the monument's marginal gloss in "a Writing in an unusual Hand" lays further emphasis upon reason and knowledge. Called upon as one who "was learned," Christian uses his rational skills of decipherment to "pick out the *meaning*" and not simply the letters (emphasis mine). What follows is a discourse based not on faith, grace, and forgiveness but on reason and legalistic conclusions of God's mercilessness. A-mazing (and distressing) consequences follow from this episode not simply because the pilgrims reveal themselves to be spiritually complacent but because they read the monument of Lot's wife epistemologically instead of "grace-fully" or, as Stanley Fish might put it, by the light of reason rather than by the light of faith.

The pilgrims reveal a somewhat disconcerting reprobate certitude in interpreting the monument of Lot's wife; moreover, according to Fish, they are supremely at fault for contriving "to turn remembering Lot's wife into a forgetting of mercy and therefore when they lead themselves out of the Way, they have no mercy left for themselves."[25] This self-enactment of the "severest Judgements" and lack of mercy, then, ultimately manifests itself in the horribly tangible form of Giant Despair and imprisonment in Doubting Castle, an episode Fish views as the natural consequence of the pilgrims' earlier severe conclusions. The pilgrims' discourse on Lot's wife inevitably leads to despair: it rationally and effectively "dis-pairs" the unity of God's justice and forgiveness, the wholeness of the Old and New Testaments made one through grace and faith.[26]

It is for this reason that Christian's re-instruction by the Shepherds in matters of mystery and interpretation is so important; nor are the Shepherds willing to let such complacency go uncorrected either in the text's protagonists or in its reader. Among the truly fearsome visions the Shepherds show the pilgrims, therefore, is one of the most powerful and terrifying emblems of spiritual a-maze-ment in all of Bunyan's works. The pilgrims are taken "to the top of another Mountain" the name of which, significantly, is "*Caution.*" From there

> they perceived, as they thought, several men walking up and down among the Tombs that were there. And they perceived that the men were blind, because they stumbled sometimes upon the Tombs, and because they could not get out from among them. (121)

These blind men are lost in an appalling spiritual wasteland. This vision represents a chilling, spatially inverted image of the Man in the Iron Cage witnessed by Christian in Interpreter's House: such blind wandering is the figure of the Man's imprisonment in despair turned inside-out. The connection is made clear when Christian asks the Shepherds "*What means this?*" to which he is, this time, given an alarmingly unequivocal answer. These blind men "came once on Pilgrimage" and, like Christian and Hopeful, trespassed into By-Path-Meadow only to be taken (as they were) by Giant Despair, who "did put out their eyes, and led them among these Tombs, where he has left them to wander to this very day" (121).

The point is registered by the use of a spatial image for spiritual distraction, despair procuring an endless wandering and a living death. The Shepherds use this vision to reinforce what may appear to be the providence of God's severest judgments—such a vision exists, apparently, to fulfill "the saying of the wise Man . . . *He that wandereth out of the way of understanding, shall remain in the Congregation of the dead*" (121). But, again, the more important point is to recognize that the blind men represent something very different from the harshness of God's judgments (or those of Calvinist predestination). The emphasis instead is finally on remaining in "the way of understanding." Here, understanding becomes a Way in itself. Consequently, there is no complacent and rationalized discourse from the pilgrims now. Rather, "*Christian* and *Hopeful* looked one upon another, with tears gushing out; but yet said nothing to the Shepherds" (121).

Notes

1. Vera Brittain, *In the Steps of John Bunyan* (London: Rich and Cowan, 1950, repr. 1987), 108–10; Vincent Newey, " 'With the eyes of my understanding': Bunyan, Experience, and Acts of Interpretation," in *John Bunyan: Conventicle and*

Parnassus Tercentenary Essays, ed. N. H. Keeble (Oxford: Clarendon Press, 1988), 194.

2. Newey, " 'With the eyes of my understanding,' " 192.

3. Donald Gutierrez, "The Labyrinth as Myth and Metaphor," *University of Dayton Review* 16, 3 (1983–84): 90.

4. John Barth, "The Literature of Exhaustion," in *The Novel Today*, ed. Malcolm Bradbury (London: Fontana Press, 1990), 71–86.

5. Thomas Luxon, " 'Other Men's Words' and 'New Birth': Bunyan's Antihermeneutics of Experience," *Texas Studies in Literature and Language*, 36 (1994): 259. See also Huston Diehl, "Into the maze of self: the Protestant transformation of the image of the labyrinth," *Journal of Medieval and Renaissance Studies* 16 (1986): 281–301, in which it is suggested that the postmodern concept of the labyrinth "has its roots in the sixteenth and seventeenth centuries, specifically in the Protestant Reformation" (283).

6. Amir Ali Nojoumian, "The Representation of Space and Time in Postmodern Narrative" (Master's thesis, University of Leicester, 1994), 26.

7. Nojoumian, "The Representation of Space and Time," 28.

8. J. Hillis Miller, *The Linguistic Moment* (Princeton: Princeton University Press, 1985), 403, cited in Nojoumian, "The Representation of Space and Time," 29.

9. See Paul Delany, *British Autobiography in the Seventeenth Century* (London: Routledge & Kegan Paul, 1969); Joan Webber, *The Eloquent "I": Style and Self in Seventeenth-Century Prose* (Madison: University of Wisconsin Press, 1968); Dean Ebner, *Autobiography in Seventeenth-Century England: Theology and the Self* (The Hague: Mouton Press, 1971).

10. See Roger Pooley, "*Grace Abounding* and the New Sense of the Self," in *John Bunyan and His England, 1628–88*, ed. Anne Laurence, W. R. Owens, and Stuart Sim, (London: Hambledon Press, 1990), 105–14; and Stuart Sim, *Negotiations with Paradox: Narrative Practice and Narrative Form in Bunyan and Defoe* (London: Harvester Wheatsheaf, 1990), 24.

11. Sim, *Negotiations with Paradox*, 24.

12. Delany, *British Autobiography in the Seventeenth Century*, 35–36.

13. R. T. Kendall, *Calvin and English Calvinism* (Oxford: Oxford University Press, 1979), 24.

14. Kendall, *Calvin and English Calvinism*, 19.

15. John Calvin, *Calvini Opera*, 47: 147, trans. Edward A. Dowey, Jr., in id., *The Knowledge of God in Calvin's Theology* (New York: Columbia University Press, 1952), 187, cited in Ebner, *Autobiography in Seventeenth-Century England*, 34.

16. John Calvin, *Institutes of Christian Religion*, ed. John T. McNeill and trans. Ford Lewis Battles, vols. 20 and 21 of *The Library of Christian Classics* (Philadelphia: Westminster Press, 1961), editor's note 36, 1: 64–65. All subsequent citations are to this edition.

17. Dayton Haskin also notes that Calvin "warned against introspection, which, he said, causes anxiety and leads even to damnation," and yet considers *Grace Abounding* to be obsessively informed by an "intense introspection" (see "The Burden of Interpretation in *The Pilgrim's Progress*," *Studies in Philology* 79 (1982): 270). Haskin believes that Bunyan follows the English Calvinist tradition of introspection established by William Perkins and, especially in Bunyan's case, gaining transmission through texts such as Arthur Dent's *Plaine Man's Path-way to Heaven* and Lewis Bayly's *Practise of Piety* (261–69). However, Rebecca S. Beal radically counters the efficacy of such texts in Bunyan's conversion (and hence

his theology), suggesting that in *Grace Abounding* these books are "spiritually soporific! . . . incapable of inculcating an awareness of [Bunyan's] true need for grace, or even of his true spiritual state" (see "*Grace Abounding to the Chief of Sinners*: John Bunyan's Pauline Epistle," *Studies in English Literature* 21 (1981): 154).

18. *Good News for the Vilest of Men* (MW, 11: 88–89). For further examples and a discussion of the image of the labyrinth in relation to the doctrines of election and assurance in the writings of Puritan divines, see John von Rohr, *The Covenant of Grace in Puritan Thought* (Atlanta: Scholars Press, 1986), 131–33, 156–58, 167, 176.

19. Calvin, *Preface to the Commentary on the Psalms, CR 31: 21*, quoted in introduction to Calvin, *Institutes of Christian Religion*, li, and id., 146.

20. Carolynn Van Dyke, *The Fiction of Truth: Structures of Meaning in Narrative and Dramatic Allegory* (Ithaca and London: Cornell University Press, 1985), 179.

21. Stuart Sim, " 'Safe for Those for Whom it is to be Safe': Salvation and Damnation in Bunyan's Fiction," in *John Bunyan and His England, 1628–88*, ed. Anne Laurence, W. R. Owens, and Stuart Sim (London and Roncenerte: Hambledon Press, 1990), 149.

22. John Stachniewski, *The Persecutory Imagination: English Puritanism and the Literature of Religious Despair* (Oxford: Clarendon Press, 1991), 207.

23. John R. Knott Jr., *The Sword of the Spirit: Puritan Responses to the Bible* (Chicago and London: University of Chicago Press, 1980), 141–42.

24. Deborah L. Madsen, *Rereading Allegory: A Narrative Approach to Genre* (London: Macmillan Press, 1995), 104.

25. Stanley E. Fish, *Self-Consuming Artifacts: The Experience of Seventeenth-Century Literature* (Berkeley, Los Angeles, and London: University of California Press, 1972), 255.

26. Maureen Quilligan makes this point effectively about Spenser's Redcrosse Knight in his encounter with Despaire in *The Faerie Queene*: "Despaire is not simply the personification of the lack of hope, which is what his name means etymologically (*de-spero*), he is one who 'dispairs' the natural wholeness of Christian teaching. By emphasizing the Old Testament virtue of justice to the exclusion of the New Testament virtue of love or mercy he [Despaire] 'dis-pairs' this true pair of testaments." See *The Language of Allegory: Defining the Genre* (Ithaca and London: Cornell University Press, 1979), 36–37.

"For the Best Improvement of Time": *Pilgrim's Progress* and the Liturgies of Nonconformity

KEN SIMPSON

IN SPITE OF BUNYAN'S CONTENTION THAT "THE WAY INTO HEAVEN IS through the church on earth" (*Solomon's Temple*, MW, 3: 497), the church has been largely ignored by readers of *The Pilgrim's Progress*.[1] The importance of what occurs in the church—the order of the Word and sacraments—has been equally neglected in studies of Bunyan's allegory. Although the centrality of Christian liturgy in seventeenth-century English literature has been clearly demonstrated by A. B. Chambers, P. G. Stanwood, and J. N. Wall, among others, these studies concentrate on the Anglican liturgical tradition rather than the Nonconformist, free church tradition in which Bunyan worshiped.[2] In fact, most readers accept the seventeenth-century Anglican view of Nonconformist worship as "liturgical chaos," what Samuel Parker called "the fiendish disorder in God's house,"[3] but as J. F. White suggests:

> Free Church worship is basically liturgical congregationalism. This does not mean liturgical chaos; indeed, the degree of predictability is usually almost as high as in other traditions of worship. But it often means that published liturgies are considered superfluous at best and idolatrous at worst. If God's word is clear to anyone who reads, each Christian community can discern what is God's will by itself and must be free to act accordingly.[4]

Liturgical chaos did reign in some gathered churches, but certainly not in all, especially after the Restoration when the more radical Protestant sects virtually disappeared. The anonymous author of *The Christian Conventicle or, The Private-Meetings of God's People in Evil Times* emphasizes orderly prayer, breaking of bread, and exhortation, assuring those framing the Second Conventicles Act that these are pure ordinances, and "nothing but what comes from an upright heart, guided and ordered according to the rule."[5] John Gifford, guiding spirit of the Bedford church and probably Bunyan's model for Evangelist in *The Pilgrim's Progress*, urges his congregation to "be constant in your Church assemblyes" and, citing 1 Corinthians 14.40, to "let all things be done decently and in order," especially in the observance of the three ordinances commanded by Christ—preaching, prayer, and the breaking of bread.[6] Although Bunyan rejects unbiblical, prescribed forms of worship as much as any Independent of his time, he also attacks the "libertine" who "pretendeth to be against forms and duties, as things that gender to bondage, neglecting the order of God" and asks rhetorically that since Christ "made himself known . . . in breaking of bread; who would not then, that loves to know him, be present at such an ordinance?" (*The Strait Gate, MW*, 5: 125; *The Desire of the Righteous Granted, MW*, 13: 130). Given that a sense of the liturgy did exist in the free church tradition, and given Bunyan's commitment to the Independent church of Bedford for about thirty-four years, eighteen as a layman and sixteen as a pastor, I will suggest that the influence of Nonconformist liturgy on *The Pilgrim's Progress*, and especially the Palace Beautiful scene, is more considerable than has been supposed. In keeping with the Nonconformist emphasis on spontaneity within a predictable order of service, Bunyan freely varied liturgical details, structures, and metaphors, turning liturgy into literature and literature into liturgy. Before turning to the liturgy, however, it is first necessary to discuss the church in which the liturgy takes place.

In *The Holy City*, Bunyan identifies two dimensions of the church that are commonplace in Nonconformist ecclesiology: the mystical church, consisting of the communion of saints in the presence of God, and the visible church, consisting of the communion of saints in each particular congregation (*MW*, 3: 173–75). The visible church is also part of the militant church which, in turn, is divided into three historical periods: a period of pure apostolic worship lasting approximately three hundred years after the crucifixion, a period up to and including the present time in which the true church must hide in the wilderness and suffer persecution, and a period in the future when apostolic worship will be restored after Christ's Second Coming. *The Holy City* depicts in great detail the restored church of the future, while the Celestial City of *The Pilgrim's Progress* corresponds to the mystical, triumphant church of elect saints, but Bunyan's abiding concern throughout the rest of *The Pilgrim's Progress* is with the persecuted militant church, a concern reflected in the guidance, fellowship, edification, and spiritual nourishment Christian receives from Evangelist, the Interpreter, Hopeful, Faithful, the shepherds of the Delectable Mountains, the Gardener of Beulah, and the holy community of Palace Beautiful.

As Richard Greaves has suggested, however, the mystical and visible churches are distinguished in Independent and separatist ecclesiology only to have their essential unity affirmed.[7] On the one hand, visible church membership is open to those who profess their conversion to Christ and their obedience to the church covenant—the "visible saints by calling" referred to by Bunyan in *The Holy City* (*MW*, 3: 174). On the other hand, membership does not ensure election and entry into the mystical church triumphant since only God knows whose conversion is sincere, but for Bunyan upstanding membership in the visible church is as close to an unambiguous and clear sign of election as is humanly possible. This is why from the Palace Beautiful Christian can see the Delectable Mountains, but only on a clear day; why from the Delectable Mountains Christian can see the Celestial City through a "Perspective Glass," but cannot look steadily because of shaking hands; and why from Beulah Christian can see the Celestial City, but still needs an "Instrument" despite being close to the end of his journey. Because of the possibility of lapsing into sin, every member of the visible church remains alienated from the full glory of God's presence (*PP*, 54, 122–23, 156).

Bunyan continued to argue that membership in the visible church was psychologically and spiritually necessary for salvation even though membership did not guarantee election. Because inward conviction and holy fellowship were the sole criteria for membership, Independent congregations of visible saints were gathered and separated from the world for comfort and edification rather than born into grace through communion in a parish church. As John Gifford states and as Bunyan reiterates in *A Confession of My Faith*, before church membership is granted a person must satisfy church elders of sincere conversion during a personal interview after which he or she should "solemnly declare (before some of the Church at least), that union with Christ is the foundation of all saintes' communion, and not any ordinances of Christ, or any judgement or opinion about externalls," including ordination and baptism.[8] Conversion narratives, public professions of faith, and church covenant ceremonies replace baptism as rites of initiation while preaching, prayer, and the Lord's Supper edify, sustain, and nourish faith rather than convey grace immediately. The public profession of membership also makes church discipline the responsibilty of each member of the church rather than the jurisdiction of the state or a church court above the congregation. This leads to a rigorously watchful discipline designed to sustain the church by encouraging faithful members in times of need and banishing members who persist in wrongdoing. The minutes of Bunyan's church in Bedford attest to the unflagging vigilance needed to maintain each member's "walke in fellowship" with the church. One need only consider where Christian would have arrived without Evangelist before Legality's house, or without Hopeful in Despair's dungeon, to realize how important church fellowship is in Bunyan's allegory. Visible church membership is necessary for Bunyan because no one can complete the journey to the mystical church without the instruction and nourishment that God provides in the ordinances, discipline, and fellowship of a particular visible church.

Bunyan also addresses the specific historical condition of the militant church in *The Pilgrim's Progress*. As the author's apology for his book indicates, writing is an extension of Bunyan's preaching ministry and issues from his pastoral concern to "perswade some that go astray, / To turn their Foot and Heart to the right way" (*PP*, 173). He also tells us in the first line of the allegory that he "walk'd through the wilderness of this world"(8), the metaphor that underlies the whole narrative. In the Bedford church minutes, "walk" is a kind of collective verb referring to the Christian life of the church as a whole: John Gifford urges his people to "Walke with the church in all love"; associating with other churches is referred to as "walking . . . with other congregations"; and in November 1668 Bunyan is sent out to rescue "many of the friends [who have] . . . in these troublous times withdrawne from close walking with the church."[9] This experience with the Bedford congregation occurs when Bunyan is probably writing *The Pilgrim's Progress* and may underlie the withdrawal of Timorous and Mistrust from the church of the Palace Beautiful. The lions scare Timorous and Mistrust just as the Conventicles Act caused some members of Bunyan's church to withdraw from fellowship.[10] "Walk," then, alerts us to Christian's corporate nature; he is not a solitary individual but a concrete universal, an individual whose lived experience represents the inner life of the church. He is no more individual than the "I" of the psalmist when his words are sung or recited by the whole congregation.

The image of the wilderness in the opening line of *The Pilgrim's Progress* also alludes to the persecuted condition of the true church. Not only does this "wilderness" refer to the wandering of the Israelites in Exodus 16 and the spiritual desolation of those outside of the church as Haller and Hill have argued, but it also evokes the struggle between the woman clothed with the sun and the dragon in Revelation 12.[11] Protestant commentators from David Pareus and William Perkins to Thomas Taylor and John Downame have glossed this text as a description of the historical state of the the militant church from the early apostolic period to the onset of reformation.[12] The woman is the true apostolic church assaulted by the Roman dragon in the wilderness where "she is nourished for a time" by God (Rev. 12:14). Christian's sacramental meal following his defeat of Apollyon may typify the precariousness of worship in the wilderness of the late 1660s: he sings a song of thanksgiving before the meal, eats bread and drinks wine provided by the Palace Beautiful community and then abruptly moves on, "sword in hand."

For Bunyan, however, another text also comes into play in the depiction of the church in its persecuted state—1 Kings 7, the subject of his elaborate typological exegesis *Of the House of the Forest of Lebanon*. Here he describes the house built by Solomon as a type of "our gospel church in the wilderness" (*MW*, 7: 126). It is a solitary, "bewildered," and afflicted church, but also one that, in due time, will be delivered from its wilderness condition because of its patience and strength. God "will make her wilderness like Eden, and her desert like the garden of the Lord" after the church is liberated "from her desert, her wilderness, her desolate, and comfortless state" (Isa. 51.3; *MW*, 7: 172). The fruitful field surrounding Solomon's house is compared to "the recovering of the afflicted church into a state most quiet and fruitful" when the church is "plant[ed] again with Christians" (*MW*, 7: 170, 171). Bunyan's identification of the church with the garden is even more explicit in *The Barren Fig Tree* where he refers to the church as the "vineyard" and "garden of God" (*MW*, 5: 18, 20). The wilderness symbolizes the historical condition of the church from the end of the apostolic period to the present. The garden is an archetype of the renewed, triumphant church in the future as well as the source of that renewal—the nourishment, strength, and comfort provided by the fellowship of saints and the ordinances of the true church, especially the Lord's Supper. In *The Pilgrim's Progress*, then, garden images allude not only to the church but to the sacrament which is the central liturgical act of the church. The sacramental gardens of the Delectable Mountains, Beulah, and the Meadow by the river of God, however, are not depicted as conveying grace but as conveying instruction and spiritual sustenance. When the sacramentality associated with eating and nourishment in these gardens is considered with the architectural analogues of the church in the House of the Interpreter and Palace Beautiful, the presence of the church can be felt throughout *The Pilgrim's Progress*. As the garden imagery suggests, the presence of the church can also be felt in the way Bunyan incorporates and transforms Nonconformist liturgical images, ideas, and structures into a liturgical event of his own.

"Liturgy" originally referred to work of or for the people, but was especially applied to public worship in the Hebrew temple by the authors of the Septuagint. Eventually, by the analogy of sacrifice evident in the Epistle to the Hebrews and other works in the New Testament, it signified the eucharistic rite of the Western church.[13] Through the repetition of a prescribed service by the sacerdotal priesthood, Christ's body and blood were made present to the church in the elements of bread and wine. The formal characteristics of this liturgy have been described most concisely by Mircea Eliade. Eliade sees in the liturgy a desire, found universally in world religions, for union with God through the creation of a sacred order of time lived in the yearly, weekly, and daily repetition of events in the life of a divine being.[14] For Christians, this redemption of time occurs in the repetition of the Christian calendar throughout the year, in the repetition of prescribed services, and, particularly, in the repetition of the Eucharist. The Eucharist is not a temporal occasion at all really, but an eternal present in which the repetition of Christ's sacrifice suspends chronological time, manifesting his real presence.

Independents like Bunyan, following Zwingli's sacramental theology, never referred to Christ's presence in the Eucharist; rather, the Lord's Supper was an ordinance, and the bread and wine were covenant seals or visible symbols through which members remembered together the body and blood given in Christ's death and resurrection. As a result, the Lord's Supper was primarily a holy and solemn ordinance for teaching and edification which united the community in Christ. Bunyan never used "liturgy" to describe the order of the Word and sacraments in his church either, but this should not keep us from acknowledging the importance of the Lord's Supper in the Nonconformist tradition or that order and predictability remained a central part of Bunyan's worship.[15] Bunyan associated "liturgy" with tyranny, idolatry, and the rote repetition of ceremonies even when he continued to be influenced by it because its meaning had both contracted and expanded to refer to prescribed rites of any kind and, specifically, to prescribed prayers such as the litanies and collects of the English church. Instead of repeating the same rite over and over again regardless of the condition of the individual church member, the true pastor, in Bunyan's view, had to move the hearts of individuals to a recognition of their dependence on Christ. To do this, creative rather than rote repetition was necessary. As John Cotton explained, prayers should be offered to God "not in any prescribed forme of Prayer, or studied Liturgie, but in such a manner, as the Spirit of grace and prayer . . . helpeth our infirmities."[16] The dissenting brethren of the Westminster Assembly also called attention to the source of the sermon in the free exercise of the Spirit: "publique Prayers in our Assemblies should be framed by the meditations and study of our own Ministers, out of their own gifts, (the fruits of Christs Ascension) as well as their sermons use to be."[17]

This attention to the Word and Spirit did not exclude the use of formal liturgies in the Nonconformist tradition; it excluded the imposition of unbiblical rites on the local congregation by authorities other than the local church and excluded those forms that stifled the gift of the Spirit in prayer and preaching. Richard Baxter's *Savoy Liturgy* (1661) is a good example of Nonconformist worship, even if the quiet fervour of its devotion is lost, at times, in Baxter's wordiness.[18] *The Westminster Directory* (1644), however, was more representative. Called by Parliament to reform the doctrine and discipline of the Church of England, the Westminster Assembly first met in July 1643 and by October they were granted the authority to create a liturgy to replace the Book of Common Prayer. The Assembly failed to produce a liturgy of set forms, however, because two Independent members on the subcommittee empowered to produce the liturgy—Thomas Goodwin and Philip Nye—refused to impose a form of prayers on the ministry. Just as preaching is the gift of the Spirit, so is prayer; as a result, only a directory, a set of guidelines for the ministry, was ratified by the House of Commons in April 1645.

The emphasis in Nonconformist liturgy, then, was on the Word and Spirit rather than on the repetition of prescribed acts. This resulted in a directory that allowed each individual pastor to address the needs of his own particular church, rather than a prescribed form that ignored individual differences between churches. The Word stipulates that worship should be based on "the apostles' doctrine and fellowship, and in breaking of bread, and in prayers" (Acts 2:42), but preaching and prayer must also be directed by the gifts of the Spirit, especially in the person of the pastor. As I have shown, this did not exclude a predictable order of divine service; rather, expressions of the Spirit in sermons and prayers allowed creative repetition within a predictable framework. According to most liturgists, preaching and Bible study illuminated by the Spirit—the liturgy of the Word—replaced the Eucharist as the focus of devotion in the free church tradition. Even though the medium of communication is different in each case, however, the purpose of the liturgy of the Word and sacraments is the same: in Eliade's terms, to redeem time by uniting believers to Christ through the repetition of sacred events.[19] This was made possible by the sanctifying and inspiring activity of the Holy Spirit, especially as the Spirit applied the Scripture to the everyday lives of believers through the preacher's sermon, through each believer's interpretation of Scripture, through the gift of prayer, and through remembered experience. The liturgy of the Word was enacted each time the Spirit revealed a biblical pattern in the life of the nation, church, and individual. This enactment created in the quietness of each believer's heart the recognition that Christ continued to speak in all details of life.

This flexibility within an accepted structure also encouraged the varied use of liturgical modes in literature. These modes range from literal references to liturgical events and ritual forms to imaginative and suggestive transformations of structures and images. Literal references are the most rare because the liturgies, to a great extent, were never written down. Several examples do exist in *The Pilgrim's Progress*, however. Before entering the Palace Beautiful, Christian participates in a rite of church admission very similar to the one described by Bunyan in *Grace Abounding* (*GA*, 78–79, §§ 253–54) and recommended by John Gifford in his last pastoral letter to the Bedford church. Christian first meets the porter Watchful who corresponds to the elder responsible for interviewing prospective church members. *Solomon's Temple Spiritualized*, Bunyan's exegesis of the Hebrew temple as a type of the perfected gospel church, confirms this. The porters of the temple are types of elders and pastors noted for their "watchfulness, diligence, [and] valour" who "look that none not duly qualified enter into the house of the Lord" (*MW*, 7: 40; cf. *The Strait Gate*, *MW*, 5: 77–78). Piety, Prudence, Charity, and Discretion symbolize the discipline of holiness expected by the church; they examine the candidate to determine his fitness for admission to the meal "according to the Law of the House" (*PP*, 47). Christian then tells his own story before he is welcomed into the family of the church and admitted to the supper, just as members of Bunyan's congregation were required to recite their story of faith as a requirement for membership and admission to the Lord's Supper. Noticeably absent from this rite is any reference to baptism as an initiation into the church, a principle of baptismal theology defended by Bunyan in the 1670s but also by Gifford twenty years earlier.

If references to baptism are rare in *The Pilgrim's Progress,* the same cannot be said of the Lord's Supper. The central symbols of the supper are, as I have suggested, communal meals, gardens, and pastoral settings where Christian receives nourishment of various kinds. If the church is a garden, the Sacrament, as the central rite of the church, is the spiritual nourishment that Christ offers members as they remember together his death and resurrection. Since, according to the Westminster Directory, the Sacraments are meant to comfort, nourish, and strengthen "weak and wearied souls," it is only fitting that Bunyan use pastoral images of food and abundance to convey the benefits of collective worship.[20] Thus, in *A Discourse of the Building, &c., of the House of God* he describes the garden of the church in sacramental terms, just as he does in Beulah and the Delectable Mountains:

> The *pomegranates* at all her gates do grow,
> *Mandrakes* and *Vines*, with other dainties mo;
> Her *Gardens* yield the *Chief*, the richest *Spice*,
> Surpassing them of *Adam's paradise*:
> Here be sweet *oyntments*, and the best of Gums;
> Here *runs* the *Milk*, here *drops* the Honey-Combs.
> (*MW*, 6: 278–79)

The signs of bread and wine nourish and sustain the church because they "teach and instruct" it about the essentials of faith; as a result, edification accompanies the representations of the Lord's Supper in Beulah, the Palace Beautiful, and the Delectable Mountains. More important, as the intricate texture of biblical allusions in Bunyan's work testifies, the source of the church's edification and nourishment is the Word of God. Bunyan transfers sacramental imagery to the Word, suggesting that the Word itself is the chief Sacrament of the church. In *The House of God* he suggests that "The Word's our ghostly Food; Food for our Faith" while in *The Strait Gate* he refers to the *Sursum Corda* before the eucharistic prayer to exhort his readers "not only to read, but to attend in reading; not only to read, but to lift up our hearts to God in reading" (*MW*, 6: 292; *The Strait Gate, MW*, 5: 73–74). In his description of the divinely inspired "opening" of Revelations 21:10–27 and 22:1–4 which became *The Holy City*, Bunyan uses imagery of bread and wine to underline the sacramental basis of reading and interpretation:

> I with a few groans did carry my meditations to the Lord Jesus for a blessing, which he did forthwith grant according to his grace; and helping me to set before my brethren, we did all eat, and were well refreshed; and behold also, that while I was in the distributing of it, it so increased in my hand, that of the fragments that we left, after we had well dined, I gathered up this Basketful. . . . Much more than I do here crush out, is yet left in the cluster. (*MW*, 3: 70)

Through the Lord's Supper, and also the Word of God which authorizes the rite, each member can "meet with God; and by them they are builded, and nourished up to eternal life" (*The Desire of the Righteous Granted, MW*, 13: 130).[21]

A more obvious sacramental meal occurs at the Palace Beautiful, but even here Bunyan transforms the rite into a uniquely literary, liturgical event. Bunyan selects only a few details of the liturgy to signify its ritual forms, creating a richly suggestive allegory while maintaining the decorum of a meal. The sacramental meal of the Palace Beautiful follows the liturgy of the Word in the House of Interpreter just as the Sacrament follows the Word in free church worship. Within the Palace, the meal follows the discipline of the House because a pure communion must be maintained. In the words of the Westminster divines, "the ignorant and scandalous are not fit to receive this sacrament of the Lord's Supper"; consequently, members must prove to be worthy of communication.[22] Bunyan refers to wine but not bread during the meal and alludes to the "Table" and the "Lord" without spelling out that this is the Lord's Table. In so doing he provides details that suggest the Lord's Supper without repeating the ritual by rote. More suggestive still is the reference to "their talk at the Table" which "was about the Lord of the Hill," "what he had done, and wherefore he did what he did, and why he had builded that House" (*PP*, 52), just as the eucharistic prayer over the gifts elaborates upon Christ's death and resurrection in the past, his redemption of the present, and his heavenly feast in the future. In fact, these heads of prayer are remarkably close to the pattern, though not the tone, of Baxter's exhortation before the prayer of consecration in the Savoy Liturgy. He speaks with great passion and devotion of Christ's redemptive sacrifice, the benefits enjoyed by the church, and the preparation of the marriage supper for the communion of saints: "See here Christ dying in this holy representation! . . . doubt not that your scarlet, crimson sins shall be made white as wool or snow. . . . And remember that he is coming."[23] Christ as mediator, redeemer, and judge is repeated with a difference in Bunyan's reference to what the Lord did, why he did it, and where he has gone. The passion in this communion scene, however, belongs not to the characters but to the narrator: breaking the decorum of the scene, the narrator imagines himself as part of the discourse at the table, commenting in his own voice that he "perceived that he [Christ] had been a great Warriour, and had fought with and slain him that had the power of death, but not without danger to himself, which made me love him more" (PP, 43). The identity of the "I" in this scene is so ambiguous that, in the paragraph that follows, Bunyan has to remind the reader in an abrupt parenthetical insertion that Christian is now the speaker not, by implication, the author himself.

The final liturgical mode of *The Pilgrim's Progress* is metaphorical, for neither specific allusions nor transformations of recognizable structures or images are employed, but the formal purpose of the liturgy—the redemption of time in the repetition of sacred events—is enacted in the act of writing itself. As Bunyan suggests in his "Apology" for the second part of *The Pilgrim's Progress*, his preaching ministry, the liturgy of the Word, is extended in time and space through print and thereby becomes an act of worship paralleling the sermon (PP, 167). Each typological reference, each biblical allusion potentially illuminates a reader's historical condition, re-creating the inner spirit of worship since present time is redeemed in the eternal pattern of Christ's life revealed in the narrative. The dream of the allegory is no mere convention either; it is a recognition of illumination and vision, the same illumination that is guided by the Spirit in prayer and preaching. Moreover, the incremental repetitions of events and narratives—what Kathleen Swaim refers to as incremental "loops" in the narrative structure, the pilgrim progressing by re-telling his story in ever widening circles of understanding—re-enact the condition of Nonconformist liturgies: the repetition of the same with the freedom of the Spirit.[24] Not only does Christian remember his experience in different ways—he recalls the experience of the cross first emotionally and then reflectively, for example—but he adds detail to each successive re-telling of his life-story as his understanding of his experience deepens. Other characters, like Faithful, literally go over the same terrain and tell their stories about similar experiences, shedding light on the progress of both characters. Faithful passes through the Slough of Dispond and proceeds to the Wicket Gate without the hardships experienced by Christian largely because he has Christian's example before him (PP, 68). In addition, many scenes and events of the first part of *The Pilgrim's Progress* recur in the second part as Christiana and her fellow pilgrims follow the same path as Christian, but, once again, many of the scenes and sequences are repeated with a difference. At the House of Interpreter, Christiana witnesses the same seven scenes as Christian, but then goes on to view seven more with each following the same order of presentation. The repetition of these circular structures replicates the conditions of the liturgy itself as the same events are repeated in the lives of worshipers at different times, creating a progressive, incrementally spiralling movement toward the holy city.

The culminating liturgical events in this mode occur as Christian and Hopeful, as well as Christiana and her community in Part Two, move from the restored, visible church of Beulah to the triumphant, mystical church of the Celestial City. In Part One, music is prominent in Bunyan's imaginative liturgy—harps, bells, even the "Sanctus" accompany the transfigured pilgrims into the city. In the justly praised approach to the holy city of Part Two, a rich texture of biblical allusion and "a marked rhythm, an almost musical pattern of recurrence and variation" prepare the pilgrims for the mystical church, the solemn procession of each character raising this event to a ritual performance of considerable power.[25] Each of the saints is called and sealed by the Word in the same order of events, but each is addressed in a way that illuminates his or her irreducibly individual condition. Each character receives a letter from the king of the Celestial City; each is spoken to by an angelic messenger; each receives a scriptural verse confirming the authority of the letter; each completes a will and offers final words before departing. In every case, however, the structure is repeated in a form appropriate for each individual just as in Nonconformist liturgies the creative repetition of divine events took place within a predictable framework. For Bunyan, as for many of his contemporaries, divine and eternal patterns repeated in limitless variations redeem the passing moment and re-create remembered experience as a liturgical act, an act of worship.

The Pilgrim's Progress, then, is an allegory of the soul, but it is also an allegory of the church.[26] The church itself receives frequent and varied depiction as Christian progresses from the liturgy of the Word in the House of Interpreter and the liturgy of the Lord's Supper in Palace Beautiful to analogues of the perfected gospel church in the garden of Beulah to the mystical church in the Celestial City. At the same time, the order of the liturgy Bunyan experienced in the Bedford church colors and enriches these depictions as literal allusions, transformed images or structures, and metaphorical applications of liturgical forms reveal a layer of the narrative that intensifies the drama and extends the reference of the allegory. Far from neglecting the order of worship, Bunyan weaves his worship into his story "for the best improvement of time" to the point where story and worship are inseparable sacramental acts in a church of imaginative and transcendent unity made possible by the printed word. As Bunyan declares in a passage from *The House of God* that alludes to the Palace Beautiful of *The Pigrim's Progress*:

> The road to *Paradice* lies by her *Gate*,
> Here *Pilgrims* do themselves *accommodate*
> With *Bed* and *Board*, and do such *Stories tell*
> As do for Truth and Profit, all excell.
>
> (*MW*, 6: 279)

Notes

1. For Bunyan and the church see the following: Richard L. Greaves, *John Bunyan* (Abingdon, Berkshire: Sutton Courtenay Press, 1969), 123–51; John R. Knott, Jr., "Bunyan and the Holy Community," *Studies in Philology* 80 (1983): 200–225; Kathleen M. Swaim, *Pilgrim's Progress, Puritan Progress: Discourses and Contexts* (Urbana: University of Illinois Press, 1993), 198–231; B. R. White, "The Fellowship of Believers: Bunyan and Puritanism," in *John Bunyan: Conventicle and Parnassus Tercentenary Essays*, ed. N. H. Keeble (Oxford: Clarendon Press, 1988), 1–19. For the church in Independent thought generally see Geoffrey Nuttall, *Visible Saints: The Congregational Way 1640–1660* (Oxford: Basil Blackwell, 1957).

2. See the following: A. B. Chambers, *Transfigured Rites in Seventeenth-Century Poetry* (Columbia: University of Missouri Press, 1992); P. G. Stanwood, *The Sempiternal Season: Studies in Seventeenth-Century Devotional Writing* (New York: Peter Lang, 1992); J. N. Wall, *Transformations of the Word: Spenser, Herbert, Vaughan* (Athens: University of Georgia Press, 1988). I am indebted to Chambers's taxonomy of liturgical modes (*Transfigured Rites*, 1–10) and Stanwood's view of metaphorical liturgy (*The Sempiternal Season*, xii).

3. Samuel Parker, "Preface" to *Bishop Bramhall's Vindication of Himself and The Episcopal Clergy, from the Presbyterian Charge of Popery* (London, 1670), sig. e2.

4. J. F. White, *Protestant Worship: Traditions in Transition* (Louisville, Ky.: Westminster/John Knox Press, 1989), 81.

5. *The Christian Conventicle or, The Private-Meetings of God's People in Evil Times* (London, 1670), 22.

6. John Gifford, "Pastoral Letter," in *The Minutes of the First Independent Church (now Bunyan Meeting) at Bedford, 1656–1766*, ed. H. G. Tibbutt (Bedford: Bedfordshire Historical Record Society, 1976), 18, 19, 20.

7. Greaves, *John Bunyan*, 124.

8. Gifford, *Church Minutes*, 19.

9. Gifford, *Church Minutes*, 18, 30, 39.

10. In *The Holy City* (*MW*, 3: 169), those who persecute the church are called "fierce lions."

11. William Haller, *The Rise of Puritanism* (New York: Columbia University Press, 1938), 131; Christopher Hill, *The Experience of Defeat: Milton and Some Contemporaries* (London: Faber and Faber, 1984), 297 ff.

12. David Pareus, *A Commentary upon the Divine Revelation of the Apostle and Evangelist John*, trans. Elias Arnold (Amsterdam, 1644), 20–24; William Perkins, *The Combate Betweene Christ and the Devill*, in *The Works of... William Perkins*, 3 vols. (London, 1612–1613), 3: 371–72; Thomas Taylor, *Christs Victorie Over the Dragon* (London, 1633), 292–93; John Downame et al., *Annotations Upon all the Books of the New and Old Testament*, 2d edn. (London, 1651), Rev. 12:1.

13. Gerhard Kittel et al., eds., and G. W. Bromiley, trans. and ed., *Theological Dictionary of the New Testament*, 10 vols. (Grand Rapids, Mich.: Eerdmans, 1967), 4: 215–29.

14. Mircea Eliade, *The Myth of the Eternal Return or Comos and History*, trans. W. R. Trask (Princeton: Princeton University Press, 1954), 20–25, 35–36.

15. It was the importance of the Lord's Supper, and especially the emphasis on moral and spiritual preparation for it, that led to infrequent celebration in the nonconformist tradition, not neglect, as is so often supposed. See *GA*, 78–79, §253–254.

16. John Cotton, *The Way of the Churches of Christ in New England* (London, 1645), 66–67.

17. Thomas Goodwin et al., *An Apologeticall Narration* (London, 1643), 12.

18. Richard Baxter, "The Savoy Liturgy," in *Liturgies of the Western Church*, ed. B. Thompson (Philadelphia: Fortress Press, 1961), 355–404.

19. White, *Protestant Worship*, 118; Horton Davies, *The Worship of the English Puritans* (Westminster, Md.: Dacre Press, 1948), 49–56.

20. Baxter, "The Savoy Liturgy," 369.

21. Cited in Greaves, *John Bunyan*, 136.

22. Baxter, "The Savoy Liturgy," 369.

23. Baxter, "The Savoy Liturgy," 397.

24. Swaim, *Pilgrim's Progress, Puritan Progress*, 25, 39–41, 142, 149–50.

25. Roger Sharrock, endnotes to *PP*, 352.

26. Swaim argues that the two parts of *The Pilgrim's Progress* inscribe two diametrically opposed genders, historical conditions, theological concerns, and biographical orientations. For example, she contrasts the soteriological emphasis of Part One with the ecclesiological emphasis of Part Two, but the importance of the church in Part One suggests that the relationship between the two parts is not oppositional but incremental—"what Christian left lock't up /... Christiana opens with her key" (*PP*, 139). See Swaim, *Pilgrim's Progress, Puritan Progress*, 198–200.

"For then I should be a Ranter or a Quaker": John Bunyan and Radical Religion

T. L. Underwood

LIKE MANY MINISTERS OF HIS TIME, JOHN BUNYAN PRESCRIBED A VERY restricted role for women in the church. Believing that in the Garden of Eden Eve "at one clap" had overthrown women's reputation forever as well as "her Soul, her Husband, and the whole World besides," Bunyan overturned his congregation's practice of allowing women to meet separately for prayer and worship without the leadership of men. In defending this action, he also declared that women should not minister in prayer before the whole church, otherwise as he put it, "I should be a Ranter or a Quaker"(*A Case of Conscience Resolved*, MW, 4: 305). His statement reminds us of the religious milieux in which Bunyan, as an admitted Baptist, found himself. He and many like him felt conflicting pressures to communicate their particular Christian identity and yet publicly distance themselves as far as possible from radicalism in order to gain respect and acceptance within society—all this in the midst of political turmoil and uncertainty as well as religious persecution.[1]

Of course, Baptists themselves were considered radical by many contemporaries. They were seen as having separated themselves from other Protestants, attacked the use of a professional ministry, and discarded Christian baptism as it had been practiced for centuries. In addition, many people associated them with the Continental Anabaptists who were widely remembered for the dreadful Münster revolution of 1534. Further, Bunyan's two imprisonments testify to the fact that he himself was perceived by some as a threat to the established order.

Sharing this radical end of the religious spectrum with Baptists were Familists, Seekers, Ranters, Quakers, and Muggletonians. Most have received noteworthy attention from historians in recent years. Indeed, Jerome Friedman has even positioned four of these groups in the "order of [their] radicalism" as follows: Seekers, Quakers, Muggletonians, and Ranters. Any such placement depends on the primary criterion chosen, of course, but all of these movements, including Familists, were further removed from the mainstream of English Protestantism than Baptists.[2] It is my intent, then, to examine some of the characteristics of these radical groups as well as their relationships to each other and to John Bunyan.

Familists, Seekers, and Ranters, however, pose problems of historicity. The question in the case of the Familists is not whether they ever existed in England but rather whether they were still present at the time of Bunyan's ministry even though they were mentioned in each of his first two publications. Familist tenets were based on the mystical writings of the Dutchman Hendrick Niclaes (c. 1502–1580). He concluded that both in the Garden of Eden and in the revelation of Christ, divine truth had been offered to but rejected by humankind. The third and ultimate divine communication was through Niclaes himself. He emphasized the importance of the inward, spiritual world. He describes Christ's death, burial, and resurrection *within* believers, and teaches that Christ's outward historical suffering was insufficient for salvation and that believers must also have a mystical transformation variously referred to as illumination, resurrection, renewal, or triple baptism. They would then be inhabited by the Godhead and reach a state of perfection. However, enemies of the Family of Love feared that such perfection gave Familists the freedom to indulge in carnal sin.

Niclaes attracted followers in the Low Countries, Germany, and France, and his ideas eventually gained attention in England. From 1573 to 1575, eighteen English translations of Familist books became available there. The existence of Familist communities was soon reported, and it was even thought that sympathizers and converts were among Queen Elizabeth's own Yeomen of the Guard. Although such communities were to be found as far south as Canterbury and Exeter and as far north as Grindleton and York, most were concentrated in parts of Huntingtonshire and Cambridgeshire, both bordering on Bunyan's Bedfordshire. However, by the time of the Interregnum the beliefs of the Family of Love may have passed into other streams of religious radicalism such as Ranterism or Quakerism. Familists as such perhaps faded into obscurity even though scattered references to them continued until near the end of the century. It is true that Familist works were reprinted during the Commonwealth and Protectorate, but this may have been for an audience generally interested in a variety of religious views rather than for or by Familists themselves. Christopher W. Marsh, the most recent historian of English Familism, has admitted that the Family of Love's "interest in spiritual illumination, the divine presence within the soul of the true believer, clearly does connect its members with later Seekers, Quakers, [and] Ranters," but he has gone on to point out that in contrast to these radicals, Familists were inconspicuous. Following Niclaes's injunctions, they became part of the social fabric, obeying magistrates, serving in ecclesiastical and public offices, being good neighbors and good citizens, but remaining secretive about their religious views and usually sharing them only within the Family. Thus, although there is clear if limited evidence of some of their activities in Elizabethan and Jacobean times, Familist existence in subsequent decades is elusive. As Marsh has pointed out, "The Family of Love, despite the best efforts of historians, will always retain many of its secrets." Its very presence during the period of Bunyan's ministry may be one such secret.[3]

The historicity of Seekers in the mid-seventeenth century has also been challenged. Early Quaker membership was traditionally thought to have drawn significantly from Seeker communities in northwest England. However, J. F. McGregor is probably correct in concluding that "there was no *sect* of Seekers in revolutionary England." Less convincing is his suggestion that Seekers be approached as merely "the personification of a point of religious debate." Some Friends like John Tomkins and Thomas Taylor, after all, remembered groups of Seekers and a time when conversions had been made from among them. Edward Burrough wrote to Margaret Fell in 1654 that Francis Howgill and Richard Hubberthorne had spoken to a meeting of "Waiters" or Seekers in London, and in 1657 William Caton wrote to Fell to report several Seekers near Lewes in Sussex. In addition, the heresiographer Thomas Edwards described and attacked Seeker beliefs and even identified William Erbery, William Walwyn, John Saltmarsh, and Laurence Clarkson as members of this supposed sect. In defending themselves, Erbery, Walwyn, and Saltmarsh described basic Seeker tenets with many of which they claimed to be sympathetic. For his part, Clarkson, who was successively a Presbyterian, Independent, Baptist, Seeker, Ranter, and Muggletonian, admitted that having been influenced by Erbery, he became a Seeker and then moved among Seekers in London, Kent, and Hertfordshire. Richard Baxter also described Seeker beliefs and even distinguished between six different types of Seekers. In addition, John Jackson, who explained and defended Seeker views in *A Sober Word to a Serious People* (1651), was considered by Baxter to be "The most rational and modest that hath wrote for this way." Thus we have a number of descriptions of

Seeker characteristics written by Seekers and Seeker sympathizers as well as detractors. In brief, Seekers believed that they lived in an age of apostasy. Thus they took a skeptical approach to current Christian faith and practice. They maintained that the true church, ministry, and worship were "lost" and that Christians were to wait for them to be restored by God's initiative.[4]

Another problem of historicity has been raised by J. C. Davis in suggesting that Ranters may have been an invention of seventeenth-century royalists, Presbyterians, and sectaries, assisted by modern historians bent on demonstrating a radical tradition in English history. On the other hand, Jerome Friedman has readily accepted the existence of Ranters and has placed them in several categories including sexual libertines, gentlemen Ranters, and philosophical Ranters. The term *Ranter* was a sobriquet used loosely and pejoratively to refer to a variety of persons. On the one hand there were men like Captain Robert Norwood and the minister John Pordage who were apparently morally upright but accused of Ranterism because of alleged theological aberrations. On the other, there was Abiezer Coppe who declared "I can if it be my will, kisse and hug Ladies and love my neighbours wife as my selfe, without sin," and John Robins whose followers were said to believe he was God and thus also the father of Jesus Christ who was then in his wife's womb. Ranter beliefs usually reflected antinomianism and a mystical pantheism, appealed to an inward spiritual authority, and sometimes embraced a denial that the spiritual person actually sinned in the commission of carnal acts. As a result, according to Baxter, "they spake most hideous Words of Blasphemy, and many of them committed Whoredoms commonly."[5]

In the case of John Robins and his supporters, blasphemy may well have been demonstrated by more than just the words and acts described above. Lodowick Muggleton reported that Robins showed to his followers many lying signs and wonders "presenting the appearance of Angels, burning shining Lights, Half-Moons and Stars in Chambers and thick Darkness, where it was Light to the Phantasies of People, when they covered their Faces in the Bed." He also reported that Robins claimed to have raised Jeremiah, Benjamin, Cain, Judas, and other biblical characters from the dead and that "I saw all those that was said to be raised by *John Robins*, and they owned themselves to be the very same Persons that had been Dead for so long [a] time."[6]

Ranter "whoredoms" may have been perceived, for example, in the activities of the minister Thomas Webb whose story has been reconstructed from Webb's own writing and from a work by Judge

Edward Stokes which included some legal records. Shortly after Webb became minister at Langley Burial in North Wiltshire, his second wife died and he then remarried. In March 1650 he and his new bride took up residence in the large manor house occupied by Henry and Mary White, husband and wife. In this more convenient setting, Webb renewed his interest in Mary White, one of several women in the area with whom he had already had sexual relations. He also became intimate with a young man whom he publicly referred to as his "male wife." Mary White, jealous of both of Webb's wives, brought legal action against the minister for sexual and religious irregularities. In the court of Justice Stokes, Webb confessed his errant ways, declared that he had turned from them, and accused Mary White of being a temptress with an insatiable sexual appetite who had been responsible for leading him astray. The case was dismissed. But a renewed intimacy with Mary White, the involvement of additional people in his irregular affairs, and the forwarding of more charges to Justice Stokes eventually brought Webb to the attention of the Parliamentary Committee of Plundered Ministers. Following accusations by his parishioners that he claimed it was lawful for him to lay with any woman and that he preached other Ranter doctrines, Webb was ejected from his living.[7]

Whereas Familists, Seekers, and Ranters, as we have seen, present problems of historicity, Quakers and Muggletonians do not. Indeed, of the radical religious groups that arose in the mid-seventeenth century only these two survived into the twentieth. By the early 1650s George Fox's experience with the inner light and his subsequent mission to "bring people off from all the world's religions, which are vain," and to "turn people to that inward light, spirit, and grace, by which all might know their salvation, and their way to God" was so successful in the north of England that Quakers were soon able to launch a major evangelistic campaign into most other parts of the country and overseas as well. By 1660 their numbers probably reached 35,000. This was alarming to John Bunyan and most others, for Friends replaced the fundamental authority of Scripture with that of the spiritual inner light, internalized and spiritualized Christ's crucifixion and resurrection, discarded the sacraments, refused to pay tithes or show deference to magistrates and social superiors in traditional ways, and sometimes went naked "as a sign" in public. In addition, Fox occasionally performed "miracles," keeping a record of them in his "Book of Miracles," and was sometimes addressed by followers with extravagant language such as "him to whom all nations should bow." James Nayler, for a time a rival to Fox for Quaker leadership in London, reportedly raised up Dorcas Erbery, widow of the Seeker William Erbery, after she had been dead for two days. More notably, in Bristol in 1656, he re-enacted Christ's triumphal entry into Jerusalem for which he was tried and punished for blasphemy. Following the Restoration, however, various means were taken by Friends to impose order, control potential extravagances, and render Quakerism more respectable. Nevertheless, such efforts did not seem to change Bunyan's decidedly negative opinion of them.[8]

As in the case of Quakers, there is no question about the existence of Muggletonians. At their beginning, the London tailor John Reeve claimed that three times in early 1652 he literally heard the outward physical voice of God appointing him as the last divine messenger and designating his cousin Lodowick Muggleton his spokesperson. The two taught that God became a man (Christ) and continued as such, standing between five and six feet tall and ruling in heaven some six miles above the earth. They also maintained that the human soul was mortal, that matter was eternal, and that the ministry and worship of the church for most of its history was void. As the two witnesses of the eleventh chapter of Revelation, their doctrines, curses, and blessings were said to be the direct will of God. Following Reeve's death in 1658, Muggleton was challenged for the leadership of the sect by Laurence Clarkson (Claxton) who, as we have seen, previously passed through several religious phases as a Presbyterian, Independent, Baptist, Seeker, and Ranter before becoming a Muggletonian. In reaction to his attempted usurpation, Muggleton wrote to Clarkson, "I do renounce [and] disown you upon any such accompt as to be a Messenger, Bishop, Or servant any more to this commission."[9] Muggleton was successful in countering this threat, was reconciled to a submissive Clarkson, and continued to be considered by his faithful followers as God's only remaining commissioned witness until his death in 1698.

Unlike the Quakers, Muggletonians did not engage in active evangelism and perhaps for that reason remained small, probably numbering only in the hundreds. Nevertheless, they were eventually to be found not only in England (mostly in the Midlands and the South) but also in Scotland, Ireland, Spain, Germany, New England, and the West Indies. Also, in contrast to Fox, Muggleton did not like to travel, although he did sometimes venture from his London home into Cambridgeshire, Leicestershire, Nottinghamshire, Derbyshire, Kent, and Essex. Much of Muggleton's pastoral care, therefore, was extended through correspondence. Among copies of his letters are many that give spiritual, financial, or marital advice, including one that conveys comfort to a dying girl and another that chastises a young man for contracting venereal disease from a prostitute.[10]

Like the organization of the sect itself, Muggletonian religious services were very informal and were usually held in a tavern or a member's house. There was no preaching, traditional worship with prayers and scripture readings, or observance of sacraments but rather eating, drinking, discussion, and the singing of songs composed by members. On a visit to his followers in Braintree, Essex, for example, Muggleton was greeted in their religious service with this song composed by William Wood:

> And now, Divine Sir, you are welcome to mee
> And to the rest of our friends by their joy you doe see
> We greet you in love as our Sheppard and pastor
> And prostrate our selves to the grace of your Master.
> (British Library Additional Manuscript 60220/29)

Reeve and Muggleton were financially assisted in some measure by their followers but they mostly supported themselves, in part by the sales of their books. The most notable of their printed works were their joint efforts *A Transcendent Spiritual Treatise* (1652) and *A Divine Looking-Glass* ([1656] 1661), and Muggleton's *The Acts of the Witnesses*, an autobiographical effort published posthumously in 1699. Among their other books were several directed against the Quakers. But Muggleton's books and beliefs resulted in his imprisonment, fine, and punishment on the pillory in 1677—a sentence imposed by George Jeffreys, best known for his part in the "bloody assizes" following the Monmouth Rebellion of 1685. Although the imprisonment experience made him more cautious, Muggleton continued his normal ministry until his death in 1698 at age 88. Whereas the Muggletonian presence in England in the two following centuries was recognized, it was not widely known until the 1980s that they had enjoyed a continuous existence until at least 1979.[11]

There were some points of similarity among Familists, Seekers, Quakers, Ranters, and Muggletonians but especially among the first four who shared a strong emphasis on an inward, spiritual authority and the inward, spiritual qualities of Christianity. Muggletonians, on the other hand, stressed outward physical religious elements. Their authority in faith and practice, for example, consisted not of an inner spiritual divine light but rather of the two divinely commissioned witnesses, Reeve and Muggleton.¹² In spite of some similarities there were skirmishes among these groups as well as attacks against Baptists. The Ranter Abiezer Coppe, for example, criticized Baptists for "damning all those that are not of thy Sect." The Seeker John Jackson warned Friends of the danger of the devil posing as an angel of light. The Quaker Edward Burrough condemned both Seekers and Ranters for not having the *true* light, and Margaret Fell denounced the latter for their lying, swearing, and drunkenness. Friends ridiculed the Muggletonian notion that God was a man five or six feet tall, and George Fox thought Muggleton had "made himself [into] a Pope." The Muggletonian Thomas Tomkinson believed "Atheistical Quakers & Ranters" were led by their own dictates of reason. Muggleton himself accused Quakers of preaching "ninny-nonies" and considered William Penn "an ignorant spatter-brain'd Quaker," reportedly declaring of Penn, "*I care not a Fart for Him, nor his Friends.*"¹³

Having examined some of the characteristics of these radical groups and their relationships with each other, we must now ask what Bunyan's connections with them were. His association with Quakers is well known, of course. Disputes with unnamed Friends in Bedfordshire launched him into print with tracts published in 1656 and 1657, censuring Edward Burrough as "an enemie to the Truth" (*Some Gospel-Truths Opened*, MW, 1: 134) and denouncing the Quakers as "blinde Pharises" (*A Vindication of . . . Some Gospel-Truths*, MW, 1: 61). Burrough replied in print as did George Fox, who condemned Bunyan's "Lies and Slanders," and rebuked Bunyan himself as a person who "had better have been silent, then to fight against the Lord, the Lamb and his Saints." In spite of Bunyan's oral and written attacks on Friends' doctrine and practice, the work of early Quaker evangelists met with considerable success in Bedfordshire. Fox himself ventured into the area, on one occasion in 1658 attending a general meeting of as many as 4,000 Friends. By 1669 the number of Quaker conventicles in Bedfordshire equalled that of Presbyterians, Independents, and Baptists combined.¹⁴ Beyond his first two printed works, Bunyan continued to denounce Quaker doctrine and practice in nine of his subsequent publications including *A Defence of the Doctrine of Justification, by Faith* (1672), *Grace Abounding* (5th ed., 1680), and *Questions About the Nature and Perpetuity of the Seventh-Day Sabbath* (1685).¹⁵ There were at least two ironies to be found in Bunyan's hostile relationship with Friends. First, his release from prison in 1672 was expedited by the addition of his name to a petition for the release of some 450 Quakers (*MW*, 1: xxx). Second, although Fox and Bunyan never met, the two antagonists both died in London within a span of twenty-nine months and were buried in Bunhill Fields within 300 yards of each other.

Bunyan documented in print something of his association with Ranters, just as he did with Quakers. In fact, he linked the two, declaring that the views of Friends "are the same that long ago were held by the *Ranters*. Only the *Ranters* had made them thredbare at an Ale-House, and the *Quakers* have set a new glosse upon them again by an outward legal holiness" (*A Vindication of . . . Some Gospel-Truths*, MW, 1: 139). Richard Baxter and Lodowick Muggleton said much the same.[16] Bunyan admitted in *Grace Abounding* that he had become familiar with Ranter views by reading some of their books, and he went on to tell of an intimate religious companion of his who "turned a most devilish *Ranter*, and gave himself up to all manner of filthiness, especially Uncleanness," and who "would also deny that there was a God, Angel, or Spirit." Bunyan also told of others "swept away by these Ranters" who believed they "could do what they would and not sin" (GA, 16–17). Condemnation of Ranter principles appeared in other works as well, including *Some Gospel-Truths Opened* (1656), *A Vindication of the Book Called, Some Gospel-Truths Opened* (1657), and *The Holy City* (1665) (MW, 1: 7, 138; MW, 3: 121). In addition, perhaps some Ranter characteristics may be seen in Mr. Atheism accused in *The Holy War* (1682) of believing it "as good to go to a Whore-house as to go to hear a Sermon." But if antinomianism led some Ranters to engage in "Uncleanness" yet "not sin," it should also be remembered that Bunyan himself was accused of antinomianism by Richard Baxter among others. The Bedford tinker maintained, however, that the Christian life was to be a holy life, although based on a free offer of grace even to the basest sort of persons.[17]

Familists were mentioned only twice in Bunyan's works. In *Some Gospel-Truths Opened* (1656) John Burton (d. 1660), his pastor, wrote "To the Reader" in which he linked the Family of Love with Quakers and Ranters, describing all three as people who "either deny Christ to be a reall man without them, blasphemously fancying him to be only God manifest in their flesh; or else make his humane nature with the fulnesse of the Godhead in it, to be but a type of God to be manifest in the saints, and so according to their wicked imagination, his humane nature was to be laid aside after he had offered it up upon the crosse without the gate at *Jerusalem* . . ." (MW, 1: 7). The Quaker Edward Burrough, in answering Bunyan's tract, protested against Burton's comparison of Quakers to Ranters.[18] In his reply to Burrough, *A Vindication of the Book, Called Some Gospel-Truths Opened* (1657), Bunyan defended Burton, repeating his pastor's comparison of *"Familists, Ranters, Quakers, and others"* and asking, "what harme is it to joyne a *Dog* and a *Woolfe* together? a fawning *Dog*, and a *Woolfe* in sheepes clothing, they differ a little in outward appearance, but they can both agree to worrie Christs Lambes" (*MW*, 1: 137–38). Thus, Bunyan did not initiate the references to Familists and, although in certain subsequent publications he attacked some doctrines that Familists, Ranters, and Quakers might have shared (see above), he never again mentioned Familists by name, perhaps because they had faded from view as previously suggested.

Whereas Bunyan recorded his association with Quakers, Ranters, and Familists by specific references to them in his publications, he did not do so with Seekers and Muggletonians. Indeed, we must ask whether Bunyan might even have known of these two groups or their views. Of course the Bedford tinker was not a Bedford isolate. He saw garrison duty in the Parliamentary Army at Newport Pagnell, Buckinghamshire, from 1645 to 1647. Thomas Edward's alleged Seekers William Erbery and John Saltmarsh were notable preachers in the Parliamentary Army and Erbery was at Newport Pagnell in late 1645. Later, the ministerial network of which Bunyan was a part extended through Bedfordshire and into the Midlands, East Anglia, and of course London. Among Bunyan's numerous contacts in London was the Independent minister John Simpson with whom Erbery disputed there in 1652. In the following year Erbery also debated with Baptists in London. Thus it seems possible, perhaps even likely, that Bunyan was aware of Erbery and of Seeker beliefs. Although there is less evidence for an awareness of Muggletonians, they may have been more visible in London than Seekers. Reeve's and Muggleton's early association there with the notorious Ranter John Robins, the many curses they pronounced on adversaries (the Quaker Thomas Loe died shortly after such a pronouncement), and Muggleton's 1677 trial at the Old Bailey and public punishment that followed, may have come to Bunyan's attention. News may also have reached him of Muggleton's visits to followers in Braintree, Essex, and in Cambridge and other parts of the county, for Bunyan also had acquaintances in these places.[19]

In any case, in *The Holy City* Bunyan seems to have described much of the central belief of Seekers when he related the idea that "this outward Gospel-Worship should be set aside while the Church is in the World, before her Lord doth come to be enjoyed by her." He went on to dismiss this notion because, he said, "it looks too like *Ranting Opinions*, and contradiction to Scripture, for me to believe" (*MW*, 3: 156–57). In addition, the Seeker characteristic of questioning, skepticism, and hesitancy with regard to current religious practice is perhaps to be seen in the Doubters of *The Holy War* who "at a distance are but like Objections refell'd [refuted] with arguments," and who "put a question upon every one of the Truths of *Emanuel*" (*HW*, 215, 227). Such characteristics possibly also appear in Mr. Feeble-mind in *The Pilgrim's Progress* (Part Two) who claimed, *"you are all lusty and strong, but I, as you see, am weak . . . so weak a Man, as to be offended with that which others have a liberty to do. I do not yet know all the Truth"* (*PP*, 270). Although there is no specific mention of John Reeve or Lodowick Muggleton in Bunyan's works, in *An Exposition of the Ten First Chapters of Genesis* (1692) he clearly rejects the belief in the eternal nature of matter held by Muggletonians, declaring, "The first thing that God made, was Time," and "Whatsoever was before Time, was Eternal; but nothing but God himself is Eternal" (*MW*, 12: 105). Similarly, in Part Two of *The Pilgrim's Progress* Prudence, catechizing Matthew, asked *"If there was ever any thing that had a being, Antecedent to, or before God?"* to which Matthew replied, "No, for God is Eternal, nor is there any thing excepting himself, that had a being until the beginning of the first day" (*PP*, 225–26). Finally, Bunyan's treatment of Revelation 11 in *Of Antichrist, and His Ruine* (1692) struck at the very heart of the Muggletonian message, for the two messengers in that chapter, he claimed, were to be interpreted "in a mystical sense" (*MW*, 13: 472–73) as the whole succession of professing saints who had borne witness for God against the Antichrist through the centuries.

In general, then, although Bunyan may have disagreed with most of the beliefs and practices of all five of these radical religious groups, the strong emphasis on inward and spiritual religious qualities on the part of the Familists, Seekers, Ranters, and Friends, as most fully developed and articulated by Quakers, stood furthest from his views. He denounced as errors in the fifth edition (1680) of *Grace Abounding*, as he had on earlier occasions, such Quaker beliefs as the following:

> 1. That the holy Scriptures were not the Word of God. 2. That every man in the world had the spirit of Christ, grace, faith, &c. 3. That Christ Jesus, as crucified, and dying 1600 years ago, did not satisfy divine justice for the sins of the people. 4. That Christ's flesh and blood was within the saints. 5. That the bodies of the good and bad that are buried in the churchyard shall not rise again. 6. That the resurrection is past

with good men already. 7. That that man Jesus, that was crucified between two thieves on Mount Calvary, in the land of Canaan, by Jerusalem, was not ascended up above the starry heavens. 8. That he should not, even the same Jesus that died by the hands of the Jews, come again at the last day, and as man judge all nations, &c. (*GA*, 39)

Indeed, his own emphasis on the outward, physical religious elements of Christianity meant that in this respect he had more in common with Muggletonians than with Familists, Seekers, Ranters, or Friends. Reflecting this affinity was a statement he made in his first printed work and repeated in his second. In arguing that Christ had outwardly, physically, visibly ascended into heaven rather than into his saints, as Quakers seemed to be saying, Bunyan asked to be shown by his adversaries "that there is in them any place called heaven, which is able to contain a man of some four or five foot long" (*Some Gospel-Truths Opened*, *MW*, 1: 79; *A Vindication of . . . Some Gospel-Truths*, *MW*, 1: 183). Edward Burrough who conceived of God and Christ as infinite spirit reacted strongly, condemning Bunyan's "Carnall sottishness." Seventeen years later the Quaker George Whitehead accused the Baptist minister Henry Grigg and Baptists in general of committing the heresy "of the present *Muggletonians*, who," he said, "imagine God to be a personal or bodily Existence circumscribed as to place, denying him to be an infinite Spirit."[20] Had Bunyan responded to such a charge, he might have done so in a manner similar to his statement about women ministering in prayer before the whole church, and may thus have concluded that he did not believe Christ or God to be only an infinite spirit, "for then I should be a Ranter or a Quaker."

Notes

1. In *The Heavenly Foot-man* (1698), *MW*, 5: 153, Bunyan warned readers not to "have too much Company with some *Anabaptists*, though I go under that name my self." I have chosen to use the admittedly anachronistic term "radical," for the defense of which see Richard L. Greaves, *Enemies under His Feet; Radicals and Nonconformists in Britain, 1664–1677* (Stanford: Stanford University Press, 1990), 7–8.

2. Jerome Friedman, *Blasphemy, Immorality, and Anarchy: The Ranters and the English Revolution* (Athens: Ohio University Press, 1987), 13.

3. Christopher W. Marsh, *The Family of Love in English Society, 1550–1630* (Cambridge: Cambridge University Press, 1994), 18–32, 259, 249 quoted. See also Alastair Hamilton, *The Family of Love* (Cambridge: James Clarke, 1981); and Jean Dietz Moss, *"Godded With God": Hendrick Niclaes and His Family of Love* (Philadelphia: Transactions of the American Philosophical Society; new series v. 71, pt. 8, 1981).

4. J. F. McGregor, "Seekers and Ranters," in *Radical Religion in the English Revolution*, ed. J. F. McGregor and Barry Reay (Oxford: Oxford University Press, 1984), 129 (the emphasis is mine), 123 quoted; John Tomkins, *Piety Promoted*, 2d ed., 3 pts. (1703–1706), 3: 119; Thomas Taylor, *Truth's Innocency* (1697), sigs. B2r, C2r; Burrough to Fell 1654, Library of the Religious Society of Friends, London (hereafter *LF*): Swarthmore Manuscripts 3/63; Caton to Fell 19 January 1656, *LF*: Swarthmore Manuscripts 1/314; Thomas Edwards, *Gangraena* (London, 1646), 73, 77–78; id., *The Second Part of Gangraena* (London, 1646), 21; id., *The Third Part of Gangraena* ([London], 1646), 75, 89–90; William Erbery, *The Testimony* (1658); William Walwyn, *A Whisper in the Eare of Mr. Thomas Edwards* (1645); John Saltmarsh, *Sparkles of Glory or Some Beams of the Morning Star* (1647); Laurence Clarkson, *The Lost Sheep Found* (London, 1660), 19; John Jackson, *A Sober Word* (1651), 34–35; Richard Baxter, *A Key for Catholicks* (London, 1659), 331–34, 332 quoted; Richard L. Greaves and Robert Zaller, eds., *Biographical Dictionary of British Radicals in the Seventeenth Century*, 3 vols. (Brighton: Harvester Press, 1982–84).

5. J. C. Davis, *Fear, Myth and History: The Ranters and the Historians* (Cambridge: Cambridge University Press, 1986); id., "Fear, Myth and Furore: Reappraising the 'Ranters,' " *Past and Present* 129 (1990): 79–103; Friedman, *Blasphemy, Immorality, and Anarchy*; Abiezer Coppe, *A Second Fiery Flying Roll* (1649), sig. B3r (faulty pagination); John Taylor, *Ranters of Both Sexes* (1651), 2; Richard Baxter, *Reliquiae Baxterianae* (London, 1696), Part I: 76; Greaves and Zaller, *Biographical Dictionary of British Radicals*. See also A. L. Morton, *The World of the Ranters: Religious Radicalism in the English Revolution* (London: Lawrence & Wishart, 1970); J. F. McGregor, "Ranterism and the Development of Early Quakerism," *Journal of Religious History* 9 (1976–77): 349–63; Nigel Smith, *Perfection Proclaimed: Language and Literature in English Radical Religion, 1640–1660* (Oxford: Clarendon Press, 1989). Friends themselves distinguished between "Civil Ranters" (antinomian Independents) and those who engaged in more objectionable behavior—see Thomas Barcroft to Margaret Fell, 26 May 1657, *LF*: Swarthmore Manuscripts 1/173; Oliver Atherton to Margaret Fell, 17 December 1660, *LF*: Swarthmore Manuscripts 1/134.

6. Lodowick Muggleton, *The Acts of the Witnesses of the Spirit, In Five Parts* (London, 1699), 21–22.

7. Friedman, *Blasphemy, Immortality, and Anarchy*, 217–35.

8. George Fox, *The Journal of George Fox*, ed. John L. Nickalls (London: Religious Society of Friends, 1975, hereafter *FJN*), 35; George Bishop to Margaret Fell, 27 October 1656, Swarthmore Manuscripts 1/188. William G. Bittle, *James Nayler 1618–1660: The Quaker Indicted by Parliament* (York: William Sessions, 1986); Winthrop S. Hudson, "A Suppressed Chapter in Quaker History," *Journal of Religion* 24 (1944): 108–18; Thomas O'Malley, " 'Defying the Powers and Tempering the Spirit': A Review of Quaker Control over Their Publications, 1672–1689," *Journal of Ecclesiastical History* 33 (1982): 72–88; Henry J. Cadbury, ed., *George Fox's "Book of Miracles"* (New York: Octagon Books, 1973); H. Larry Ingle, "George Fox as Enthusiast: An Unpublished Epistle," *Journal of the Friends Historical Society* 55 (1989): 266–70; and id., "George Fox, Historian," *Quaker History* 82 (1993): 28–35.

9. John Reeve and Lodowick Muggleton, *A Transcendent Spiritual Treatise* (1652), 5, 23, 34; id., *A Divine Looking-Glass* ([1656] 1661), 100–103; Lodowick Muggleton, *An Answer to Isaac Penington* (London, 1669), 16; id., *A Discourse Between John Reeve and Richard Leader* (1682), 7; Lodowick Muggleton to Lau-

rence Claxton (Clarkson), London, 25 December 1660, British Library Additional Manuscript 60168/6-7.

10. Lodowick Muggleton to Robert Pierce, 2 August 1680, British Library Additional Manuscript 60168/30-39; Lodowick Muggleton to Elizabeth Dickenson, Junior, 6 March 1674, British Library Additional Manuscript 60171/134; Lodowick Muggleton to William Cleve, 1665, British Library Additional Manuscript 60171/73.

11. Christopher Hill, Barry Reay, and William Lamont, *The World of the Muggletonians* (London: Temple Smith, 1983), 1-5.

12. Muggleton, *An Answer to Isaac Penington*, 20; id., *The Answer to William Penn* (London, 1673), 120; William Penn, *The New Witnesses Proved Old Hereticks* (1672), 65; George Fox, *Something in Answer to Lodowick Muggleton's Book* (London, 1667), 9; *FJN*: 96-97.

13. Abiezer Coppe, *A Fiery Flying Roll* (1649), 14; John Jackson, *Strength in Weakness* (1655), 12-14; Edward Burrough, *A Trumpet of the Lord Sounded Out of Sion* ([London], 1656), 28-29; Margaret Fell, *A Testimonie of the Touch-Stone* (1656), 27; Penn, *The New Witnesses Proved Old Hereticks*, 39-40; Muggleton, *An Answer to Isaac Penington*, 16; Fox, *Something in Answer to Lodowick Muggleton's Book*, 27; Thomas Tomkinson, to Brethren and Sisters in Ireland (1674), British Museum Additional Manuscript 60180/11-16, 13r quoted; Muggleton, *The Answer to William Penn*, title-page; Penn, *The New Witnesses Proved Old Hereticks*, 41.

14. George Fox, *The Great Mistery of the Great Whore Unfolded* (1659), 8, 211. *Some Gospel-Truths Opened* was answered by Edward Burrough's *The True Faith of the Gospel of Peace Contended For....* (1656), to which Bunyan replied with *A Vindication of the Book Called, Some Gospel-Truths Opened*. To this Burrough responded with *Truth (the Strongest of All) Witnessed Forth* (1657). George Fox also replied to Bunyan's two tracts in his collection of polemical pieces, *The Great Mistery of the Great Whore Unfolded* (1659). *FJN*, 219, 226-27. George Lyon Turner, ed., *Original Records of Early Nonconformity Under Persecution and Indulgence*, 3 vols. (T. Fisher Unwin, 1911-14), I: 63-68. T. L. Underwood, *Primitivism, Radicalism, and the Lamb's War* (New York: Oxford University Press, 1997).

15. See also *The Doctrine of Law and Grace Unfolded* (1659); *Light for Them That Sit in Darkness* (1675); *The Strait Gate* (1676); *A Case of Conscience Resolved* (1683); *Israel's Hope Encouraged* (1692); *The Heavenly Foot-man* (1698, perhaps composed in the late 1660s).

16. Baxter, *Reliquiae Baxterianae*, Part I, 77; Muggleton, *An Answer to Isaac Penington*, 20.

17. Richard Greaves, ed., *MW*, 11: xxxi; Richard Baxter, *The Scripture Gospel Defended* (London, 1690), sig. A2r; John Child, *The Mischief of Persecution Exemplified* (1688), 36.

18. Burrough, *The True Faith*, 4.

19. Richard Greaves, *John Bunyan and English Nonconformity* (London: Hambledon Press, 1992), 71-99; B. R. White, "William Erbery (1604-1654) and the Baptists," *Baptist Quarterly* 23 (1969-70): 114-25; Christopher Hill, *A Tinker and a Poor Man: John Bunyan and His Church 1628-1688* (New York: Knopf, 1989), 50; Muggleton, *The Acts of the Witnesses of the Spirit*, 20-22, 34-37, 45-47, 86-90, 115-20, 130-33, 153-79; William Wood to Lodowick Muggleton, 9 February 1692, British Library Additional Manuscript 60168/42-43.

20. Burrough, *The True Faith of the Gospel of Peace Contended For*, 23; George Whitehead, *The Christian Quaker* (1673), 102.

Bunyan's Sisters: "Unfolding of [their] Secret Things"

PATRICIA DEMERS

I WANT TO EXPLORE SOME DISCURSIVE TANGENTS THAT COULD LINK BUNyan's classic, canonical spiritual autobiography with lesser-known forerunners by women. I am also suggesting a bold bond of kinship, attitudinal if not sanguineal, or, strictly speaking, denominational or sectarian. I am less interested in unearthing genealogical facts about actual female siblings from his father's three marriages and more intrigued by the fact that many women, decades before Bunyan, were examining "secret things": the "fearful dreams" and "dreadful visions," the sense of being "cast down and afflicted in . . . mind," of "not knowing which way [to] tip," and fluctuating between the comfort and torment of "diverse frames of spirit" (*GA*, 53, 6, 54, 66).

Because the work of these proposed spiritual siblings has not been subject to the same scrutiny as Bunyan's, some underlying assumptions need to be clarified at the outset. The very idea of examining an established, recognized text alongside neglected or, more accurately, rarely unearthed ones introduces the prickly issue of comparison. Is it better to treat women's writing as a genre unto itself, as Hilda Smith, Elaine Hobby, and Phyllis Mack have done, with its own constructions of selfhood, voice, and subjectivity? Or should their work be situated in the same milieu and within the similarly volatile, unstable politics of the 1640s and 1650s as Bunyan's? I am opting for the latter, for it seems to me that Bunyan shares many ideological and discursive positions with vocal, often vilified female contemporaries. The so-called distinction between private and public spheres proves to be very permeable in seventeenth-century spiritual writing, where "the languages of what we might call the private and the public spheres were interchangeable and interdependent."[1] Not only was all life "public" in early modern England, but religious ritual with its easy movement "from domestic to sacred space" became "the nexus between family and community as well as between (wo)man and God."[2] Social action was ultimately the stage on which people constructed identities and performed themselves. The speech of this performance—recorded, transcribed, re-presented—is an important element in discursive self-construction. In emphasizing her appeal to attend to the unexamined "rhetorical decorum" of much of early modern women's writing, Lisa Jardine returns to "the standard schoolboy's text on rhetorical public self-presentation," Aphthonius's *Progymnasmata*, whose eleventh exercise about "imagined first-person, emotionally charged speech of intense self-presentation" cites examples of "highly emotionally charged *female* speech."[3]

The intricate nexus between seventeenth-century spiritual speech and writing, between oral and print cultures, reveals an overwhelming concern with language and modes of orthodox, or allegorical, or satirical interpretation. The major "communication shift" of printing and its "fundamental alterations in prevailing patterns of continuity and change" permanently altered "the way Western Christians viewed their sacred book and the natural world."[4] As Elizabeth Eisenstein observes, "it made the words of God appear more multiform and His handiwork more uniform."[5] Just as the physical product of the book necessitated a blending of practical and rarefied, quotidian and scholarly, and artisanal and literary considerations, so the text itself—and particularly in a genre where claims of personal and divine authority are preeminent, the clash of the "politics of the congregation and the politics of the nation"—yields a language remarkable for its "combination of the experiential and the cosmological."[6]

It is easy and possibly most accommodating of current feminist theories of agency to look to female spiritual writers who were indomitable, opinionated, and politically active. Among them would be Elizabeth Warren, whose learned yet hard-hitting meditations, *Spiritual Thrift* (1647), likened the "Civill War" and its "unnaturall divisions" to a "tumour"[7] in need of lancing, and Mary Cary, whose prophetic, utopian discourse, *A New and More Exact Mappe or Description of New Jerusalems Glory* (1651), forecast the operation of the Spirit preserving "Saints from being so snared & in us overtaken with the temptations of the world."[8] The fearless testimony of Elizabeth Hooton from the prison in York Castle[9] or "the victorious hymns, songs, and praises"[10] of Katherine Evans and Sarah Chevers from their confinement in Malta could complement Esther Biddle's jeremiads against Oxford and Cambridge as "full of . . . filth" and "polluted in thy blood" and against London as a "Treacherous and Backsliding City" whose clergymen's "loathsome

Robes . . . are like unto a menstrous Cloth before the Eye of the pure Jehovah."[11] In contrast to these assertively didactic exempla and their reforming, corrective purposiveness, I wish to examine three works of great and apparent vulnerability. Quivering between dejection and hard-won hope, they are the ventriloquizing of Sarah Wight's voice by her transcriber and champion Henry Jessey in his *Exceeding Riches of Grace Advanced by the Spirit of Grace* (1647), the ambivalent image of honey tipping the rod of correction and also signifying the arms of grace in Elizabeth Major's "comfortable contemplation for one in affliction," *Honey on the Rod* (1656), and Rebecca Travers's zealous combination of autobiography and reproof, *Those that meet to worship at the Steeplehouse* (1659). Such troubled narratives, reflecting psychic, spiritual, and political turmoils, correspond in time to the period when Bunyan himself was approaching relief and awakening. The pattern of *Grace Abounding* was, as Nigel Smith remarks, "set in the congregations of the late 1640s and early 1650s."[12] Although Bunyan's notorious shyness with women, his shrinking even from a handshake, might cause some to reject any sense of kinship outright, I propose that the voices of these female speakers—an adolescent, a woman in her twenties, and a middle-aged matron—are as familiar as Bunyan with the miry bog of sin and corruption, the swoon of joy and peace, and the fearful sense of brokenness and pendant doubt. In designating this female circle a sisterhood and speculating about Bunyan's place within it, I borrow from Virginia Woolf's obsequies for Judith Shakespeare and from Gilbert and Gubar's first-generation feminist essay collection. Examining such a circle closely could shed more light on these women and their contemporaries and on us and our postmodern hesitations. The autobiographies of Bunyan's spiritual sisters could alert us to the cultural capital of this literature of anxious gloom and the speed with which the orthodox elite called their religious enthusiasm madness and branded "the vexations of tender consciences religious melancholy."[13] They also underline the difference between late twentieth-century "fairly rigid standards of self-control and self-integration" and a conception of the self that "turns our modern archaeology of the personality virtually upside down" by believing that "the deepest, most hidden, most authentic aspect . . . was something akin to conscience, . . . a shard of universal truth, God's voice embedded in the self."[14]

Critical opinion, though limited, varies widely about the effect of Sarah Wight's voice as ventriloquized or transcribed by the Independent Baptist minister Henry Jessey. While Dorothy Ludlow maintains that the sinstruck fifteen-year-old, suffering from blindness, lameness, and dumbness, was "never a threat to civil authorities,"[15] Barbara Ritter Dailey draws an illuminating parallel between Wight's seventy days of catatonic numbness and the period of national and municipal crisis from April to July 1647; during this interval Parliament denied the soldiers in the New Model Army, who themselves wanted to delimit the power of Parliament and the King, the right to petition.[16] Accordingly, the issue of voice, presented as a dichotomous struggle between weakness and strength, emptiness and abundance, abandonment, and joy, and as internalized and instructively externalized dialogism, is central to *The Exceeding Riches of Grace Advanced by the Spirit of Grace, in an Empty Nothing Creature, viz. Mris Sarah WIGHT, Lately hopeles and restles, her soule dwelling as far from Peace or hopes of Mercy, as ever was any. Now hopeful, and joyfull in the Lord, that hath caused Light to shine out of Darknes: that in and by this Earthen Vessell, holds forth his Own eternall love, and the Glorious Grace of his dear Son to the Chiefest of Sinners.*

Jessey not only documents Sarah Wight's struggles to speak, declare, and name her sinfulness; he makes this "holy innocent"[17] an enabling counsellor of other distressed souls, who are all women. Numerous dramatic suicide attempts—stabbing and scorching her body, pounding her head until it bleeds, jumping off a roof, throwing herself to the dogs on Lambeth Marsh—are punctuated with declarations of worthlessness:

> *I am a reprobate, a castaway, I never had a good thought in all my life. I have been under sinne ever since I can remember, when I was but a childe &c. . . . My earthly Tabernacle is broken all to pieces; and what will the Lord doe with me?*[18]

But Jessey also relates exchanges that dwell on the superiority of her despair. Consider this "conference" between Sarah and another young gentlewoman:

Mris. A.	I must be damn'd.
Mris. S.	I am damn'd already, from all eternitie, all eternitie. . . .
A.	I was a great professor, but I was but an hypocrite, and an hypocrites hope shall perish.
S.	I have been an hypocrite, a revolter, a backslider.
A.	I know it shall be well with you.

S.	As well as it was with Judas, who repented and hang'd himselfe: which I must doe before I shall be free from these torments.

(*Jessey*, 44)

Both Michel de Certeau and Natalie Zemon Davis have commented that in the genre of spiritual autobiography "it is precisely the lack of dialogue which . . . sets a limit to spiritual advancement."[19] Although there is a certain staginess about Jessey's recreation of Sarah Wight's counselling of others, there is also an adroit point-for-point echo and sermonic advantage in the way Wight's reported responses stretch doubt to determination and transform depression to hope. Interrogated by disbelieving critics anxious to corroborate or perhaps nullify her inability to eat or sleep for such an extended period and sought out, too, as a spiritual psychoanalyst, Sarah both withstands these external tests and, through grace, overcomes the terror of beholding herself "in hell locally" (*Jessey*, 78). As Bunyan "preached what [he] felt, what [he] smartingly did feel" (*GA*, 85), so Sarah counsels from experience.

Maid.	I am puld up by the roots.
Mris. S.	Christ will root you out of your sin, and root you out of your selfe: and plant you in himselfe. He will doe it.
Maid.	But I cannot beleeve.
S.	I lay in unbeliefe and could beleeve nothing but that there was no God, and no Devil and no Hell: till he made me beleeve in himselfe. . . .
Maid.	I had a glimpse of God, but I have backslidden from him.
S.	Say this to God; Turn me, and I shall be turned.

(*Jessey*, 63)

Sarah Wight experienced transformation. The only other work attributed to her is a lament for her brother, who predeceased her, although he had expected his sister to die during this spiritual collapse.

The shifting register of the self, which can range from dejection to jubilation, which can be uprooted or replanted, is also a central issue in Major's *Honey on the Rod*. Elaine Hobby finds it a treatise on submission, with the "recurrent simile . . . portray[ing] the author as an erring child or poor scholar" and the text's sense of "Passivity . . . [being] based in female powerlessness."[20] The rare autobiography of this young serving woman, lamed and therefore unemployed, returned home to her father after a "resort to those that pretended skill in lameness,"[21] is a two-part work. The first section is a continuous prose dialogue between Consolation, font of biblical paraphrases, and the envious, rebellious yet confessional Soul. Outlining her *"Apprenticeship"* in the prison of lameness, where she considers herself "one of the poor Scholars in the School of the lowest form"(*Major*, A4), of a rank comparable to Bunyan's "meanest" (*GA*, 5), Major through the afflictions of the Soul confesses her sins of pride, blasphemy, and Sabbath-breaking. What she emphasizes is not the submissiveness but the stubbornness of her will.

> I took no notice of sinning till the rod was sadly on me; and then I mourned, but not as an humble childe for offending a good Father but as a froward childe for being crost of my will. (*Major*, 19)

This rod of correction and sweetness is as riddling and complicated as Samson's discovery of honey in the lion's carcass and his subsequent test about sweetness coming forth from strength (Judg. 14). For me it has a ferocious and problematic potency similar to Bunyan's image of the "Horseleach at the vein" (*GA*, 15) to illustrate his early and insincere preoccupation with heavenly things. The voice that emerges in *Honey on the Rod* is deeply inflected with humility at the same time as it is conscious of a pedagogic mission. As an allegorist Major takes pains to delimit yet explain her work: coming from "a little (but a full) Hive," being "more wax than Honey" with "honey (the Divine part)" and "wax (the moral part) . . . clarified from the dross (that is, the faults & failings through weakness)" (*Major*, A3). Because Major is as aware as Bunyan of the need to emphasize the "practic" part of faith, especially evident in her distinguishing of working and idle, fruitful and barren, "particular" and "onely a general" (123) faith, she willingly enlists as a prophetic emissary. Divine sanction will not only inspire her voice; it will make it truly orotund: "O Lord enable me, and then I shall breake out into the mention of thy great goodness, and sing aloud of thy righteousness, and speak of thy power, and of thy fearful acts" (84).

The second section, titled *Sin and Mercy Briefly Discovered: or The Vail taken a little from before both. Together with the Authors Accusation, Confession and Belief*, blends poetry and prose in the extended dialogue where public penitence is the dominant mode:

> 'Tis reconcilement to my offended God
> (Whose sins deserv'd a sword, although a rod
> He pleas'd to take) a free discharge from all
> My sad offences, under the which I fall.
>
> *(Major,* 163)

Indicative of the purposiveness of this public voice is the appearance of "Eccho" who, entering into conversation with the Soul, exhorts: "Out from thy self, thy senses recollect, / And then what's said may prove to good effect" (192). Recognition of the rod or, as Echo advises, "husband[ing] well this evening-tide of grace" (193) involves no quiescent calmness, no utter docility. On the contrary, as Major's closing "particular Application of the Book of Jonah" clarifies, she sees herself reacting to kindness and mercy with inveterate recalcitrance ("alas for I / Do *Nineveh* out-sin, for which I die" [209]) and therefore in constant need of guidance. Her image of the rod as a corrective (in the sense of Proverbs 13: 24) and as the inhibiting control against which she chafes captures with candor the complexity of the seventeenth-century self that strives to be God-centered in the midst of an acute recognition of corruption and perversity.

> . . . unless he send
> A rod me to prevent, then for a time
> I may observe his will; but if my minde
> He's pleas'd to cross, I'le grumble, fret, nay cry,
> And in that passion wish of him to die:
> My nature's grown so bold, that I with him
> Dare expostulate, nay plead it is no sin
> To wish not to be, rather then to lie
> Under his rod; no, sooner let me die;
> If he in mercy me my errors tell,
> My answer is, I know that I do well;
> I sin and grieve thee, still thou wilt be kind,
> Wilt mercy shew, though oft against my minde.
>
> *(Major,* 209)

In the genre of spiritual autobiography, where the Pauline propensity to sin while vowing to do the opposite is the norm, it seems to me misguided to search for statements of powerfulness and independence, and especially wrongheaded to do so with seventeenth-century texts. Though the asseveration runs counter to a post-Freudian, post-Lacanian view of the self as the repository of curative, directional, affective energy, the Soul in Major's dialogue searches in vain within for "the Antidote, that Balsom pure, / That will not fail but make a perfect cure" (197). In direct contrast to postmodern autobiography's concept of the self as a walking text only as convincing as its latest construction, she finally judges the inadequacy of the worldly, creaturely self:

> Assist me Lord, I in my self may see
> All dung and dross, grant faith to rest on thee.
> For I confess a will I have, 'tis true,
> But 'tis for evil, no good that I can do:
> When I would good, then evil shews his face,
> The good I leave, the evil I imbrace.
>
> (*Major,* 198)

In place of the dialogism, the "internal I and you" so characteristic of "spiritual discoveries . . . made through dialogue,"[22] a continuous spiritual tension permeates Major's work. She denies, denigrates, abases the body in order to affirm, illustrate, and quite literally incorporate the soul's affinity with the creator. The reduced, twisted, maimed body nevertheless still houses the chastened, restored, invigorated spirit.

Although Rebecca Travers, widow of a London tobacconist, Baptist convert to Quakerism, prominent worker for Morning Meetings, and prolific writer, did not emphasize the dross of self, she did, like Sarah Wight, call on her own experience to illustrate the need to mortify and empty the self. In the place of voice, she offers silence; in place of works, stillness; in place of interpretations, an inner light, which tenets Phyllis Mack has seen as consonant with "the mortification of the intellect" and the disavowal of "political ambitions"[23] characteristic of Quakerism. In some ways Travers is the most challenging of these autobiographers: the most assertive, doctrinally precise, and exposed, and therefore the most vulnerable. Unlike Sarah Wight she speaks in her own voice, directly declaring "the blindness of your teachers, with their blasphemous and idolatrous doctrines, whereby they deceive the simple, lead captive silly women, which are always learning, but never come to the knowledge of the truth."[24] Unlike Elizabeth Major, she is not expiating guilt or wracked with doubt. Instead, she is confident that, in interrogating the minister of the Steeplehouse of John the Evangelist, "for the Seed's sake" (*Travers,* 3), she has made public his idolatry and deception, even though this act caused her to be scorned and vilified by the other parishioners. As she relates,

> But he hasting away as hirelings used to do, his people fell on me as so many devouring Wolves, railing, tearing, thrusting, haling, and pushing

me down several times, yet a hair of my head they could not hurt; . . . some . . . near related to me in the outward, stood by, & said they thought I was a mad woman, in which I can rejoyce, being no other then what was done, and said unto my Lord, The servant is not greater then his Master and him I serve [Acts 26.24; Job 15.20]. (*Travers*, 3)

Travers deems that the principle of discerning the "intentions of the heart . . . is not ink and paper, or words, . . . but it is spirit, life and power, killing and making alive" (8); yet she makes these declarations through the very deliberate, self-conscious medium of her own words and stories. Further, she admits having been "a reader of Scriptures . . . from a child of six years old, as constantlie as most" and confesses that "when by the power of the eternal Gospel [she] was turned from darkness to light [she] saw things unutterable, and the Scriptures . . . plain without a meaning" (17–18); yet Travers buttresses her own breathlessly paratactic condemnations of false prophets, sects, and opinions with flanks of marginal biblical glosses. The lengthy reproof of her attackers and accusers is ostensibly a praise of stillness:

> . . . your best works are but self-righteousness, dead works, and to be repented of [Heb. 6:1], but we who have gained to that which shewed us the evil of our wayes, and the vanity of the world with the glory thereof, have been brought to cease from our own works and words [Ps. 4:2] and come to stillness, in which the still voyce hath been heard of God. (*Travers*, 29)

Many similar binaries, involving mortification and publication, appear in *Grace Abounding*. But in this commodification of spiritual realities, what unites Bunyan and his sisters—all daring, revealing, purposively self-absorbed authors—is not a focus on the marketplace. However self-deprecating or self-emptying, their sights are on an eschatological and not, in the first instance, a political reality. With the possible exception of Travers's overt Quakerism, the doubts, torments, and joys experienced and described by these female autobiographers correspond to many troughs and peaks in Bunyan. Sarah Wight would understand intimately his attempts to avoid sinning against the Holy Ghost by leaping "with my head downward, into some Muckhil-hole or other, to keep my mouth from speaking" or blessing "the condition of the Dogge and Toade . . . [as] far better then this dreadful state of mine" (*GA*, 33). Elizabeth Major would recognize the perversity of his early rashness in vowing to be "damned for many sins, as . . . damned for few" (*GA*, 11). Setting aside doctrinal differences, Rebecca Travers might be charmed into seeing the applicability of Bunyan's simile for enlightenment as beholding "the Lord Jesus look[ing] down from Heaven through the Tiles upon me, and direct[ing] these words unto me" (*GA*, 65).

My suggestion of a seventeenth-century filiation of spiritual autobiographers is not an attempt to delimit their uniqueness or deny the particularities of cultural provenance. The women cited were all Londoners. Although a London congregation "maintained connexions with the Bedford separatist Church during Bunyan's membership and pastorate, receiving Bedford brethren into communion,"[25] I am certainly not proposing a free and open exchange or unproblematized transferability among Bunyan and Wight, Major and Travers. I am also not promoting the idea of judging these women—strictly, solely, or even appropriately—according to a male, canonical rhetorical standard. The passionate strength and directness of these virtually unknown women's texts mean, for me, that they deserve to be studied in tandem with Bunyan. Their voices do not falter; they evoke experiences vividly; their accounts have a pellucid intensity.

It is as instructive to realize what connects this spiritual sisterhood to Bunyan as to recognize the traits they share with one another. These Londoners were definitely women on the margins—removed from the exercise of political, royal, or civic power and excluded from formal centers of learning and institutions for cultural definition. Unlike the three seventeenth-century women, Glikl bas Judah Leib, Marie de l'Incarnation, and Maria Sibylla Merian, whom Natalie Zemon Davis has characterized as appreciating or embracing "a marginal place, reconstituting it as a locally defined center," Sarah Wight, Elizabeth Major, and Rebecca Travers neither journeyed so extensively nor did they undertake such macrocosmic projects as "real power relations with non-European peoples."[26] But the self they probed within admittedly limited geographical confines shares the "seventeenth-century European motifs" Davis has outlined in the lives of the Hamburg widow and merchant, the Ursuline nun and ethnographer, and the German divorcée and entomologist: "melancholy, enhanced sense of self, curiosity, eschatological hope, the pondering of God's presence in and intentions for the universe."[27]

The sense of self in Wight, Major, and Travers—pain-filled, emptied, mortified—may not strike twentieth-century readers as particularly enhanced. The unremitting intensity of their microcosmic confessions points to an expiatory rather than triumphalist faith. Whether a gendering of spiritual autobiography occurred in the seventeenth century is not clear. Within the hierarchical ideology of this time women were considered to be "of a different order of being"[28] from men. In *Christian Behaviour* (1663) Bunyan explicitly directed the wife to take "her warrant, licence and authority from [the husband]" (*MW*, 3: 33). Although Wight's experience was transcribed by a minister and Major was introduced with approbation by the censor, there is little sense that these unmarried or widowed women were controlled by men. As a genre spiritual autobiography was equally compelling for men and women. It appears to have offered sustaining and salvific attractions which transcended gender, illuminating how and why spiritually questing, anxious, exuberant women as well as men were inclined—for a variety of personal and cultural reasons—to document their search for wholeness in a fractured and hostile yet needy society.

Notes

1. Kevin Sharpe and Steven N. Zwicker, eds., *Politics of Discourse; The Literature and History of Seventeenth-Century England* (Berkeley and Los Angeles: University of California Press, 1987), 9.

2. David Cressy, "Private Lives, Public Performance, and Rites of Passage," in *Attending to Women in Early Modern England*, ed. Betty S. Travitsky and Adele F. Seeff (Newark: University of Delaware Press, 1994), 187–88.

3. Lisa Jardine, "Unpicking the Tapestry: The Scholar of Women's History as Penelope among Her Suitors," in *Attending to Women in Early Modern England*, ed. Betty S. Travitsky and Adele F. Seeff (Newark: University of Delaware Press, 1994), 138.

4. Elizabeth L. Eisenstein, *The Printing Press as an Agent of Change; Communications and Cultural Transformations in Early-Modern Europe*, 2 vols. (Cambridge: Cambridge University Press, 1979), 703.

5. Eisenstein, *The Printing Press as an Agent of Change*, 703–4.

6. Nigel Smith, *Perfection Proclaimed; Language and Literature in English Radical Religion, 1640–1660* (Oxford: Clarendon Press, 1989), 342, 344.

7. Elizabeth Warren, *Spiritual Thrift; or, Meditations Wherein humble Christians (as in a Mirrour) may view the verity of their saving Graces, and may see how to make a spirituall improvement of all opportunities and advantages of a pious proficiencie (or a holy Growth) in Grace and goodnesse* (London: Henry Shepherd, 1647), 35.

8. M[ary] Cary, *A New and More Exact Mappe or Description of New Jerusalems Glory when Jesus Christ and his Saints with him shall reign on earth a Thousand Years, and possess all Kingdoms* (London: Printed by W. H., 1651), 305.

9. Emily Manners, *Elizabeth Hooton: First Quaker Woman Preacher (1600–1672)* (London: Headley Brothers, 1914), 12.

10. Katherine Evans and Sarah Chevers, *A Short Relation of the Cruel Sufferings for the Truths Sake of Katharine Evans and Sarah Chevers, in the Inquisition in the Isle of Malta* (London: Robert Wilson, 1662), 45–48.

11. See Esther Biddle, *The Trumpet of the Lord, Sounded forth unto these*

Three Nations, As a warning from the Spirit of Truth (London, 1662) and her *Wo to thee town of Cambridge* (London, [1655]) and *Wo to thee city of Oxford* (London, [1655]), 3, 16.

12. Smith, *Perfection Proclaimed*, 346.

13. Michael MacDonald, *Mystical Bedlam; Madness, Anxiety, and Healing in Seventeenth-Century England* (Cambridge: Cambridge University Press, 1981), 9.

14. Phyllis Mack, *Visionary Women; Ecstatic Prophecy in Seventeenth-Century England* (Berkeley and Los Angeles: University of California Press, 1992), 135–36.

15. Dorothy P. Ludlow, "Shaking Patriarchy's Foundations: Sectarian Women in England, 1641–1700," in *Triumph over Silence: Women in Protestant History. Contributions to the Study of Religion*, ed. Richard L. Greaves (Westport, Conn., and London: Greenwood Press, 1985), 102.

16. Barbara Ritter Dailey, "The Visitation of Sarah Wight: Holy Carnival and the Revolution of the Saints in Civil War London," *Church History* 55 (1986): 451.

17. Dailey, "The Visitation of Sarah Wight," 451.

18. Henry Jessey, *The Exceeding Riches of Grace Advanced by the Spirit of Grace, in an Empty Nothing Creature, viz. Mris Sarah WIGHT* (London: Henry Overton and Hannah Allen, 1647), 14. All subsequent citations are to this edition.

19. Natalie Zemon Davis, *Women on the Margins; Three Seventeenth-Century Lives* (Cambridge: Harvard University Press, 1995), 7.

20. Elaine Hobby, *Virtue of Necessity; English Women's Writing 1649–88* (Ann Arbor: University of Michigan Press, 1989), 63, 64.

21. Elizabeth Major, *Honey on the Rod: Or, a Comfortable Contemplation for one in Affliction; with sundry Poems on several subjects* (London: Tho. Maxey, 1656), h2. All subsequent citations are to this edition.

22. Davis, *Women on the Margins*, 6–7.

23. Mack, *Visionary Women*, 149, 319.

24. Rebecca Travers, *Those that meet to worship at the Steeplehouse, called John the Evangelist, in London* (London, 1659), 2. All subsequent citations are to this edition.

25. Roger Sharrock, "Introduction" in *GA*, xiii.

26. Zemon Davis, *Women on the Margins*, 210, 211.

27. Zemon Davis, *Women on the Margins*, 212.

28. N. H. Keeble, ed., *The Cultural Identity of Seventeenth-Century Woman; A Reader* (London: Routledge, 1994), xi.

"Baffled, and Befooled": Misogyny in the Works of John Bunyan

Aileen Ross

THERE ARE THOSE WHO MAY BE DISTRESSED AT THE SUGGESTION THAT John Bunyan is a misogynist. Nevertheless, the treatise *A Case of Conscience Resolved* (1683) and the second part of *The Pilgrim's Progress* (1684) lend credence to the charge, as do his depictions of women in other works. Whether he presents women in treatises or prose fiction they generally fall into two categories: a Madam Bubble or a Christiana. This is not particularly surprising; Bunyan inherited a long tradition of such thought about women. The words "Baffled, and Befooled" in the title of this essay refer, as one might expect, to women, and they are taken from what Professor Ted Underwood calls "a curious piece among Bunyan's many printed works" (*MW*, 4: xlii). *A Case of Conscience Resolved* was published some five years before Bunyan's death, and one year prior to the publication of the second part of *The Pilgrim's Progress*. The title of the tract seems innocuous enough, the subject matter in keeping with many other treatises published by Bunyan.

Paradoxically a conservative country artisan as well as a radical Nonconformist preacher, Bunyan demonstrates in his works his solid belief in a hierarchical societal order. In *Christian Behaviour* (1663) he says "it is amiable and pleasant to God when Christians keep their Rank, Relation and Station, doing all as become their Quality and Calling" (*MW*, 3: 10). Bunyan's application of this structure to women is apparent in the comparatively few works where women's roles are dealt with to any great degree, and Christopher Hill draws attention to the fact that in the above mentioned treatise, "the duties of wives [occupy] twice as many pages as the duties of husbands."[1] Toward the end of *A Case of Conscience Resolved*, Bunyan admits to having "laboured to keep them [women] in their place" (*MW*, 4: 329), and he believes that his labors are genuinely in accordance with God's will for the advancement of

Christ's church on earth. It might be observed, in passing, that today there are a great many Christian churches that still strongly and sincerely adhere to the principles regarding women's place in the church of Christ that Bunyan steadfastly endorses.

In the second part of *The Pilgrim's Progress*, societal order colors the piece to a significant extent. This accounts in part for what is taken as its sedateness compared to the earlier part's liveliness; the latter includes, for example, the episode where Giant Despair, to his later chagrin, heeds his wife's advice. Roger Sharrock points out that this episode is an afterthought added to the second edition, and one cannot help but wonder if the unhappy experience involving Agnes Beaumont had any bearing on Bunyan's decision to underline the dangers inherent in listening to women's advice (*PP*, xliv).[2] Sedate as the second part of Bunyan's best known work may be, it remains a fictive work of remarkable power, patches of sermonizing and emphasis on the group rather than the individual notwithstanding. The description of the idealized female characters Christiana and Mercy is so thoroughly compelling that they have been held up as female masochism.

A Case of Conscience Resolved is not a well-known work, and perhaps Bunyan's women readers would be less approving of Christiana's and Mercy's characters had they access to this earlier tract. It is certainly an odd treatise; in it Bunyan singles out a particular group in his church, namely, the women, which is entirely contrary to his ordinary practice of designating works "For Young, for Old, for Stag'ring and for Stable" (*PP*, 170). Addressing the women as his "Honoured Sisters" in Christ, he assures the female members of his congregations that they are to be highly commended as being "eminent for piety," their "Holiness of life has gone out of many of the Brethren" (*MW*, 4: 295). Bunyan's sincerity is unquestionable. As was often the case in the dissenting congregations, the women in Bunyan's gathered churches outnumbered the men by some two to one.[3] When backslidden, members of both sexes were treated equally: they were unhesitatingly taken to task for their misdemeanors of various kinds and sometimes even excommunicated if the sins were not amended (*MW*, 8: xxv). However, it is the brethren who are reprimanded for misconduct far more often. The reason for Bunyan's specific address to the women in this case is that some two years earlier they had taken the unprecedented step of having prayer meetings without their menfolk. As Christians "eminent in piety" they had found the practice spiritually uplifting, and there had been answers to prayers. Bunyan, as their pastor, showed them in his treatise that there was no scriptural justification for such a practice, and these women willingly, it would seem, gave it up.

That might have been the end of the matter, but for a certain "Mr. K." Hearing of Bunyan's objections, he wrote to the women giving some persuasive arguments for going on with the meetings. We do not know for sure who this Mr. K. was, although there has been speculation that he was the Baptist minister William Kiffin, with whom Bunyan had been at odds a decade earlier in a controversy over Christian baptism. Mr. K.'s arguments in favor of the women's prayer meetings were in circulation in the Nonconformist churches around Bedford. Bunyan was given a copy and asked to reply. The sometimes intemperate wording of the reply is some indication of how threatening Bunyan perceived these meetings to be. It is to be readily understood that he is justifiably irritated by Mr. K.'s audacity in again interfering in the Bedford gathered churches. In asking Bunyan to answer Mr. K., however, the women themselves were challenging their own pastor's authority, for he assumed the matter to be already settled.

Yet they were asking for little. They did not aspire to preach, nor did they aim for church eldership. They had the time and inclination to seek fellowship with each other and to pray. Vera Camden, in editing *The Narrative of the Persecutions of Agnes Beaumont* (1674), draws our attention to the loneliness experienced by many country women. Conversion to a gathered church would have alleviated some of this, and meetings with fellow adherents might have freed them from some "domestic domination," but it would have further inhibited free interchanges with family and neighbors. It is understandable that Agnes Beaumont declares, "It was like death to be kept from such a meeting."[4]

The case Mr. K. advances rests on the premise that prayer is enjoined on the entire church, male and female alike. Thus in his estimate, there is nothing untoward in godly sisters meeting together for that purpose. Among other arguments, he cites Old Testament precedents in Miriam ("and all the Women . . . went out after her" [*MW*, 4: 310]) praising God for the Israelites' delivery at the Red Sea. He also mentions that Esther and her maidens prayed and fasted together before Esther approached King Ahasuerus, and the New Testament instance of Lydia and the faithful women whom Paul and Silias found praying by the riverside in Philippi.

Bunyan is unimpressed by these arguments, claiming that in Mr. K.'s injunctions to the women "there is, not only Boldness, but Flattery. *Boldness*, in *Fathering* of his mis-understanding upon the Authority of the Word of God, and *Flattery*, in Soothing up Persons in a way of their own, by making of them the Judges in their own cause" (*MW*, 4: 299). The implied criticism of the "Holy Sisters" here is severe, and their inherent subordination made plain. Mr. K.'s role, of course, is worse. He is abusing "those Holy Words of God . . . to make them stand" (*MW*, 4: 317). This calumny is unusual for Bunyan who is much more interested in building up believers in the faith than indulging in the all-too-common seventeenth-century vituperation. In his anger, he goes on to deliver an especially vindictive gibe at Mr. K. for his sponsoring of "the Sisters, the Women, the Womens Meetings, and the like, and how they have prevailed with Heaven." He goes as far as calling Mr. K. "*Nunnish* in such a day as this" (*MW*, 4: 307). To use the word "nunnish" is to impugn the solidity of Mr. K.'s Protestantism. To be fair to Bunyan, however, he concedes later in the treatise, and this is surprising given his more common anti–Roman Catholic stance, that, "Without doubt the *Fryers* and *Nunns*, and their Religious Order, were of a good intent at first, as also compulsive vowes of chastitie, single life, and the like: But they were all without the Word, and therefore, as their bottom wanted divine Authority, so the Practise wanted Sanctity by the Holy Ghost" (*MW*, 4: 322). Thus Mr. K. is more thoroughly rebuked by the sting in the tail, and, along with Mr. K., just as surely rebuked are the upstart sisters.

Bunyan vigorously justifies his own position mainly by an appeal to Pauline authority. In his turn, he cites New Testament instances of assemblies for divine worship that consisted of both men and women, of mixed gathering of saints and sinners, or church elders and principal brethren of the church, "men the more noble part in all the Churches of Christ" (*MW*, 4: 317). Having reviewed New Testament practice, Bunyan goes on to claim "in all the Scripture, I find not that the Women of the Churches of Christ, did use to separate themselves from their Brethren, and as so separate, perform Worship together among themselves or in that *their* Congregation" (*MW*, 4: 301). His claim has a ring of assurance, an assurance that he works out more palatably but just as firmly in the second part of *The Pilgrim's Progress:*

> The Holy Ghost doth particularly insist upon the inability of Women, as to their well managing of the Worship *now* under Consideration. . . . They are forbidden to teach, yea to speak in the Church of God. And why forbidden, but because of their inability. They cannot orderly manage that Worship to God that in Assemblies is to be performed before him (I speak now of our Ordinary believing ones, and I know none Ex-

traordinary among the Churches.) They are not builded to manage such Worship, *they are not the Image and Glory of God*, as the Men are, I Cor. 11.7.

They are placed beneath, and are *called the Glory of the Man*. Wherefore they are weak, and not permited [sic] to perform Publick Worship to God. When our first Mother, who was not attended with those weaknesses, either Sinful, or Natural, as our Women now are, stept out of her place but to speak a good Word for Worship, you see how she was baffled, and befooled therein; she utterly failed in the performance, tho she briskly attempted the thing. Yea she so failed thereabout, that at one clap she overthrew, not only (as to that) the reputation of Women for ever, but her Soul, her Husband, and the whole World besides. (*MW*, 4: 306)

Given Bunyan's familiarity with the Bible, and his more usual sound exegesis, this gross oversimplification of the account of the Fall in Genesis comes as a shock. Notably lacking is the scriptural emphasis on Satan's role and Adam's deliberate choice of sin: there is more than just a hint of medieval misogyny here. If the Bedford preacher sounds respectful of "ordinary" women, calling them "Holy and Beloved Sisters" and stating "They are an Ornament in the Church of God on Earth, as the *Angels* are in the Church in Heaven," the Sisters are also reminded of their status: "For the Angels are inferior to the great Man *Christ*, who is in Heaven; and the Woman is inferior to the Man, that Truly Worships God in the Church on Earth" (*MW*, 4: 325).

We find the same word "Ornament" bestowed approvingly on Christiana in *The Pilgrim's Progress*. For the female pilgrims are, in John Brown's words, "queenly in their passive meekness."[5] Graciously accepting of their position, they are grateful to be pilgrims well-guarded by Mr. *Great-heart*. We scarcely register the fictive working out of Bunyan's blunt words to the women in his congregations, as he enjoins them to be content with their inferiority "since the cause thereof, arose at first from your selves" (*MW*, 4: 325). Women may, nevertheless, find consolation in that their inferiority is not to last forever. It "will last but a little while: When the day of Gods Salvation is come, to wit, when our Lord shall descend from Heaven, with a shout . . . these distinctions of Sexes shall be laid a side" (*MW*, 4: 323). The difference that Christ's coming has made to the here and now, that in Him "There is neither bond nor free, there is neither male nor female; for yea are all one in Christ Jesus" (Gal. 3:28), is apparent to the devout pastor and poet George Herbert, but escapes John Bunyan.

That being Bunyan's position, the first question we might ask is whether or not Bunyan's view on women's role in seventeenth-century gathered churches is a typical one, and the answer is a qualified yes. With regard to society in general, Professor Ted Underwood has this to say:

> Women's place in society was clearly secondary, but was also perceived as deteriorating in some respects. The roles of midwife, partner in family farming, and skilled artisan, among others, were lessening. And within the upper class, the useful function of women in family estates was declining. With respect to women's general role in marriage, the difficulties suffered by wives and mothers were recognized by [the well-known Presbyterian preacher and writer] Richard Baxter, who wrote that "*Women* especially must expect so much suffering in a married life, that if God had not put into them a natural inclination to it, and so strong a love to their children, as maketh them patient under the most annoying troubles, the world would ere this have been at an end, through their refusal of so calamitous a life." Yet he did not advocate change. There were feminist writers, however, who objected to the secondary role of women in marriage and society in general as well as to the decline in certain specific positions, and who perceived social change as necessary for the restoration of appropriate opportunities for women. (*MW*, 4: xxxvii–xxxviii)

Earlier in the seventeenth century, George Herbert, the devout Anglican preacher and poet mentioned above, was one such person. He not only advocated marital equality but practiced it by putting half the management of his affairs into his wife's hands. He also recommended other Christians do the same, on the grounds men and women are "joint heirs together of grace." Even he, however, reserves the right of the husband to keep an overall eye on the family affairs.

The Protestant Reformation of the sixteenth century had, of course, wrought change and turmoil in Europe generally, and in England women as well as men suffered for their beliefs. As an avid reader of Foxe's *Actes and Monuments*, Bunyan was well aware of this. In *A Case of Conscience Resolved*, Bunyan is at pains to concede that some "extraordinary" women "shewed Christian valour and fortitude of minde, when called of God to bear witness to, and for his Name in the World" (*MW*, 4: 295). That the ordinary women of his own group, among others, had been subjected to ongoing persecution with little respite from 1660 on, he seems not to take account of, perhaps judging only those actually imprisoned, as he himself had been, or put to death for their faith as being "extraordinary." Yet suffering and sacrifice were the lot of all who worshiped in the Nonconformist churches. The *Church Book* of Bedford Meeting contains some harrowing accounts of women persecuted for their beliefs. The widowed Mary Tilney, for example, had all her goods distrained and acted with great courage and cheerfulness while her neighbors wept for her.[6]

Among more radical groups, such as Ranters and Quakers, women were often allowed to preach in worship services. Bunyan consistently attacks Ranters and Quakers in his publications, including *A Case of Conscience Resolved*, where he claims that his acceding to the request for prayer meetings would make him one with them: "I do not believe they [women] should Minister to God in Prayer before the whole Church, for then I should be a Ranter or a Quaker" (*MW*, 4: 305). Underwood points out that among the more conservative churches "prophesying" by women either in separate groups or together with men was not uncommon, but Baptists of any stripe tended to the more traditional Pauline view, and women were "not permitted at all to speak in the church, neither by way of praying, prophecying nor enquiring" (*MW*, 4: xl). They were, however, allowed to "confess their faith in requesting membership, and speak as witnesses or in acts of repentance" (*MW*, 4: xl–xli). This latter view would reflect practice in the Bedford churches. Given Bunyan's hearty dislike and fear of the unorthodox theology of Quakers and Ranters, it is quite reasonable to surmise that it reinforced his opposition to women taking on any more active a role in church affairs. Even so, the *Church Book* of Bunyan's Bedford congregation shows that, occasionally, devout women were given the duty of visiting female backsliders for the purpose of bringing such to repentance, although this task was, as a rule, allocated to the elders, all of whom were men.

While obedience to the male church elders was obligatory for both male and female church members in Nonconformist congregations, including Bunyan's, it is most surprising that the widely accepted society norm for women to obey their husbands in all things was waived by some of the Baptist churches and even by Bunyan's own churches where attendance was required. Threats made by a husband furnished no excuse for a wife to miss church services, and the commonplace physical violence against wives was frowned upon by Bunyan's congregation. In March 1679 an entry in the *Church Book* reads "our brother John Stanton was admonished by the Church of his evill in abuseing his wife and beateing hir often for very light maters. Hee promised us reformation and seemed sory for his fault."[7] However, one cannot help but wonder if a beating was in order for very grievous faults.

Obedience to church-ruling elders was often a problem when a female believer was married to an unbeliever. In 1668 the General Assembly of the General Baptist Churches (with whom Bunyan's congregations were not associated) went as far as to declare that "in the marriage of a believer and an unbeliever, 'for those so married yet to live together as man and wife when repented of, is a sin.' "[8] This exceeds the Pauline injunction by far, but such a rule would have provided a welcome relief for a woman like the wife of Bunyan's character Mr. Badman, whose history Bunyan traces in his second work of prose fiction published in 1680. Badman's wife married without seeking advice from the church elders and experienced the unhappiest of married lives.

It was taken for granted that a good wife would obey and support her husband in all things, but when he was absent from the home then she, according to Bunyan in *Christian Behaviour*, is to be treated as head of the house, for she is the queen consort. She is, says, Bunyan, "a husband's yoak-fellow, not his slave" (*MW*, 3: 22–28). Children are enjoined to obey both parents, but they, too, have the right to opt out of this obedience when it conflicts with their commitment to Christ. Adult children risked economic ruin by so doing, particularly females, for women had fewer means of economic survival should they be disinherited. In the case of Agnes Beaumont, her spiritual equanimity is seriously disturbed when her father threatens to cut her out of his will without the proverbial penny if she continues to worship with Bunyan's congregations. She is distraught and wonders what will become of her: "To go to service and work for my living is a new thing to me; and so young as I am too."[9] Willful disobedience to parents is not countenanced by the church. There are records in the *Church Book* of adult children being sternly reprimanded, but when it comes to church attendance, they, like married women, have no choice but to hazard parental wrath, as Agnes Beaumont does, rather than compromise their souls.

Bunyan himself accepted this, and indeed, because of it, got himself into a grave situation that could have permanently damaged his ministry. The ingenuous and enthusiastic Agnes Beaumont had a call on Bunyan's conscience because he was her pastor. She was the first member of the Gamlingay congregation (a sister church of Bedford Meeting), which Bunyan had entered into the *Church Book* in 1672 just after being released from prison. Although he knew of her father's express disapproval, he yielded to Agnes's brother's importunity to take his sister on horseback to a prayer meeting, she herself having first entreated him to no avail. It resulted in the scandal recounted in *The Narrative of the Persecutions of Agnes Beaumont*. There is no doubt that this sorry incident had an effect on the Bedford preacher, for in 1680 he added some material about the episode to the fifth edition of his spiritual autobiography, *Grace Abounding* (1666). His hot denial of wrongdoing suggests that rumors were still running rampant six years after the event.[10]

In the introduction to *The Holy War* (1682) Sharrock and Forrest draw attention to the "striking gap" in Bunyan's publications between 1680 and 1682 and surmise that the time may have been spent on that "carefully constructed work" (*HW*, xix). Underwood postulates that William Kiffin's *A Sober discourse of Right to Church-Communion* (1681) is aimed specifically at Bunyan and those who, like him, advocated open membership of the gathered churches, based on belief in Christ and a holy life. Underwood points to the "moderate and subtle, yet dramatic, expression of Bunyan's position . . . in the second part of *The Pilgrim's Progress*" seen in the pilgrims' cleansing bath at the House of the Interpreter. The aftermath of the so-called Popish Plot of 1678 and the attempt to exclude Charles II's Roman Catholic brother, James, from the succession had made for a volatile political situation where dissenters' positions were precarious to say the least. No wonder that Bunyan is irascible when the "Holy Sisters" who should know better seem to be adding to his burden.

A Case of Conscience Resolved is a stinging enough rebuke to bring the devout "godly sisters" around to Bunyan's way of thinking, but Bunyan's pastoral care for them is plain enough. It is shown to even more advantage in the second part of *The Pilgrim's Progress*, which is often said to be a compliment to the women of Bedford Meeting after the remonstrance in the earlier tract. Christopher Hill sees it as making "some amends."[11] However, given Bunyan's assiduous care for his flock, his resolute opposition to the closed-communion Baptists, and strong views on female inferiority—the latter vigorously reiterated in his posthumously published *An Exposition on . . . Genesis* (1692) where women are still designated as the "simple and weak sex" who must not "perk it and Lord it over their Husbands" (*MW*, 12: 147)—it is equally, if not more possible that his primary intent was not to compliment but to reinforce the lessons in *A Case of Conscience Resolved*, albeit in a more genial way.

Christiana's undertaking to follow Christian to the Celestial City starts out as "a desperate adventure" (*PP*, 205), and some of the breathless excitement present in the earlier part is felt until the pilgrims reach the House of the Interpreter. Once Christiana's authority has been handed over to the male characters, notably Mr. Great-heart, and the women made thoroughly aware of their weak status, any adventure becomes a male prerogative even when the outcome is not in doubt. The females may weep, admire, or thank their doughty protectors, but participate they may not. Many have remarked that Christiana's pilgrimage, in contrast to her husband's, has the atmosphere and excitement of a Sunday School outing: pleasant enough in its way, and sometimes deeply moving, but lacking in suspense (*MW*, 4: 317).

Christiana is depicted throughout as the economically stable widow who even Bunyan countenanced to assist in good works in the Bedford churches. Her freedom in this state is underlined: she needs no permission from a male relative to leave the City of Destruction. Her position as Christian's widow enhances her status as part of the pilgrim group, at the same time that it shows her contentedness and dignity in her essentially inferior female position. The depiction is all the more readily accepted by the reader since Christiana is filled with self-recriminations which she considers only too well fully justified. She mourns and confesses her disobedience to her four sons because she had failed to heed her husband, thus depriving her four sons, as well as herself, of the chance to accompany Christian to the Celestial City. Her now aroused conscience responds readily to her two dreams and to the letter brought by the visitor named Secret. Prayer is part of her preparation to leave, and she is not deterred by her neighbors' arguments about unwomanly or mad behavior. Economic and societal independence, along with the transformed personality, are seen in the extraordinary and beautiful promise given to Mercy that the younger woman can travel as her servant, but that they "will have all things in common" (*PP*, 185).

For her part, Mercy shows an equal independence in unhesitatingly leaving behind her parents, friends, and kindred, although her deep affection for them is demonstrated later as she thinks of their unsaved condition. The gaiety of her youth is seen in the reason she gives the prying neighbors for accompanying Christiana: it is a "Sun-shine morning" and she will go only "a little way . . . to help her"(*PP*, 183). Mercy wants to find "Truth and Life" for her soul, and if she does (for she is by no means certain that she will), she "would never go near the Town any more" (*PP*, 183, 185). Unsure of her salvation, untried by life's vicissitudes, surprisingly, it is Mercy who takes the lead in crossing the Slough of Dispond which gave Christian so much trouble and now is in an even worse state.

On reaching the Wicket Gate, it falls to Christiana's lot as "eldest" of the party to have the responsibility of knocking. By this time, the pilgrims are all frightened by the "heavy" barking of a great dog. As soon as Christiana and the boys enter, the older woman starts to intercede for Mercy, but the younger woman's own determination has her battering feverishly on the door. Mercy's fears of rejection and of the "most cruel *Dog*" cause her to faint. The warmth of the reception and the forgiveness "by word, and deed" fill the pilgrims with gladness, but even amidst the delights, they have questions that they want answered, and they are willing to ask these questions directly. Sensible, and ever conscious of hierarchy, Mercy mentions to Christiana first that she intends to ask the "Lord at the head of the way" when the pilgrims next see him "why he keeps such a filthy Cur in his Yard." The Dog, it turns out, "has another Owner" and its "barking [is turned] to the Profit of the Pilgrims" (*PP*, 190–93). Women are dealt with by the Lord just as attentively as was Christian: "he fed them, and washed their feet, and set them in the way of his Steps." As they leave the Wicket Gate with "the weather very comfortable to them" (*PP*, 193), Christiana's hymn acknowledges her indebtedness to her husband. Nevertheless, she is still very much the leader of the little group.

As the would-be rapists approach, it is a formidable woman who commands "Stand back, or go peacably as you should." As the men attempt to touch the women, Christiana is prepared to make it a physical resistance, and "waxing very wroth, spurned at them with her feet" (*PP*, 194). It is after this ugly incident that the women are urged by their male rescuer from the Wicket Gate to petition the Lord at the head of the way for a Conductor. While agreeing this would be a good idea, Christiana has questions and is still sufficiently assertive to remark that "since our Lord knew 'twould be for our profit, I wonder he sent not one along with us" (*PP*, 196). Her thought is reasonable. But *Reliever*'s gentle chiding has reminded them of their status—they are "*but weak Women*" (*PP*, 196). Now Christiana reproaches herself that one of her dreams had warned her of this danger and she "did not provide for it where provision might have been had" (*PP*, 197). The reader readily accepts Christiana's blaming of herself. The thought of rape in this situation is one that readily occurs, perhaps more on the literal than allegorical level. The episode works well enough, and Christiana's prescient dream is given satisfying fulfillment. The raw nature of such a physical attack, however unsurprising, deflects our attention from the issue that Bunyan is going to pursue: the utter necessity of female subordination in a well-ordered Christian church. The narrative gradually works toward it, until the two heroines are firmly relegated to the secondary roles that demonstrate the beauty of their "queenly submissiveness."

Womanly weakness and woman's place in the overall scheme of things are astutely handled in the House of the Interpreter. Christiana and Mercy are shown many more "*Significant*" rooms than was Christian. Part of this, of course, is to avoid needless repetition of the first part's scenes, but part allows for the driving home of the lesson about woman's place. Christiana is initially commended for her response to the room with the "great *Spider*: as being a "Woman quick of Apprehension," yet in the very next room Interpreter says "I chose, my Darlings, to lead you into the Room where such things are, because you are Women, and they are easie for you" (*PP*, 202). The compliment followed by the overt instruction is neatly accomplished, and now the emphasis falls on submission. The fact that it is a Sheep that "took her Death patiently" (*PP*, 202) links the image of Christ as the Lamb of God to the women. They are told, "You must learn of this Sheep, to suffer: And to put up wrongs without murmurings and complaints" (*PP*, 202). Order and hierarchy are stressed in the garden, Bunyan employing almost the same words that he had used in *Christian Behaviour*: "the Flowers are divers in *Stature*, in *Quality*, and *Colour*, and *Smell*, and *Virtue*, and some are better then some: Also where the Gardiner has set them, there they stand, and quarrel not one with another" (*PP*, 202).

We can see the kind of fruit that the new pilgrims are expected to produce in their lives in order that they "condemn not [them]-selves," and in the ingenious *Robbin* emblem of the false professor who may be "pretty of Note, Colour and Carriages" in order to "frequent the House of the Godly" (*PP*, 202, 203), we can catch the image of a Mr. K. The pilgrims' stay at the House of the Interpreter feeds an appetite for "Profitable" things, especially in Christiana, and he tells her, "Thy beginning is good, thy latter end shall greatly increase" (205); with the lessons shown, Christiana can be under no illusion about her role. Where Mercy is concerned, Interpreter's attitude is determinedly avuncular: he calls her "sweet-heart" and "dear-heart" in a way that brings Agnes Beaumont's interlocutors to mind. Her blushing modesty seems to be the accepted norm for young women converts who know their place in the garden.

The Interpreter's kindliness extends to giving Mr. Great-heart to the little party to protect them as far as the House Beautiful. He guards and guides them. Guidance includes answering their questions and delivering eagerly sought after sermons. He proves his manly worth by killing the giant Grim who is blocking the way to the House called Beautiful, but it is to be noted that Christiana also challenges Grim's right to impede those on the King's Highway. Having fulfilled his master's commission, Mr. Great-heart prepares to return immediately to the House of the Interpreter, much to the dismay of the women and children. Mercy asks, "How can such poor Women as we, hold out in a way so full of Troubles as this way is, without a Friend, and Defender?" (220). Her vulnerability after the near rape had been displayed when the usually tender-hearted woman rejoiced in the sight of the three hanged men seen by the wayside: "who knows else what they might a done to such poor Women as we are?" (214).

Yet, once again, the pilgrims have failed. According to Mr. Great-heart, they should have been aware that a request for his services for the entire journey had to be made, but their fault will be overlooked if they remedy the omission, and they can expect his return when they send for him. Here, the necessity for Christians to "continue constant in prayer" is made, but the narrative hardly sustains the allegory. Prior warning has not been given. Mr. Great-heart's reproach seems arbitrary, more a guise for insisting on women's inability to manage their pilgrim walk without male guidance than anything else. It does not, however, detract from the welcome given the pilgrims at the House Beautiful. Christiana, in particular, is feted as Christian's wife, and she herself requests to sleep in "that Chamber that was my Husbands" (221).

Bunyan now enlarges the action to have the damsels at the House Beautiful and Christiana's sons play increasingly important parts, but neither Christiana nor Mercy quite loses her sturdy independence within this environment. Mercy deals astutely with Mr. Brisk's courtship. Her intuitions about his character are bolstered by Prudence's sought advice. Christiana's teaching of her sons is much commended by the inhabitants of the House Beautiful. Also, when Matthew falls sick, it is Christiana who decides to send for Dr. Skill, and she pays for the requisite medicines that will be useful both now and later in the pilgrimage. The women are busy and happy here, and their actions are applauded; but all these actions fall within the realm of what is permitted and encouraged in the gathered churches. Christiana's role is subtly diminished in that it takes a son to remind her to send for Mr. Great-heart when they are ready to leave. The women now deport themselves very much like the idealized wife and mother who merits the gracious speech by Gaius as he recites scriptural instances of women's commendable actions which, significantly, "take away their Reproach" (261).

That this accolade comes after Christiana makes no demur about Gaius's forthright suggestion that Mercy should marry Matthew, with, of course, the young woman's consent, is also well calculated to depict proper female submission. They fade imperceptibly into the background, responding, as required, to the decisions made by the males.

Bunyan's powerful depiction of the ideal growing church with the weaker members well taken care of is a deeply moving one. What happens to the now sheltered female characters, however, hardly squares with the reality of women's seventeenth-century conversions as they are shown in many spiritual autobiographies, where their uncertainty and anguish often equal Bunyan's own. The second part of *The Pilgrim's Progress* shows a knowledgeable pastor's awareness of different kinds of conversion experiences and his firm grasp of how a growing church might be best governed. Mr. Great-heart is the ideal pastor, and he leads the ideal flock, with strong young men to help him kill giants, slay dragons, and demolish the castle of Giant Despair. Mercy bears children for the growing church and continues to make an economic contribution to the party; Christiana continues to be the person through whom some problems can be resolved. One might see in them exactly the kind of "ordinary" women that Bunyan hopes to have in his churches: caring, kind, but above all, obedient.

In the real life of the Bedford churches, Bunyan's attitude towards women shows ambivalence. On the one hand, women are encouraged to seek salvation above all things and to live the Christian life, sometimes at the expense of a natural obedience to parents and husbands. On the other hand, when they elect to obey Christ first and receive the gifts of the Holy Spirit, it seems that very few of the gifts are for "ordinary" women. They may teach their children and do charitable works. They are not their husbands' slaves and may take command in a situation where there is no male to do so. But they remain weak, blushing, and unfit to lead. Bunyan has no faith that there are any "extraordinary" women in his congregations, but the fact that he realizes there may be such women elsewhere is some encouragement.

It might seem to us that he has known a number of exceptional women, and, indeed, been married to two of them. Certainly his young second wife, Elizabeth, displays a courage, eloquence, and knowledge of the Scriptures that enable her to counter fearlessly arguments from the learned justices on the bench in seeking her husband's release from prison. As her pastor, Bunyan knew of Agnes Beaumont's testimony that being able to withstand public censure and legal proceedings with a fine spiritedness was the consequence of her lively faith. Had she failed to convince the justices of her innocence, she would not have suffered alone: Bunyan would have been arraigned as well. Bunyan also owed much to that nameless first young wife who brought to the marriage the dowry of Lewis Bailey's *Practice of Piety* and Arthur Dent's *The Plaine Mans Pathway to Heaven*, along with her testimony of her father's godly life. Then there is the nameless old woman who reproves the young man for his blaspheming tongue, as well as the old women sitting in the sunshine whose exchanges on the nature of their spiritual walk move Bunyan toward John Gifford and spiritual maturity in the Bedford Meeting.

Many circumstances led to women's second-class status in society and in most churches. It is plain, however, that by allowing women the New Testament privilege of being joint heirs together in Christ, and free access to the Scriptures, the churches create the possibility that women like Elizabeth and Agnes, emulating the New Testament Priscilla, may teach men "the better way." In *The Pilgrim's Progress* it is thoroughly ironic to find that after the stubborn insistence all along on the frailty of the female pilgrims and the utter necessity of a Protector, the women are casually left on the road with only Mr. Feeble-mind and Mr. Ready-to-halt as guards when Mr. Great-heart decides to fight Giant Despair and tear down Doubting Castle. The assurance is given that since they are in the Road, "A little Child might lead them" (*PP*, 281). John Bunyan would not entertain the possibility, even here, that the women might survive and even thrive on their own. The least male is to be preferred to the best female. He says in *A Case of Conscience Resolved*, "When Women keep their places, and Men manage their Worshipping God as they should, we shall have better days for the Church of God, in the World" (*MW*, 4: 329). And it is that world he so compellingly portrays in the second part of *The Pilgrim's Progress*.

Notes

1. Christopher Hill, *A Tinker and a Poor Man: John Bunyan and His Church 1628–1688* (New York, Knopf, 1989), 297.
2. Roger Sharrock, "Introduction" to *PP*.
3. Hill, *A Tinker and a Poor Man*, 297.
4. Vera Camden, ed., *The Narrative of the Persecutions of Agnes Beaumont* (East Lansing, Mich.: Colleagues Press, 1992), 15.

5. John Brown, *John Bunyan: His Life, Times and Work* (Hamden, Conn.: Archon Books, 1969), 263.
6. Brown, *John Bunyan,* 207.
7. Brown, *John Bunyan,* 303.
8. T. L. Underwood, ed., "Introduction" in *MW,* 4: xli.
9. Camden, *The Narrative of the Persecutions of Agnes Beaumont,* 52.
10. W. R. Owens, ed., "A Note on the Text," *Grace Abounding to the Chief of Sinners,* (London: Penguin Classics, 1987), xxv.
11. Hill, *A Tinker and a Poor Man,* 300.

"Christiana and her train": Bunyan and the Alternative Society in the Second Part of *The Pilgrim's Progress*

Melissa D. Aaron

THE SECOND PART OF *PILGRIM'S PROGRESS* HAS BEGUN TO ATTRACT ITS own critical commonplaces. Perhaps the most famous of these is "Christian goes upon a quest, Christiana upon a walking tour."[1] Critics have noted the high incidence of female pilgrims (including Christian's wife and female counterpart, Christiana), the reduction in violent incidents, and the larger number of pilgrims, and have generally drawn the conclusion that the second part is milder and more politically conservative than the first part.

The communitarian nature of the second part is clearly related to its female protagonists. To counter or challenge more conservative implications, I shall argue that Bunyan the Baptist pastor postulates an alternative Puritan society in the second part of *Pilgrim's Progress*. He creates an extended family structure, where "the last shall be first." Humility becomes the critical value, and the model for humility is female. Christiana, the Nonconformist woman, "and her train," provide the means for a Christian society—catechesis, marriage, children, and church service—and they finally are shown to be, through Christiana, the Church itself.

After 1672, Bunyan had primary responsibility for the congregation of the Bedford Church as their pastor. Even as a preacher, Bunyan had felt tremendous responsibility, as he records in his autobiography, *Grace Abounding to the Chief of Sinners*: "He hath also cause to walk humbly with God, and be little in his own Eyes, and to remember withall, that his Gifts are not his own, but the Churches; and that by them he is made a Servant to the Church, and that he must give at last an account of his Stewardship unto the Lord Jesus; and to give a good account, will be a blessed thing!" (92). Now his Puritan community depended upon him, especially once the persecutions were renewed in 1675. The result is a shift in the emphasis of his works, from individual grace and salvation

(*Grace Abounding* and the first part of *Pilgrim's Progress*) to the community of the elect and its struggle in a hostile world (*Mr. Badman*, the second part of *The Pilgrim's Progress*, and *The Holy City*). This naturally produces an effect of "social realism."[2] Along with this emphasis upon community life comes an emphasis upon the role of women.

Women had always played an important role in Bunyan's religious life.[3] Bunyan's first wife was perhaps indirectly responsible for his conversion experience:

> Presently after this, I changed my condition into a married state, and my mercy was to light upon a wife whose father was counted godly. This woman and I, though we came together as poor as poor might be, not having so much household stuff as a dish or spoon betwixt us both, yet this she had for her part, *The Plain Man's Pathway to Heaven*, and *The Practice of Piety*, which her father had left her when he died. In these two books I should sometimes read with her. . . . She also would be often telling of me, what a godly man her father was. (GA, 8, §9)

Later Bunyan was to be deeply moved by the sight of "three or four poor women sitting at a door in the sun, and talking about the things of God" (GA, 14, §15). Women, for Bunyan, are associated with humility. In the context of the oppressed Nonconformist churches, such a symbol would be evocative of the promise that "the meek shall inherit the earth," with concomitant political implications.

The importance of women in remaking the world—this world, and preparing for the next—formed a major controversy in many radical sects. Richard Greaves has described the large contribution that women made to the radical sects. Their activities included writing and publishing Nonconformist literature, extending patronage and support to Nonconformist ministers, and participating in protests and underground activity. Perhaps the most controversial activities included preaching and prophesying. Few sects outside the Quakers fully supported this practice, and it had many opponents. Thomas Lamb's General Baptist congregation had separate prayer meetings for women,[4] a practice that Bunyan opposed in his pamphlet *A Case of Conscience Resolved*.[5] Bunyan may in fact have rethought his position. Women appear as the prototype of the Church in *Pilgrim's Progress*, Part Two, but they also have several roles in the church, as catechists, as protesters and resisters, as role models, and as the servant to the Church as a whole—Phoebe.

Despite the Pauline injunction against women teaching in

church, women were influential teachers, especially in the home.[6] While the Sunday School generally traces its roots to Robert Raikes and his "ragged schools" in the eighteenth century, the informal catechesis of children and servants requiring at least biblical literacy and the "dame schools" of the Puritan colonies of New England may be considered the ancestors of both modern religious education and the public school system. This catechetical function of women is illustrated in both parts of *The Pilgrim's Progress*.

Cotton Mather, in the New England colonies, was under no illusions as to the value of the women in his church. Calling them the "Hidden Ones," "People, who make no Noise at all in the World," he recognized that his church membership was chiefly composed of women, a demographic reality echoed in England.[7] In many cases women joined Nonconformist churches without their husbands or families. Mercy's position in the second part of *Pilgrim's Progress* may be a reflection of this fact. Women Nonconformists served an important function in the church. In turn, the church was to play an important role in Puritan family life.

There are several schools of thought about the role Protestantism played in affecting family life.[8] The situation is further complicated by the many fluctuations in marriage law and practice in the seventeenth century and the wide variety of opinions on marriage and the family held by the various radical sects during that period. At the most basic level, Protestantism involved a questioning of many social institutions, and this included marriage and the family. On the other hand, this same subversive potential may have produced a backlash that necessitated the subjection of women by Puritan writers and ministers, including Bunyan himself. The church in Bunyan's formulation both replaces and buttresses the Puritan family unit, regulating marriages, raising children in the reformed faith, and controlling the damage caused by church members who leave.

Community influence in the radical sects made itself felt in many aspects of everyday family life. Church members intervened in matters of family discipline and personal behavior. All church members were cared for, particularly vital in a time of increased persecution, but there was a corresponding loss of privacy and autonomy. Church discipline required that offenses be brought to the attention of the entire church. Penitent members had to admit their fault in public; unrepentant sinners were excommunicated, sometimes involving elaborate social shunning or being "sent to Coventry." While public penitence had been a feature of church life prior to the Reformation, the novelty lay in being tried by one's peers in the aggregate, rather than by an ecclesiastical court. Since offenses were brought to light by the report of church members to the officers of the church, this led to a system of surveillance that in a small village may have felt nearly as intrusive and continual as a Foucauldian panopticon.

This certainly was the case in Bunyan's own church. H. G. Tibbutt, the editor of the minutes of the First Independent Church of Bedford, has noted this: "Many church members seem to have had a propensity for spying on others and reporting offenses, real or imagined, to the church officers."[9] After these reports, a delegation was usually sent to talk to the accused. Bunyan often served in such a capacity, both before and after his imprisonment. After this, the offense was brought to the attention of the entire church, discussed and disciplined, a process that occasionally took several months.

The church was, as Sharrock suggests, under great pressure to maintain an appearance of respectability.[10] The effects of the bad public behavior of church members were well known to Bunyan, who remembered his impressions in his own youth: "yet, even then, if I have at any time seen wicked things by those who professed goodness, it would make my spirit tremble. As once above all the rest, when I was in my height of vanity, yet hearing one to swear that was reckoned for a religious man, it had so great a stroke upon my spirit, as it made my heart to ake" (*GA*, 7, §11). The two possible responses of the unregenerate—loss of respect and ridicule—were equally unwelcome.

This would not account, however, for church knowledge about and discipline of private behavior. Sexual behavior is a case in point. It is difficult to imagine who found out about Elizabeth Bisbie, and how:

> A church meeting . . . the 10th of the 2nd month '74. . . . At the same meeting was our sister, Elizabeth Bisbie openly rebuked for an immodest lieing in a chamber several nights wherein also lay a young man, nobody being in the house but them two. (*Minutes*, 76)

Sister Bisbie refused to repent or to desist and was withdrawn from the church (77). This particular meeting was very busy: Sister Landy was reported for chronic card playing, a social fault; and Elizabeth Maxey for "disobedience to her parents . . . for calling her father lier," a domestic fault (76). Sister Maxey's rebuke and discipline is a particularly interesting case. It is clear that the church protected her father's authority. However, in the process of asserting his authority, it was undermined by the mere presence of a larger communal authority—the church. His authority did not, and could not, exist in a vacuum.

In addition, the church did not support unlimited patriarchal authority. A number of men were disciplined for violent behavior to their wives and children:

> 12 March 1678 . . . our brother John Stanton was admonished by the church of his evill in abuseing his wife, and beateing hir often for very light maters. Hee promised us reformation and semed sory for his fault. (*Minutes*, 84)

When Brother Stanton had not amended his ways in October of that same year, the Bedford church cast him out (84). The Bedford church also had no tolerance for a sexual double standard. When William Man confessed to committing fornication first with one woman, then with several, the church excommunicated him in the strongest of language:

> we did then and ther cast him out of the Church, and deliver him up to Satan, for the destruction of the flesh, and that his spirit may be saved in the day of the Lord Jesus. (*Minutes*, 83)

Marriage, the beginning of a new family and a continuance of the old, was a critical issue for radical sectaries. It is not surprising, therefore, to find conflicting views reflected in the Puritan marriage manual, as well as in the second part of *Pilgrim's Progress*. Most marriage manuals comment upon the duty of parents to marry their children properly:

> Disposition in marriage is (for Parents) the highest duty, and for Children (being well discharged) the happiest.[11]

> Here by the way, let me exhort parents and other governours of children, both to traine up their owne children in true piety & feare of God, and also to seeke such matches for them, as they may have some assurance that they are of the same faith, and of the same mind and heart: thus shall they procure to their children much happiness in their marriage as *Abraham* did to *Isaak*.[12]

The trope of Rebecca and Isaac is a common one in Puritan marriage manuals. While it is used to demonstrate parental care in selecting mates and the child's right of approval or veto, embedded within this biblical story is an ideology of endogamy. In Genesis 24, Abraham determines that his son will not intermarry with the Canaanites, but instead sends for Rebecca, Isaac's cousin. Among radical sectaries, this would certainly have been interpreted as a prohibition of marriage with nonprofessors, and a commandment to marry within the church. William Gouge insists upon this point elsewhere: "it is requisite that as a Christian be maried to a Christian, and a professor of the true faith to a professor of the same faith; so one that in truth feareth God, to one of the same minde and disposition."[13] This is not so much a prohibition of exogamy, as a requirement of endogamy. Endogamy was vital if the church was to be "protected against contamination from outside."[14] In *The Life and Death of Mr. Badman*, Bunyan includes a cautionary tale against exogamy. In the second part of *Pilgrim's Progress*, endogamy reaches its apotheosis when Mercy marries Christiana's son, Matthew; literally into the "family of Christians," and becomes the daughter of Christiana, the Church. The individual family unit, if forged within the church, becomes a subset of the church, with a consequent check on patriarchal authority.

The de-emphasis of the family unit and emphasis on the church may seem puzzling when viewed in the light of the marriage manuals, which seem to advocate parental responsibility and authority. I believe the marriage manuals to be untrustworthy, implying greater individual and less community prerogative in the making of marriages than was truly the case. This can be seen best in a Quaker pamphlet by William Smith, "Joyfull Tidings to the Begotten of God." In the pamphlet Smith suggests that individual couples should make up their minds to marry according to inward guidance from God. Paradoxically, the language which he uses suggests that there was in fact a high level of community interference:

> let not any Friends make way one for another by speaking to any party, *except they feele a necessity layed upon them from the Lord*, . . . but let all wait to feele their own movings in Gods counsell and leadings, and so to manifest their own minde in his fear and wisdome . . . & *then lay it before some weighty friends that are endued with heavenly wisdom* (emphasis mine).[15]

It appears that there were no marriages of Bedford church members to nonmembers during Bunyan's tenure as pastor. His concern about this issue may have arisen from incipient marriages of this type that he had helped to prevent. The seriousness with which the Bedford congregation regarded this type of lapse is recorded in the Church Book a decade after Bunyan's death, 1698, when Mary Gates married a "carnall man" (*Minutes*, 115). Sister Gates had been discouraged by her parents and also by Brother Chandler of the Bedford congregation. Despite this, she married out of the church, which sent her an admonition on April 27:

> We understand that you lately gave yourself to [blank in the manuscript], a person of whom there is no grounds as we can heare to hope that there is a work of grace wrought in him . . . and that this was expressly contrary to the repeated intreatyes and persuasions and therefore consent of your parents . . . as well as a direct breach of the rule of God's word of which (together with the many evills attending such a marriage) you were plainly informed aforehand by our brother Chandler. (*Minutes*, 116)

The church is not merely disappointed in her marriage. Clearly, they feel responsible for her behavior and her decision in a quasi-parental manner:

> This action of yours we deem to be highly offensive to God . . . as well as a griefe to us. . . . We look on ourselves bound for this your sin in faithfullness to Christ and your own soul, and to ourselves. (*Minutes*, 116)[16]

The Bedford church, like other sectarian churches, was fearful that such marriages would destroy the structure of their community. In this case, their fears were justified: Mary Gates went on to attend Anglican services and to speak disparagingly of the Independent Church and its members.

Bunyan was clearly worried about such marriages and their effects, for, in addition to his treating the subject in *Pilgrim's Progress*, he devotes a considerable section of *The Life and Death of Mr. Badman* to the subject of a professor marrying a nonprofessor. In *Mr. Badman*, Bunyan juxtaposes the portrait of an unregenerate man with the threat he poses to society. Every bad action committed by Badman affects the community adversely. Even his drinking, which would seem to be a private fault, is linked to theft in order to obtain the necessary money. Badman's first wife is a "godly maid," and her marriage to him causes her great misery and difficulty in her religious life (*Badman*, 65). Hers is not merely an individual misery, for Badman threatens to inform on her and the conventicle she belongs to, thus endangering an entire religious community: "he . . . sware moreover that if she did go, he would make both her, and all her damnable Brotherhood (for so he was pleased to call them) to repent their coming thither. . . . You may easily guess what he meant: he meant, he would turn Informer" (79). Badman is a threat not only to his wife but to the entire religious community to which she belongs. Perhaps most threatening, however, is the means by which Badman puts himself in a position of power: infiltration. Badman wants money, but he is advised that the best way to win the affections of the girl is to pretend to be religious himself. This he has no difficulty in doing, since he was brought up in a religious family:

> after a while, [he] went as boldly to her, and that under a Vizzard of Religion, as if he had been for Honesty and Godliness, one of the most sincere and upright-hearted in England . . . and quickly obtained her too; for natural parts he had . . . and his Religion was the more easily attained; for he had seen something in the house of his Father, and first Master, and so could the more readily put himself into the form and show thereof. (*Badman*, 66–67)

This passage is very revealing of the anxiety that many sectarians must have felt concerning each other. In a time of increased persecution, when loyalty and reliability were vitally important, danger was increased by the number of nonprofessing children of professors. Like Talkative in the first part of *Pilgrim's Progress*, these people would have no difficulty in feigning the mannerisms of nonconformism. They might be insincere, or actual informers. Badman personifies a serious threat: the absence of clear distinctions between those in and outside the church, an issue of particular concern to the open communion policies of Bunyan's church in Bedford.

This threat requires a unified reliable church "family," which is the solution presented in *Mr. Badman* for this particular problem. The girl to whom Badman pays court is especially vulnerable, since her parents are dead (67). The auditor of Badman's history, Attentive, expresses his pity for her misfortunes, whereupon Wiseman, the narrator, points out the alternative course of action she should have taken:

> What if she had acquainted some of her best, most knowing, and godly friends therewith? What if she had engaged a Godly Minister or two to have talked with Mr. Badman? Also, what if she had laid wait round about him, to espie if he was not otherwise behind her back than he was before her face? And besides, I verily think (since in the multitude of Counsellors there is safety) that if she had acquainted the Congregation with it, and desired them to spend some time in prayer to God about it, and if she must have had him, to have received him as to his

godliness, upon the Judgement of others, rather than her own. (*Badman*, 72–73)

In this case, the church would serve *in loco parentis* to the young people of the congregation. Better still, of course, would be marriages arranged within the church itself. Mercy, in the second part of *Pilgrim's Progress*, takes the advice proffered by Wiseman. She asks advice of other women, rejects a match like Badman, and ultimately marries within Christiana's "family," the church.

Pilgrim's Progress, part two, offers an anodyne for worldly corruption: an extended family, an alternative society.[17] These new pilgrims, consisting of women, children, and feeble men, are able to live in Vanity Fair for years without being tainted by it in any way. They have in effect set up a new society. This book is not *The Pilgrim's Progress*; it is *The Pilgrims' Progresses*, and its chief danger to the world lies in its desire to replicate the society it describes: "*Go then, my little Book and shew to all / That entertain, and bid thee welcome shall, / . . . may make them chuse to be / Pilgrims, better by far, than thee or me*" (*PP*, 172). This evangelization by replication forms the structure of the book—the gradual increase of "Christiana's train," the Church.

The second part is relational from its beginning.[18] Its ethic can be summed up in the phrase "Bowels becometh Pilgrims" (*PP*, 186), and the desire to share the joys of salvation, to spread the Christian society, is deeply embedded in the book. The invitation that Christiana receives gradually spreads to her children, her neighbor Mercy, and the many pilgrims they meet upon the way. This has rather curious theological implications. Christian spends much of his journey agonizing about his election. Sharrock points out that Mercy, on the other hand, actually sets off without a roll of election.[19] Mercy worries about her right to go on pilgrimage, but is reassured by the Gatekeeper: " 'I pray for all them that believe on me, by what means soever they come unto me' " (*PP*, 190). Mercy's primary emotion is at first a love of Christiana, and only later a love of pilgrimage. In this episode, affection among women in worldly society is transformed into Christian society. The natural humility and affection of women pose a potential threat to the social order. Finally, community of goods, reminiscent of the earliest Christian community described in Acts, is initiated naturally by women in the very beginning of the second part, for Christiana decides to share everything with her companion: "Yet we will have all things in common betwixt thee and me" (185).

Christiana, in bringing her children along, adds an important qualifier to the other-worldly orientation of Bunyan's book. The chief good of children is that they continue the life of Christians here on earth, a point made explicit by Gaius later in the book. In this sense the book is not millenarian: the expectation is that Christians will continue to be in the world, but not of the world, for at least another generation. Paradoxically, this makes this society potentially a larger threat than other extreme millenarian sects, since they know they will have to resist the corrupt Anglican royalist society around them for years to come.

The importance of the children is immediately recognized at the House of Interpreter, the book's first representation of church society. The attendants come out to see them:

> And one smiled, and another smiled, and they all smiled for Joy that *Christiana* was become a Pilgrim. They also looked upon the Boys, they stroked them over the Faces with the Hand in token of their kind reception of them: they also carried it lovingly to *Mercie*, and bid them all welcome into their Master's House. (*Old Saints glad to see the young ones walk in God's ways, PP,* 199)

The preparation of the women by the significant rooms, the Bath, and the seals serves several purposes. The women are prepared by biblical instruction to live the Christian life. They are also ready to teach the children, vital in the House Beautiful episode.

Great-heart accompanies the party to the House Beautiful. Some critics feel that as Christian is an autobiographical figure in Part One, Great-heart, the Congregational minister, is the autobiographical figure of Part Two. Bunyan may also be making the polemical point that the women cannot and should not travel alone: a reference to *A Case of Conscience*, though I will later elaborate the reasons I think Bunyan shifted his point of view. In either case, Bunyan is not suggesting that women do not have the intelligence or the emotive capability to respond correctly. He goes to some trouble to demonstrate that they possess both: the former by the intelligent questions that the women ask Great-heart, and the latter by Christiana's deep response to the spot where Christian's burden fell off. Significantly in this communitarian book, her first thought is of her neighbors: "O Mercie, that thy Father and Mother were here, yea, and Mrs. Timorous also. Nay I wish now with all my Heart, that here was Madam Wanton *too*" (*PP*, 212).

Great-heart is fully armed, not merely to suggest a Pauline metaphor, but because the pilgrimage is dangerous.[20] In some ways, it is more dangerous than it was before: the lions are awake and giant

Grim is in the road. Christiana is defiant: *"Now I am Risen a Mother in Israel"* (*PP*, 219). Gender was no protection against religious persecution in the 1680s: pregnant women were thrown into prison. Quaker women were particularly highly represented among the persecuted, probably because they were most likely to have preached publicly.[21] Grim is the first of the types of aristocratic or Catholic religion that threaten the pilgrims. Great-heart, in his role as spiritual figurehead, becomes the primary target for violent attack and persecution. His job is to make it possible for Christiana, Mercy, and the children to "hold on their way" (*PP*, 219). But the real revolution is not the violent action or reaction undertaken by Great-heart; revolution need not be bloody. It is quietly being effected by the women. The parallel to real Puritan churches, in which women were keeping things together with instruction and hiding Nonconformist ministers, is no accident.[22]

The women's value is seen in the catechesis episode that follows at the House Beautiful. The boys have learned from their mother, and their catechist is one of the wise maidens of the house, Prudence. She is not merely curious about the children themselves: her stated purpose is to "see how *Christiana* had brought up her Children" (*PP*, 224). As she proceeds, she compliments Christiana on the quality of her instruction: "You are to be commended for thus bringing up your Children" (*PP*, 224). After she has finished, she tells the children that they can expect further instruction from women:

> Then said *Prudence* to the Boys, You must still hearken to your Mother, for she can learn you more . . . I for my part, my Children, will teach you what I can while you are here, and shall be glad if you will ask me Questions that tend to Godly edifying. (*PP*, 226)

The women's catechesis is vital to society's transformation. The educating of the children leads to the inculcation and maintenance of the new radical Christian ideology. By altering education and ideology, these women are turning the world upside down permanently.

Bunyan moves from issues of education to issues of marriage in the church. While Christiana and Prudence are educating the next generation of pilgrims, Mercy is facing a situation not unlike that of Mr. Badman's first wife. She is courted by a Mr. Brisk, "a man of some breeding, and that pretended to religion, but a man that stuck very close to the world," a cousin of By-ends no doubt, perhaps by marriage. While Mercy is physically attractive, her primary attraction for Mr. Brisk is clearly economic. Since she is always making clothing, Mr. Brisk assumes that in acquiring Mercy, he will be acquiring a lucrative cottage industry: "I will warrant her a good huswife quoth he to himself" (227). Like Mr. Badman, his chief motivation in marriage is pecuniary gain.

Mercy, however, is wise enough to ask the maidens of the house about Brisk "for they did know him better than she" (227). She is following the advice of Wiseman set forth in *Mr. Badman*: "what if she had acquainted some of her best, most knowing, and godly friends therewith?" (*Badman*, 72). She discovers that he is in fact only a pretender to religion. There is also a sly hint that discovery of Mercy's true economic status will end his interest, and that proves to be the case:

> What always at it? Yes, said she, either for my self, or for others. And what canst thee *earn* a day? quoth he. I do these things, said she, *that I may be Rich in good Works, laying up in store a good Foundation against the time to come, that I may lay hold on Eternal Life:* Why prethee what dost thou with them? said he; Clothe the naked, said she. With that his Countenance fell. So he forebore to come at her again. And when he was asked the reason why, he said *That* Mercie *was a pretty lass; but troubled with ill Conditions.* (PP, 227)

Mercy is aware that to marry a man that does not share her values is to invite misery upon herself and the Christian society, and tells the story of her sister Bountiful, which parallels that of the first Mrs. Badman. Prudence asks Mercy: "And yet he was a Professor, I warrant you? Mer. *Yes, such a one as he was, and of such as he, the World is now full; but I am for none of them all*" (228). Here again the caution is given against those who seem to be professors. The need for consultation with the church is made doubly vital. This episode demonstrates how marriages ought not to be made: later Bunyan will demonstrate how marriages should be made.

The Christian society will be formed explicitly at the house of Gaius. Before this occurs, the values of this society need to be made clear. The next episode, the Valley of Humiliation, is one of the most radical in the book. It explicitly sets forth a view in which the last are first. Since this requires a re-writing of the Valley of Humiliation from the first part of *Pilgrim's Progress*, it can be argued that Bunyan has become more, not less radical in his views. In the first part, the Valley of Humiliation is a fearful place. Christian experiences one of his most terrible struggles there, the battle with Apollyon. Little attention is given to the landscape, and the valley itself runs directly into the Valley of the Shadow of Death. In the second part, Bunyan has rewritten this so that instead of an epic struggle, it is a pastoral idyll.[23]

The landscape of the Valley of Humiliation is a literalized Magnificat; the mighty are put from their thrones, and the humble exalted, the hungry filled with good things and the rich sent empty away: "I have also known many laboring Men that have got good Estates in this Valley of *Humiliation* (For God resisteth the Proud but gives *more, more* Grace to the Humble)" (*PP*, 237).[24] This is most clearly seen in the song of the shepherd boy: "*I am content with what I have, / Little be it, or much: / . . . Here little, and hereafter Bliss, / Is best from Age to Age*" (238). Bunyan's radicalism must therefore be seen in the context of his otherworldly orientation. Bunyan is not a radical in one sense: his chief good lies in the life after death, and he describes material wealth as a hindrance to pilgrims. The poor simply acquiring the goods of the gentry therefore is not of interest to him. However, throughout both books of *Pilgrim's Progress* Bunyan has been at pains to demonstrate the injustice perpetrated by various types of wealthy elite: the landowner Giant Despair, the gentrified hireling minister Mr. Worldly Wiseman, and the merciless buying and selling at Vanity Fair.

Pilgrims must move through the world: "the way is the way, and there's an end," as Great-heart comments (*PP*, 237). There is no reason that pilgrims need be of the world, however, and this can be demonstrated in their attitude toward worldly goods. Christiana and Mercy have been holding their goods in common since the beginning of the book. Once again, they are Cotton Mather's "Hidden Ones," teaching Christian doctrine and sharing goods because they are naturally humble. The shepherd boy's song is an echo of their own status. If this is not made explicit enough, Mercy draws attention to the natural affinity of the Valley and her own nature:

> I think I am as well in this Valley, as I have been any where else in all our Journey: The place methinks suits with my Spirit. . . . Here one may think, and break at Heart, and melt in ones Spirit, until ones Eyes become like the *Fish Pools of Heshbon*. (*Humility a sweet grace, PP*, 239)

What comes naturally to Christiana and Mercy is for Great-heart an acquired trait. If indeed Great-heart is an autobiographical figure, it is significant that Bunyan felt especially troubled by the cardinal sin of pride. The ease of their journey through the Valley does not reflect the women's weakness, but their strength.

It is after the Valley of the Shadow of Death and the meeting with Honest that the "church" begins to be formed. Honest's commentary upon the different sort of pilgrims can be read as the experience of an old professor who has seen many types of member: one thinks of Bunyan writing up the commentary in the Church Book. The inn that they come to is a New Testament inn. Sharrock notes that the host, Gaius, is from *Romans:* "the host of himself and of the whole church."[25] Christian's genealogy is related by Gaius. The "family" is from Antioch, the place where "the disciples were first called Christians" (*Acts* 11:26).[26] Its continuance for posterity is important: Christian's sons are urged to marry and have children. Bunyan here portrays the proper making of marriage within the church. Gaius puts forth the suggestion in his ministerial capacity:

> And *Christiana,* said *This* Inn-keeper, I am glad to see thee and thy Friend *Mercie* together here, a lovely Couple. And may I advise, take *Mercie* into a nearer Relation to thee. If she will, let her be given to *Mathew* thy eldest son. 'Tis the way to preserve you a posterity in the Earth. So this match was concluded, and in process of time they were married. (*PP*, 261)

Mercy marries into the church, which is Christiana's family. While the purpose of marriage is to breed more Christians, the family is primarily Christiana's. Christiana is thus revealed as a type of the Church. Bunyan knew that the Church ought to be female: "This is one of God's chief ends in instituting Marriage, that Christ and his Church, under a figure, might be wherever there is a Couple that believes through Grace" (*Christian Behaviour*, MW, 3: 27). Since the Church had to be female, it was necessary for the main protagonists of the second part of *Pilgrim's Progress* to be female. Bunyan chose to portray female pilgrims not primarily because he wished to display the peculiar difficulties of the female professor, but because in Christiana and Mercy he sets forth a type of the pilgrim Church on earth. The Church is weak, her "husband" is in heaven, and she is beset by difficulties; yet in the end she triumphs through humility. Corporate Christianity, Bunyan's primary subject, had to be represented by women.

Gaius's eulogy of women, which follows the betrothal, should be read as eulogizing Christian virtue. Women are not privileged over men at the end: they are sharers in the "Grace of Life" (*PP*, 261). Christian society ought to be egalitarian. But since humility is made the cardinal virtue of Christianity, it neatly undercuts any concept of female church leadership. If to be a "Hidden One" is virtuous, the implied corollary is that the more hidden, the more virtuous. Bunyan, however, does seem to retreat from his earlier position on female church leadership. His position is modified, not merely by the eulogy to women, but by the second betrothal, that of James to Phoebe.

Phoebe, like Gaius, is from the Epistle to the Romans. She is not, like Dorcas or other New Testament women, a type of domestic benefactor: "I commend to you our sister Phoebe, a [minister/servant/deacon—gr. *diakonos*] of the church at Cenchrae, so that you may welcome her in the Lord as is fitting for the saints, and help her in whatever she may require from you, for she has been a benefactor of many and of myself as well" (*Rom.* 16:1–2). Phoebe is a woman with a ministerial role. By selecting her in particular as a mate for James, Bunyan gives approval to a certain level of church leadership for women.

The Christian society has a future, symbolized by the children of the new marriages, and a communitarian ethic of its own. While in Vanity Fair the pilgrims are able to operate as an alternative society. Vanity Fair is in general less dangerous than it was before, but the sectarian church needs to keep itself separate: "He that lives in such a place as this is, and that has to do with such as we have, has need of an Item to caution him to take heed, every moment of the Day" (*PP*, 275). Through separation it keeps itself free of the taint of the Fair, apparently for years. The church is also growing. Old pilgrims fall in by the wayside, and new children are being born to the four "fruitful" wives of Christian's daughters. Its size makes it more threatening and harder to extinguish. The rapid growth of the church is noted by the Shepherds in the Delectable Mountains. The size of Mr. Great-heart's company surprises them. Since Christiana is the Church, Great-heart's introduction of "Christiana and her train" could apply to the entire company. By the time they reach the Delectable Mountains, Christiana's company is beyond the reach of the threatening worldly society.

The communitarian society depicted by Bunyan, an idealized version of Bedford Meeting, suggests a threat to the Stuart state. Unlike Christian, the company does not merely survive monsters, but utterly defeats and overwhelms them. While it is tacitly acknowledged that pilgrims will have to continue to live "in the Fair" for some time to come, by marriage and propagation, education, community of goods, and a secure alternative society, the pilgrims will not only be safe, but slowly transform the threatening Vanity Fair into Beulah. Christiana's train will become the Church Triumphant, and the meek, many of them women, will literally inherit the earth.

Notes

1. Roger Sharrock, ed., "Introduction" to *PP*, 23.
2. N. H. Keeble, "Christiana's Key: The Unity of the Pilgrim's Progress," in *The Pilgrim's Progress: Critical and Historical Views*, ed. Vincent Newey (Liverpool: Liverpool University Press, 1980), 3.
3. See Monica Furlong, *Puritan's Progress* (New York: Coward, McCann & Geoghegan, 1975), 116–17. She argues that women in Bunyan are associated with refinement.
4. Richard L. Greaves, "Foundation Builders: The Role of Women in Early English Nonconformity," in *Triumph over Silence: Women in Protestant History, Contributions to the Study of Religion*, ed. Richard L. Greaves (Westport, Conn., and London: Greenwood Press, 1985), 77.
5. Roger Sharrock has postulated that the Second Part of *Pilgrim's Progress* may have partially been intended to give recognition to the women in Bunyan's congregation after the publication of this pamphlet. See Roger Sharrock, *John Bunyan* (London: Hutchinson's, 1954), 140. Greaves argues that while the second part of *Pilgrim's Progress* should not be read as a retreat from his earlier position, the two positions may be read as complementary: women are godly because they are lowly and humble. See Richard L. Greaves, "Conscience, Liberty, and the Spirit: Bunyan and Nonconformity," in *John Bunyan: Conventicle and Parnassus, Tercentenary Essays* ed. N. H. Keeble (Oxford: Clarendon Press, 1988), 39.
6. Greaves, "Foundation Builders," 75–92.
7. Gerald F. Moran, " 'The Hidden Ones': Women and Religion in Puritan New England," in *Triumph over Silence*, 127.
8. Ralph Houlbrooke points out three basic opinions among modern historians. The first, whose primary proponent is Lawrence Stone, asserts that Protestantism gave the husband greater authority. The second is that Protestantism raised the status of wives. A third view "first expressed during the Reformation, has stressed Protestantism's subversive potential. By emphasizing the importance of individual faith and understanding, by asserting the priesthood of all believers, and by insisting that the Scriptures were the property of all Christians, the Reformer tended to encourage the use of individual judgement, as their opponents claimed" (*The English Family 1450–1700*. [London and New York: Longman, 1984], 79).
9. H. G. Tibbutt, ed., *The Minutes of the First Independent Church (now Bunyan Meeting) at Bedford, 1656–1766* (Bedford: Bedfordshire Historical Record Society 55, 1976), 10. All subsequent citations are to this edition.
10. Sharrock, *John Bunyan*, 109.
11. William Thomas of Ibley, *Christian and conjugall counsell* (London: 1661), 81.
12. William Gouge, *Of domesticall duties* (London, 1622), 192.
13. Gouge, *Of domesticall duties*, 191.
14. Sharrock, *John Bunyan*, 109.
15. William Smith, Quaker of Besthorp, *Joyfull tidings to the begotten of God* (London, 1664), 8.

16. Warning against sinful behavior is enjoined on believers by Bunyan several times in *Pilgrim's Progress*. See, for example, Faithful: "I have dealt plainly with him; and so am clear of his blood if he perisheth" (133).

17. See Brainerd P. Stranahan, who reflects that in the Second Part, "the pilgrims exhibit a greater affection for the world . . . They remind us that, even in New Testament times, Christians were able to find a measure of comfort and hospitality in the world." "Bunyan's Satire and Its Biblical Sources," *Bunyan in Our Time*, ed. Robert G. Collmer (Kent, Ohio: Kent State University Press, 1989), 57.

18. N. H. Keeble notes that when Christiana goes on pilgrimage "it is natural affection for her husband, self-recrimination at her treatment of him and the encouragement of his example which prompts her. . . . In other words, Christian has quite literally saved his family by abandoning it." "Christiana's Key: The Unity of the Pilgrim's Progress," in *The Pilgrim's Progress: Critical and Historical Views*, ed. Vincent Newey (Liverpool: Liverpool University Press, 1980), 10–11.

19. Sharrock also suggests that this is part of "some extremely clever open-communion propaganda." *John Bunyan*, 140–41. The Slough of Despond, for example, is "rather worse than formerly" (*PP*, 187) because the King's laborers (presumably other professors) keep making it worse.

20. Brean S. Hammond points out the connection between the militant Pauline metaphor of Ephesians and the social satire in the book. "*The Pilgrim's Progress*: Satire and Social Comment," in *The Pilgrim's Progress: Critical and Historical Views*, ed. Vincent Newey (Liverpool: Liverpool University Press, 1980), 125. Hammond goes on to disagree with Christopher Hill, suggesting that the social satire is "conservative" because it is focused on another world. I am not convinced that these points of view are irreconcilable. While Bunyan may not be advocating social insurrection, he is surely advocating social resistance.

21. Dorothy P. Ludlow, "Shaking Patriarchy's Foundations: Sectarian Women in England, 1641–1700," in *Triumph over Silence: Women in Protestant History. Contributions to the Study of Religion*, ed. Richard L. Greaves (Westport, Conn., and London: Greenwood press, 1985), 112.

22. This reading counterbalances that of Margaret Thickstun, who maintains that the feminine is completely subsumed in the book. See "From Christiana to Stand-fast: Subsuming the Feminine in *The Pilgrim's Progress*," *Studies in English Literature, 1500–1900* 26 no. 3 (Summer 1986): 439–53. Perhaps it can be argued that feminine virtue is valorized, but separated and rendered less visible as a protective gesture. While this may be paternalistic, I do not feel that it is excessively repressive in historical context.

23. Christopher Hill has noted the similarity between Bunyan's Delectable Mountains and Celestial City and the "medieval peasant's Land of Cokayne, or . . . Fifth Monarchist visions of a material heaven on earth." See *A Tinker and a Poor Man: John Bunyan and His Church 1628–1688* (New York: Knopf, 1989), 220. The similarity lies, as Hill points out, in the implied or overt social criticism of the landed wealthy.

24. It is at this point that the scholarly debate between Hill and Hammond upon the relative conservatism or radicalism of Bunyan's text crystallizes. The social criticism of the mighty and the valorization of the humble are at their strongest here, which would seem to support Hill. Hammond's argument would seem to be supported by the desire of the pilgrims to have nothing.

25. Roger Sharrock, ed., "Introduction" and notes in *PP*, 405, n. 63.

26. Sharrock, *PP*, 405, n. 64.

Pilgrims' Progresses: Derivative Texts and the Seventeenth-Century Reader

Susan Cook

I INTEND TO EXAMINE THE RELATIONSHIP BETWEEN *THE PILGRIM'S Progress* and the seventeenth-century writers and readers of devotional fiction; I will focus on the derivative texts spawned by Bunyan's text in the first thirty years of its existence. These versions of the pilgrimage story have often attracted bibliographical attention—first and comprehensively by John Brown in his late nineteenth-century biography of Bunyan[1]—and also passing critical acknowledgment.[2] I would like to make a case for the reassessment of their worth as partners with, and not merely followers of, Bunyan within a religious culture that valued the sharing of narratives and looked to the solidarity of repeated patterns in conversion and the Christian life. While I am aware of the poetic versions of *The Pilgrim's Progress* to emerge at the end of the seventeenth century I have chosen to concentrate on prose fiction.[3] There are close and important links between the derivative texts that follow the prose framework of *The Pilgrim's Progress* and that treat poetry and hymns as one part of the whole expression of faith, and their great precursor.

The pilgrimage tale forms, in the late seventeenth century, a small but distinct subgenre of devotional literature. Its popularity was pronounced enough for other types of text to coin titles that suggest connections, such as Francis Bugg's *The Pilgrim's Progress from Quakerism to Christianity* (1698), a text purporting to expose the evils and methods of Quakerism, or John Dunton's satire on contemporary economic life, *An Hue and Cry after Conscience: or The Pilgrim's Progress by Candle Light* (1685). The first text in which the pilgrimage form was popularly revived in the late seventeenth century was not actually Bunyan's, but that of Bishop Symon Patrick, whose *Parable of the Pilgrim* was published in 1665. He hails the revival of this old form: "That I send one to wait upon you in the habit of a Pilgrim, which hath been so long out of fashion . . . may seem a thing very strange and surprising to you. But when you shall consider that old fashions are wont to come about again, and that we are much in love with Antiques . . . it may abate a little of the wonder."[4] However, it is Bunyan who has become the focus for this form of narrative. As early as 1768, Augustus M. Toplady could proclaim:

> What a stiff, sapless, tedious piece of work is that written by bishop Patrick! How does the unlearned tinker of Bedfordshire outshine the bishop of Ely! I have heard, that his lordship wrote his Pilgrim, by way of antidote against what he deemed the fanaticism of John Bunyan's Pilgrim. But what a rich fund of heavenly experience, life and sweetness does that latter contain! How heavy, lifeless, and unevangelical is the former![5]

Thus within a century Bunyan has superseded an author of the established church. He provides the definition against which others come to be judged, though not always as harshly as Symon Patrick. Amongst his contemporaries, Bunyan provides a prototype by which subsequent developments and copies would be evaluated; the prototype, moreover, both anticipates and expects progeny.

Although the scope of this essay cannot encompass a thorough history of the eight authors here discussed, a brief contextualization illustrates the diversity and yet the interrelatedness of their pilgrimage texts. When tracing the chronology of these derivative texts, it is helpful to bear in mind the publishing dates of 1678 and 1684 for each part of *The Pilgrim's Progress*, as this highlights just how rapid some of these responses were.

In 1683 two pilgrimage tales by men of the Baptist tradition were published: Benjamin Keach's (1640–1704) *Travels of True Godliness* and Thomas Sherman's (n.d.) *Second Part of the Pilgrim's Progress*. Their religious affiliation is shared by Bunyan, but the range of Baptist belief is vast, and this is reflected in their narratives. In theory, the groups divided into General and Particular Baptists, tending toward Arminianism and election, respectively. There were also two smaller groups of Seventh-Day Baptists (Sabbatarians) and a loose group that held to higher culture and the possibility of performing God's will in the world as it stood.[6] In practice, however, there were almost as many shades of Baptist as there were individual church groups. In the context of this essay, Bunyan is considered a separatist Puritan, more keen on purity of Christian faith in general than upholding one particular sect.[7]

Keach was a Baptist who had made a transition from General to

Particular beliefs.[8] His career parallels Bunyan's in his history of persecution, particularly for pastoral work,[9] and in his writing life that shares polemic, verse (specifically hymn-writing in Keach's case),[10] and popular fictional tales that produce sequels (Keach's *Travels* is followed in 1684 by *The Progress of Sin*, a reprobate's tale that mirror's Bunyan's own first choice as a sequel to *The Pilgrim's Progress, Mr Badman*). Although it has been suggested that each spurred the other on in new endeavors of composition, no personal links between the two have emerged.[11] *Travels* does not depict an empathetic protagonist but chronicles the journey of the celestial figure True Godliness across time and into the seventeenth century in search of a true convert to Christianity. Sherman's work, as I will discuss, is not a literal sequel to Bunyan's first part in the sense of continuing the adventures of the same clan, but rewrites the plot to reform its style and theological emphasis. His is the first "improvement" of Bunyan's text to emerge. Though Sherman himself is described in *A Baptist Bibliography* as a General Baptist,[12] Sherman's text shows the obvious liturgical influence of the *Book of Common Prayer*: before discovering the reference to Sherman as a Baptist I had diagnosed the text as an Anglican one. This is a warning against cut-and-dried definitions of Nonconformists in a period when their new cultural identities were still being established.

The popularity of this religious form was such that by 1684 the authors John Dunton (1659–1733) and a pseudonymous "J.B." had both published plagiarisms of a kind. John Dunton, a London publisher and bookseller prominent in the 1680s and '90s, has been described both as an important figure in the seventeenth-century book trade and as a "hackmaster."[13] He offered the public a "cut-and-paste" production, *The Pilgrim's Guide,* a book compiled of almost literal extracts from other pilgrimage stories, relying most heavily on Bunyan, but also using the work of Keach and Symon Patrick.[14] He then claims the whole enterprise to be that of his conveniently deceased father, though the Rev. Dunton had passed away before the texts he is supposed to have copied were ever written.[15] "J.B." wrote an accepted form of abridgement, the chapbook *The Pilgrim's Progress to the Other World*, condensing Bunyan's tale into twenty-two pages for a poorer buying public, such publications generally costing only a penny or two.[16] This proved a popular form for Bunyan's work. For example, *The Pilgrim's Progress* was abridged in the eighteenth century by two evangelists, John Wesley and Hannah More; the latter specifically chose it as a text for her *Cheap Repository Tracts*.[17]

Invoking the persona of Bunyan was obviously a popular ploy for texts aimed at a wider section of purchasers. In 1693 another "J.B." wrote his version, *The Third Part of the Pilgrim's Progress [Pilgrim's Progress III]*. This is in the spirit of a true sequel, and although it concerns a new hero, Tender Conscience, it has the same geographical setting as Bunyan's text and relates the continuing history of some of Bunyan's characters. The enterprise is considered legitimate; the spirit of the story rests with Bunyan, and acknowledgment of this is meant to enhance the texts rather than proclaim them as fakes.

The last two books I consider were both printed in the eighteenth century, though one was composed in the seventeenth. Stephen Crisp (1628–1692), a preacher and writer as well known in his Quaker circles as Bunyan and Keach were in their Baptist ones, wrote *A Short History of a Long Travel from Babylon to Bethel* in 1692, though it was published only posthumously in 1711. A rare piece of Quaker fiction (the only true Quaker fictional work I can find for this period), it is a rendering of a spiritual journey that is faithful to Friends' doctrine.[18] It portrays the search of the individual whose perseverance is rewarded upon conversion. Unlike all the others here, the story is written from the point of view of the narrator's sojourn at his destination, and is in the first person, symbolic of the spiritual fulfillment Quakers found within themselves in their mortal life.[19]

The final text under consideration is Henry Wilson's (n.d.) *The Spiritual Pilgrim*, published in 1710. It forms the more partisan versions of earlier authors into a tale whose theology is intended to be more ecumenical and whose plot is described as being more "pertinent" than Bunyan's now slightly outdated piece (though Bunyan is Wilson's inspiration). His biographical preface invokes memories of Bunyan's own history of *The Pilgrim's Progress* as a text of which he is uncertain and which is shown to friends for advice, claiming a biographical as well as literary inheritance for his work.

I am aware that imitation of Bunyan did not stop with these authors, but I have chosen these parameters because the texts within them may legitimately be said to constitute a loose writing group. Wilson's text is the pivotal point between derivative texts that are also consciously intertextual and those of the eighteenth century that are solely derivative. His text also marks a much more internalized view of pilgrimage and spiritual struggles. *The Spiritual Pilgrim*, as its title suggests, is removed from a situation of remembered and continuing actual religious conflict and from the migrations, both forced and voluntary, of Nonconformist groups.

Central to the importance of these texts is their interrelatedness. Although they follow *The Pilgrim's Progress*, they are not merely copies or new versions, but are designed to initiate intertextual dialogue. This may be through the alteration of the doctrinal base, as with Thomas Sherman's *The Second Part*, through the development of Bunyan's narrative, seen in *Pilgrim's Progress III* (where we find that Atheist was the victim of enchantment and is restored to the band of the elect as Convert[20]), or through borrowings from Bunyan and others seen in the chapbook *Pilgrim's Progress to the Other World* and in John Dunton's collection of pilgrimage stories.

In illustration I would like to turn first to Thomas Sherman, whose opinion of Bunyan is occasionally found reprinted in Bunyan criticism.[21] He acknowledges *The Pilgrim's Progress* as "that necessary and useful tract, which hath deservedly obtained such an universal esteem and commendation,"[22] and yet he sees a "fourfold defect" in Bunyan:

> First there is nothing said of the *State of Man* in his first Creation. Nor Secondly, of the Misery of Man in his Lapsed Estate before Conversion. Thirdly, a too brief passing over the Methods of Divine Goodness, in the Convincing, Converting, and Reconciling of Sinners to himself. And Fourthly, I have endeavored to deliver the Whole in such serious and spiritual phrases, that may prevent that lightness and laughter which the reading some passages therein, occasion in some vain and frothy minds.[23]

Sherman's attitude toward Bunyan is well intentioned but rather condescending; however, he does seek to engage with Bunyan on his own terms. Though his text purports to differ from Bunyan's, he assumes the same readership, which was perhaps seduced by the promise of the title only to be faced with a new evangelism. Sherman overtly demands comparison with Bunyan's "tract," as he terms it, and assumes a pastoral rather than recreational purpose for their work. In order to reform "vain and frothy minds," Sherman works on the understanding of the intellect before that of the soul, producing a more meditative text. Bunyan's introduction to *The Pilgrim's Progress* is brief and simple: "As I walk'd through the wilderness of this world, I lighted on a certain place, where was a Denn; And I laid me down in that place to sleep: And as I slept I dreamed a Dream" (8). Sherman, in contrast, begins:

> The Spring being far advanced, the Meadows being Covered with a Curious Carpet of delightful Green . . . I one Day took a Walk in the fields, to Feast my Eyes with the Variety of Delightful Objects which that Sea-

son of the Year, wherein the Universe bears the nearest resemblance to the happy state wherein the Immortal God at first created it, liberally offers to the view of the Admiring Beholders.[24]

He proceeds to take eleven pages before his narrator finally falls asleep. There is no quarter for the frothy-minded Christian here: doctrine is soundly taught before it is entertainingly illustrated.

In contrast, Henry Wilson, writing at the beginning of the eighteenth century, demonstrates not a doctrinal reform of *The Pilgrim's Progress,* but an awareness of the burden Bunyan has placed on other authors using this theme (rather like the spiritual burden Bunyan places on Christian's back in the story). In his poetic preface he defends himself against dual charges of mere plagiarism and of disrespect for Bunyan's achievement:

> First I suppose some Persons may object,
> 'Tis just the *Pilgrim's Progress* in effect. . . .
> It is in Style and Method answerable,
> But much more pertinent and applicable.
> But yet mistake me not, I will not lend
> My Pen or Tongue to argue or contend
> Against the *Pilgrim's Progress,* nor to grace
> My own by casting Dirt upon its Face.
> Nay, and so far have I been from despising
> The *Pilgrim's Progress,* or yet from devising
> A Work to contradict it, that I never
> Thro'out the Book did purposely endeavour
> To alter or avoid Names or Expressions
> If representative of the Professions
> Of the' Person speaking, merely on the ground
> Because they're in the *Pilgrim's Progress* found. . . .[25]

He acknowledges the continuing popularity of *Pilgrim's Progress,* and suggests that *The Spiritual Pilgrim* is a progression rather than a usurpation of Bunyan's work. To take up motifs used by Bunyan is to acquiesce to their universality and to provide links between the texts; this suggests an adherence to a basically Puritan code of conduct that, though appearing in many forms, underlies all these texts.

Although Sherman and Wilson provide two opposite attitudes toward Bunyan's work, each demonstrates the fluidity of his text. *Pilgrim's Progress* is present in each piece. Though the pilgrimage theme can be altered, it is an eternal narrative, taking its theme from Scripture, which itself deals with it as a typological scenario

(Heb. 11; 1 Peter 2:1). This notion is taken to its extreme in Dunton's homogenized anthology, where texts flow into each other to produce a coherent story. That Dunton used two different Baptist texts and an Anglican one to produce his basic story, with only minor changes, is an illustration of the compatibility of different versions of this genre.

One reason why these texts can be fluid and find room to develop intertextual debate is that they call on the tradition of oral literature. This is the natural environment for narrative change, where different situations or the social make-up of the audience dictate the style and content of the delivery. These are also the criteria for sermon delivery, an oral form that bridges the gap between folk tales and this devotional literature.[26] *Pilgrim's Progress* has its roots firmly in this mixed soil. It is a rewritten folk tale, focusing on a Puritan protagonist. It is still scattered with giants, monsters, and demons fought by heroes of the people, but it articulates a Christian heroism in which the protagonist wins by the spirit as much as by the sword, and it depicts a Christian hero whose reward is to attain riches and status of a different kind, in heaven. Rhetorical devices of sermons and folk tales, episodes and repetition, are found within these texts as well as between them. Benjamin Keach's *Travels* is built around a recurring pattern of the actions and outcomes of the visits True Godliness makes to various characters such as Riches, Poverty, Youth, and Old Age. Formal disputes are set up, and all arguments are refuted by True Godliness, who is nevertheless driven from each home to continue his wanderings.

Recent scholarship has highlighted the fact that ballad, broadsheet, and even chapbook literature is conscious that it moves within a culture that is both oral and printed: a typical address on a table (a moral broadsheet) might be "to thou that these Lines dost eyther heare or reade."[27] Less attention, however, has been paid to the situation of a larger text being read to the household, even though we understand that this happened. Even as late as 1786, a text of *Pilgrim's Progress* edited by George Burder was recommended for just such an educational purpose.[28] A pertinent scene takes place in *Pilgrim's Progress*, where Hopeful finds the monument to Lot's wife, but needs Christian's help in spelling out the letters of the inscription. Much Christian devotional literature accepts this scenario of the literate conveying Christian instruction to the illiterate.[29] To complete the scene, one needs to bring in the idea, assumed by Bunyan's successors, that readers and listeners would be familiar with *Pilgrim's Progress* and would therefore not only participate with the text presented to them, but enter into an intertextual debate. An intertextual way of reading and understanding is encouraged by biblical references that direct the reader to make a critical comparison of devotional texts with the one text they all purport to be interpreting. The pamphlet and tract warfare of the seventeenth century has certainly aroused interest, but I believe that more could be made of what these patterns of debate between fictional pieces reveal of the newly or semiliterate ranks who absorbed and reacted to them.[30]

In this overview I am moving toward a definition of the particular textual aesthetic that underpins the writings of these pilgrimage authors, one that allows for and encourages derivative texts. To a great extent it is determined by the religious culture in which they moved, the Puritanism and Nonconformism that directed its efforts toward the middling and lower ranks. Isolated by their own beliefs and the attitude of many conformists toward their doctrines, this peculiar style of fiction was developed. It takes the building blocks of Puritanism—conformity, repetition, and similarity—and makes them the characteristics of their literature. In many seventeenth-century conformist churches conversion was affirmed by a declaration of one's experience to the congregation, and this might be written down or even published for the edification of others.[31] *Grace Abounding*, Bunyan's spiritual autobiography, is an expanded form of his supposed declaration to the church at Bedford, and bears the marks of the rules and teachings laid down by his pastor, John Gifford. For example, Gifford's repeated exhortation to search Scripture for confirmation of all decisions and visions is manifest in Bunyan's overanxious search for confirmation of his revelations (*GA*, 37). Homogeneity of both spiritual experience and the style of its presentation was encouraged as a mark of sincerity in the convert. A typical pattern seen in Baptist or Congregational sects would include a revelation of the evils of one's early years, a description of early awakenings to piety (which are soon recognized as a superficial conversion), a lengthy spiritual struggle to attain conviction of salvation, and the final victory as the individual attains true conversion and rests within a particular denomination.

These codes are often inscribed in church covenants. In Bunyan's church this took the form of the death-bed letter of their founder, Gifford.[32] The emphasis on patterns of conformity is striking: order is frequently cited as the most important trait of the church.

> Let all things be done decently and in order according to the Scriptures. . . . Let the gifts of the Church be exercised according to order. . . .

Come together in time, and leave off orderly, for God is a God of order amongst his saints.[33]

It also significantly sets in motion a vocabulary of journeying. The convert must "declare, whether a brother or sister, that through grace they will walke in love with the Church," and "Salute the brethren who walke not in fellowship with you, with the same love and name of brother or sister as those who do."[34] The vocabulary itself moves through different texts, first into the church book itself where new converts are described as being "received to walke in fellowship," then into autobiography, and finally into the similitudes of *Pilgrim's Progress*. The pilgrimage motif, couched in the vocabulary of different denominations, moves from its scriptural base in Exodus and Hebrews through all genres of literature, consciously invading the lives of believers so that they might act out spiritually in daily life. The ways in which standards of speech may be altered by social attitudes and then reflected in both vocabulary and literature are particularly apparent in Quaker writing.[35]

Scripture, covenants, and testimonies are all developed into a narrative framework for pilgrimage texts through narrative theology, the practice of finding within Scripture the elements of a story that are read into one's own life. This conflation of Scripture and life is subsequently perceived as a coherent text into which day-to-day events are fitted. For the Christian this process is particularly informed by the life of Christ; he or she is invited in the Gospels to take this story as a structure for the imaginings of their faith.[36] For these seventeenth-century authors, their autobiographies (Bunyan, Dunton, and Crisp have left us their life stories[37]) and their fictional works become theology, reflecting a belief that the lives of the saints are to be understood as part of the life of Christ who is in them as they are in him.[38] In a more general context, it allows the individual to read appropriate parts of Scripture into his own life. As George Herbert explains in "Holy Scripture (II),"

> This verse marks that, and both do make a motion
> Unto a third, that ten leaves off doth lie:
> Then as dispersed herbs do watch a potion.
> These three make up some Christians [sic] destinie.[39]

Alternatively, members of a New England Puritan convention, prompted by the journey across seas to a type of fulfillment in a new land, were to read Scripture into their own lives in a more strictly linear way, just as Scripture can be read with a connective thread that ends with redemption in the New Testament.[40] The everyday spiritual examinations of Nonconformists, and many conformists, included a critical interpretation of Scripture into their own lives.[41] These skills were read back into their literature in order to produce works that proclaim a similar pattern of narrative theology.

Originality of composition was not the aim of these authors, for they were conducting a literary search to recover the original truth set forth in the Bible, that is, to reclaim a biblical framework for their narrative. Roger Sharrock has suggested that *Pilgrim's Progress* is an inverted sermon, where the application is the story and the scriptural exegesis the marginal notes; it also resembles the Geneva Bible in reverse, with the action of the text providing the interpretation of the biblical reference in its margin, which is placed in the position of a gloss.[42] Other texts may provide a gloss on both *Pilgrim's Progress* and Scripture: *Pilgrim's Progress III* even has a page reference to an episode in Bunyan's work. Stephen Crisp's *Short History* does not overtly comment on any other pilgrimage texts, but uses the narrator's search for spiritual fulfillment to negate the doctrines of mainstream Nonconformist churches. Its transposition of the pilgrimage theme to the key of Quaker doctrine, however, constitutes an implicit discussion of other texts. For Quakers, the process of patterning texts was taken one step further: homogeneity in official Quaker writings was established by a board of censors, The Second Day Morning Meeting, who examined texts before publication.[43] *Short History* itself fell short beneath the scrutiny of the Meeting, and was omitted from Crisp's collected works of 1694 on grounds of its disparity with the rest of his canon. This censure ties the text even more firmly within the idea of a writing group bound by a theme that transcends individual doctrines.

The aesthetic of reading literature into Scripture was extended to the material of other authors, which could be adapted and adjusted to prove the credentials and sincerity of another's endeavor. Both the "J.B."s, for example, consciously invoke the reputation of Bunyan as a background to their own work. This is not intended to excuse or disguise their enterprises, but to justify them and to ask the audience to approach the text in the spirit they would bring to Bunyan. The use of the pseudonym "J.B." implies that Bunyan's popularity has spread far enough for this to be a possible assumption. *Pilgrim's Progress* is not the first text to be abridged for general readership; it joins popular texts that Bunyan himself condemned, such as tales of St. George or Bevis of Southampton (*MW*, 1: 333). In contrast to Sherman's *The Second Part,* the chapbook concentrates on action rather than explanation, giving only a brief sense of the development Bunyan's pilgrims make through interpretation of their own narratives. *Pilgrim's Progress III* has an elegy and biography of Bunyan appended.[44] The latter is a mixture of Puritan hagiography and journalistic sensationalism, often copied from *Grace Abounding*, that overstates both Bunyan's supposed spiritual powers and his temptations to join the Ranters, a group whose sexual license is emphasized. It also talks of *The Pilgrim's Progress* in terms of a saga, referring to Bunyan's "First part of his Pilgrim's Progress . . . which, a Second Part, and now this Third is extant, completing the whole."[45]

Even Bunyan's immediate editors took up this attitude: the eighteenth century saw as many copies of the three parts published together as of Bunyan's two parts on their own.[46] Authorship, too, becomes blurred, and all three parts are eventually presented as Bunyan's.[47] One such text is sold by D. Bunyan. It would be interesting to know whether this was a cynical relative, or someone benefiting from an assumed connection. For authors who write in groups such as this, it is more than a case of influence or emulation, and marks a distinctive approach to narrative and authorial integrity that is fostered within the religious community. This pattern of dedication to a model that is set, and yet that allows for personal interpretation or even reinterpretation, is a mark of this group. The members of this group prove their adherence to a different literary code. They are allied to religious views that demand that real lives be lived in accordance with preordained forms of conduct that are reiterated in their every encounter with the written and spoken word.

The last strand of this survey, and the one that is perhaps the most intriguing, has already been touched upon in my brief examination of intertextual dialogue and a literary aesthetic: namely, a reassessment of the audience these texts reached. I would like to suggest that the reader of the "middling godly sort" had a more sophisticated critical apparatus with which to approach a text than is often assumed. Religious fiction demanded the ability to interpret critically the text into the reader's own life while reading it as an interpretation of Scripture itself. Knowledge of the Bible could be immense; we see Scripture verses taking a life of their own in the autobiographies of many believers in this period. In *Grace Abounding*, verse vies with verse for Bunyan's soul. In the autobiography of another Bedford Baptist, Agnes Beaumont, Scripture appears as comfort and prophecy for the trials to face her.[48] Even those who were not of the godly factions would have familiarity with forms of the parable or allegorical example in sermons. Scripture provided the believer with a typology that transcended time and even allowed him or her to read one's own history back into the patterns provided.

Acquaintance with different forms of narrative theory and of the historiography that underlies it was varied. Although mystery plays had practically died out, where they were still performed, audiences learned of an all-encompassing view of time as a preplanned narrative from Chaos to Judgement Day was enacted.[49] These types of cycles were reenacted liturgically within Anglican and Roman Catholic churches.[50] Medieval mystery cycles had been born from the dramatic renditions of the Resurrection, and services such as Anglican Communion commemorated Christ's death and saw in it the future of the Judgement.[51]

One might add to this contemporary debate on theories of history. Achsah Guibbory isolates three main theories of history in the seventeenth century: those of decay, progression, and the cyclic theory. The dominant theory was cyclic and was influenced by the newly revived classical historiography.[52] Seen as parallel to the natural cycles of the world, it very often incorporated the two other theories. Keach's *Travels* encapsulates the idea of a cyclic movement as True Godliness travels through history from the beginning of the world and encounters repeatedly the same forms of resistance to his message, and the same views that promote this reaction. It is also progressive in the sense that he finally finds an individual who responds to his arguments. His sequel, *The Progress of Sin*, presents an example of degenerative cycles that end with the first phases of the apocalyptic Judgement. The two books together represent the paths of both the elect and the reprobate.

I am not suggesting that all readers of a pilgrimage author sat down and made a full critical interpretation of the books they read, but I am certain that they had a wide range of tools readily available to them, and that for many Nonconformists, reading signs—in books, history, the natural world, and their own lives—was a matter of course.[53] Bunyan's emblematic *Book for Boys and Girls* (1686), for example, provides us with homilies on objects as diverse as a pebble in a stream, the sun, or a snail. There is a key episode in Bunyan's autobiography where he comes across "three or four poor women," as he terms them, sitting on a doorstep engaging in an intense discussion of the theology of conversion (*GA*, 14). Such possibilities were open for even the poor; lack of secular education need not exclude a thorough grounding in spiritual education.

Although Bunyan has been transferred to the realms of literature, he has, of course, long been read in the context of devotional works. He shared his popularity in this area with Crisp and Keach, the other two authors who were well-known pastors and whose work continued to be printed into the eighteenth century. In the true spirit of pilgrimage stories, all three were transported into the New World. Keach's work was appropriated and abridged by American Methodists in the late eighteenth century, and Crisp's book continued to be printed in the Quaker state of Pennsylvania.[54] The stories moved and changed within a religious sphere that encouraged the growth and development of literature to reinforce and restate a Puritan creed in different times and circumstances.

I have drawn out some of the assumptions and skills brought to these texts by my mythical average reader of Bunyan, which includes the authors themselves. All the pilgrimage stories put into practice the Protestant belief of access to the printed Word in personal Bible study as the key to salvation. Here, they have Scripture and each other as referents. In the practice of reading one's own life as a text through Scripture is found the ability to approach a prose fiction as something that can be transformed within the same genre, or transposed into another textual genre such as devotional literature or scriptural exegesis. These pilgrimage texts are aware that they do not stand in isolation to this tradition, and one should not treat them in such a manner. The riches of *The Pilgrim's Progress* are to be found not only in the text itself, or in Bunyan's other works, but in the whole group of tales that articulate this vision of life.

Notes

1. John Brown, *John Bunyan: His Life, Times and Work* (London: Hulbert, 1928), 456–60.
2. See most notably, W. R. Owens, "The Reception of *The Pilgrim's Progress* in England," in *Bunyan in England and Abroad: Papers Delivered at the John Bunyan Tercentenary Symposium* (Amsterdam, 1988), ed. M. van Os and G. J. Schutte (Amsterdam: Vrije University Press, 1990), 91–102; James Turner, "Bunyan's Sense of Place," in *Pilgrim's Progress: Critical and Historical Views*, ed. Vincent Newey (Liverpool: Liverpool University Press, 1980), 91–110; Luella M. Wright, "John Bunyan and Stephen Crisp," *Journal of Religion* 19 (1939): 95–109; id., *The Literary Life of the Early Friends 1650–1725* (New York: Columbia University Press, 1932), 137–39; Stephen Parks, *John Dunton and the English Book Trade: A Study of His Career with a Checklist of His Publications* (London: Garland Press, 1976).
3. For example, Ager Scholae, *The Pilgrim's Passage in Poesie* (1697); SM, *The Heavenly Passenger, or, The Pilgrim's Progress, From this world to that which*

is to come (1687); Francis Hoffman, *Pilgrim's Progress . . . Done into verse* (London, 1706).

4. Bishop Symon Patrick, *Parable of the Pilgrim* (London, 1665), sig. A3r. *Parable* had six editions between 1665 and 1687.

5. *The Works of Augustus M. Toplady*, rev. ed., 6 vols. (London: William Baynes & Son; Edinburgh: H. S. Baynes, 1825), 1: 40; cited in R. L. Greaves and John F. Forrest, eds., *John Bunyan: A Reference Guide* (Boston: G. K. Hall, 1982), 18.

6. Robert C. Walton, *The Gathered Community* (London: Carey Press, 1946), 71.

7. I base my interpretation upon Bunyan's declarations of tolerance and ecumenism in *A Confession of my Faith and a Reason of my Practice* (1672), MW, 4.

8. Walton, *The Gathered Community*, 66.

9. Thomas Crosby, *History of the British Baptists from the Reformation to the Beginning of the Reign of King George I*, 4 vols. (1738–42), 2: 185–209.

10. Carey Bonner, "Some Baptist Hymnists," *Baptist Quarterly* NS 8 (1936–37): 256–62.

11. W. T. Whitley, "The First Hymnbook in Use," *Baptist Quarterly* NS 10 (1940–41): 374.

12. W. T. Whitley, *A Baptist Bibliography*, 2 vols. (London: Kingsgate, 1916), 1: 115.

13. Parks, *John Dunton and the English Book Trade*, 4–5; C. A. Moore, "John Dunton: Pietist and Imposter," *Studies in Philology* 22 (1925): 267. See also *Dictionary of National Biography* (Oxford: Oxford University Press, 1937–38), 6: 236–38.

14. I have not yet uncovered the full extent of his borrowings, but they also definitely include Richard Bernard's *The Isle of Man*, the hymn "Jerusalem my happy home," and George Herbert's poem "The Pilgrimage," the latter in the material that is a companion to *The Pilgrim's Guide*.

15. Rev. Dunton died in 1676: *Alumni Cantabrigiensis* (Cambridge: Cambridge University Press, 1922), pt. 1, 2: 76.

16. Margaret Spufford, *Small Books and Pleasant Histories: Popular Fiction and Its Readership in Seventeenth-Century England* (London: Methuen, 1981), 198.

17. Robert C. Monk, *John Wesley: His Puritan Heritage* (Nashville, Tenn.: Abingdon Press, 1966), 256–62; M. G. Jones, *Hannah More* (Cambridge: Cambridge University Press, 1952), 140.

18. The nearest form of literature might be the few volumes of verse written between 1660 and 1725, for example, Thomas Ellwood's epic *Davideis* (1712); Wright, *The Literary Life of the Early Friends*, 114–19.

19. Hugh Barbour, *The Quakers in Puritan England* (New Haven: Yale University Press, 1964), 104–10.

20. JB, *The Pilgrim's Progress From This World to that Which is to Come, The Third Part* (London: E. Millet for J. Deacon, 1693), 133–38.

21. For example, Owens, "The Reception of *The Pilgrim's Progress* in England," 92–93.

22. Thomas Sherman, "The Author's Apology for his Book," in *The Second Part of the Pilgrims Progress From This Present World of Wickedness and Misery To An Eternity of Holiness and Felicity* (London: Tho. Malthus, 1683), sig.[*4]r.

23. Thomas Sherman, "The Author's Apology for his Book," *The Second Part of the Pilgrims Progress From This Present World of Wickedness and Misery To An Eternity of Holiness and Felicity* (London: Tho. Malthus, 1683), sigs. [*4]v–[*5]r.

24. Sherman, "The Author's Apology," 1–2.
25. Henry Wilson, *The Spiritual Pilgrim*, vii–viii.
26. G. R. Owst, *Literature and Pulpit in Medieval England* (repr., Oxford: Blackwell, 1966), 149.
27. Tessa Watt, *Cheap Print and Popular Piety 1550–1640* (Cambridge: Cambridge University Press, 1991), 227.
28. Owens, "The Reception of *The Pilgrim's Progress* in England," 99–100.
29. For example, Symon Patrick, in *A Book for Beginners*, instructs the head of the household to "read to [the illiterate] their duty" (12th ed., London, 1692), 132.
30. Most recently, Sharon Achinstein has explored assumptions about reading in her work on political pamphlets, *Milton and the Revolutionary Reader* (Princeton: Princeton University Press, 1994), 115–16, 144–45.
31. Patricia Caldwell, *The Puritan Conversion Narrative* (Cambridge: Cambridge University Press, 1983), 76–78.
32. H. G. Tibbutt, ed., *The Minutes of the First Independent Church (now Bunyan Meeting) at Bedford, 1656–1766* (Bedford: Bedfordshire Historical Record Society 55, (1976).
33. Tibbutt, *The Minutes of the First Independent Church*, 19–20.
34. Tibbutt, *The Minutes of the First Independent Church*, 19, 21.
35. Richard Bauman, *Let Your Words be Few: Symbolism of Speaking and Silence among Seventeenth-Century Quakers* (Cambridge, Cambridge University Press, 1983), 22, 45–46.
36. John Navone, *Towards a Theology of Story* (Slough: St. Paul's, 1977), 21.
37. Bunyan, *Grace Abounding* (1666); *A Journal of the Life of Stephen Crisp*, in *A Memorable Account of the Christian Experiences . . .* (1692); John Dunton, *Dunton's Remains* (1684) and *The Life and Errors of John Dunton* (1705); amongst other autobiographical pieces.
38. Navone, *Towards a Theology of Story*, 21–22.
39. *The English Poems of George Herbert*, ed. C. A. Patrides (London: Dent, 1991), 77.
40. Caldwell, *The Puritan Conversion Narrative*, 31.
41. Chana Bloch, *Spelling the Word: George Herbert and the Bible* (Berkeley: University of California, 1985), 131.
42. Roger Sharrock, *John Bunyan* (London: Hutchinson's, 1954), 96.
43. Wright, *The Literary Life of the Early Friends*, 97.
44. *An account of the Life and Death of Mr. John Bunyan* was first published separately a year before *Pilgrim's Progress III*. The authorship of both this and the elegy is unclear.
45. *An account of the Life and Death of Mr. John Bunyan*, 29.
46. The Eighteenth Century Short Title Catalog (ESTC) lists forty-five printings of Bunyan's text and forty-seven of the three parts together.
47. The first I have found is the edition sold by D. Bunyan (1760); this trend continues into the nineteenth century.
48. *GA*, e.g., 33; "The Life of Mrs Agnes Beaumont," in *The Trial of John Bunyan and the Persecution of the Puritans*, ed. Monica Furlong (London: The Folio Society, 1978), 123–24, 129.
49. C. A. Patrides, *The Grand Design of God: The Literary Form of the Christian View of History* (London: Routledge & Kegan Paul, 1972), 38–39.
50. Mircea Eliade, *Myth and Reality* (London: Allen & Unwin, 1964), 169.
51. T. R. Wright, *Theology and Literature* (Oxford: Blackwell, 1988), 174.

52. Achsah Guibbory, *The Map of Time: Seventeenth-Century English Literature and Ideas of Pattern in History* (Urbana: University of Illinois, 1986), 8.

53. N. H. Keeble, *The Literary Culture of Nonconformity in Later Seventeenth-Century England* (Leicester: University of Leicester Press; Athens: University of Georgia Press, 1987), 253.

54. There were fourteen printings of *Travels* in Britain and America in the eighteenth century, and three abridgements by the American Methodist Society (1793, 1796, and 1799); there were ten editions of *A Short History* printed in England by 1787 and ten editions in Pennsylvania, which underwent continual reprintings.

Bibliography

Achinstein, Sharon. *Milton and the Revolutionary Reader*. Princeton: Princeton University Press, 1994.

———. "*Samson Agonistes* and the Drama of Dissent." *Milton Studies* 33 (1996): 133–58.

Anon. *A True and Impartial narrative of some illegal and arbitrary proceedings*. London, 1670.

———. *Mirabilis Annus, or the year of Prodigies*. 1661.

———. *The Christian Conventicle or, The Private-Meetings of God's People in Evil Times*. London, 1670.

Augustine. *The City of God*. Translated by John Healey. Revised by R. V. G. Tasker. 2 vols. London: J. M. Dent, 1945.

Bagshaw, Edward. *The Doctrine of the Kingdom and Personal Reign of Christ Asserted and Explained*. London, 1669.

Ball, Bryan W. *A Great Expectation: Eschatological Thought in English Protestantism to 1660*. Leiden: Brill, 1975.

Barbour, Hugh. *The Quakers in Puritan England*. New Haven: Yale University Press, 1964.

Barth, John. "The Literature of Exhaustion." In *The Novel Today*. Edited by Malcolm Bradbury, 71–86. London: Fontana Press, 1990.

Bauckham, Richard. *Tudor Apocalypse*. Abingdon, Berkshire: Sutton Courtenay Press, 1978.

Bauman, Richard. *Let Your Words be Few: Symbolism of Speaking and Silence among Seventeenth-Century Quakers*. Cambridge: Cambridge University Press, 1983.

Baxter, Richard. *A Key for Catholicks*. London, 1659.

———. *The Scripture Gospel Defended*. London, 1690.

———. *The Glorious Kingdom of Christ, Described and Clearly Vindicated*. London, 1691.

———. *Reliquiae Baxterianae*. London, 1696.

———. "The Savoy Liturgy." In *Liturgies of the Western Church*, edited by B. Thompson, 355–404. Philadelphia: Fortress Press, 1961.

Beal, Rebecca S. "*Grace Abounding to the Chief of Sinners*: John Bunyan's Pauline Epistle." *Studies in English Literature* 21 (1981): 147–60.

Beaumont, Agnes. "The Life of Mrs Agnes Beaumont." In *The Trial of John Bunyan and the Persecution of the Puritans*, edited by Monica Furlong. London: The Folio Society, 1978.

Bernard, Richard. *The Isle of Man*, 14th ed. London, 1668.

Besse, Joseph, ed. *A Collection of the Sufferings of the People Called Quakers*. 2 vols. London, 1753.

Beverley, Thomas. *A Sermon Upon Revel. 11. 11. &c. Summoning the Expectation of the Witnesses Rising: And of the Great Concurrent Works Daily Shewing Forth Themselves, and to be Compleat by 1697*. London, 1692.

———. *The Good Hope Through Grace*. London, 1700.

Biddle, Esther. *The Trumpet of the Lord, Sounded forth unto these Three Nations, As a warning from the Spirit of Truth*. London, 1662.

———. *Wo to thee city of Oxford*. London, [1655].

———. *Wo to thee town of Cambridge*. London, [1655].

Bittle, William G. *James Nayler 1618–1660: The Quaker Indicted by Parliament*. York: William Sessions, 1986.

Bloch, Chana. *Spelling the Word: George Herbert and the Bible*. Berkeley: University of California, 1985.

Bonner, Carey. "Some Baptist Hymnists." *Baptist Quarterly* NS 8 (1936–37): 256–62.

Bousset, Wilhelm. *The Antichrist Legend: A Chapter in Christian and Jewish Folklore*. Translated by A. H. Keane. London: Hutchinson and Co., 1896.

Brittain, Vera. *In the Steps of John Bunyan*. London: Rich and Cowan, 1950. Repr. 1987.

Brown, John. *John Bunyan: His Life, Times and Work*. London: Hulbert, 1928; Hamden, Conn.: Archon Books, 1969.

Bunyan, John. *A Mirrour or Looking Glass for both Saints and Sinners*. 1671.

Burrough, Edward. *A Trumpet of the Lord Sounded Out of Sion*. [London], 1656.

———. *The True Faith of the Gospel of Peace Contended For. . . .* 1656.

Cadbury, Henry J., ed. *George Fox's "Book of Miracles."* New York: Octagon Books, 1973.

Caldwell, Patricia. *The Puritan Conversion Narrative*. Cambridge: Cambridge University Press, 1983.

Calvin, John. *Institutes of Christian Religion*. Edited by John T. McNeill. Translated by Ford Lewis Battles. 2 vols. *The Library of Christian Classics*. Philadelphia: Westminster Press, 1961.

Camden, Vera, ed. *The Narrative of the Persecutions of Agnes Beaumont*. East Lansing, Mich.: Colleagues Press, 1992.

Capp, B. S. *The Fifth Monarchy Men: A Study in Seventeenth-Century Millenarianism*. London: Faber, 1972.

———. *Astrology and the Popular Press*. London: Faber, 1979.

Cary, M[ary]. *A New and More Exact Mappe or Description of New Jerusalems Glory when Jesus Christ and his Saints with him shall reign on earth a Thousand Years, and possess all Kingdoms*. London, 1651.

Chambers, A. B. *Transfigured Rites in Seventeenth-Century Poetry*. Columbia: University of Missouri Press, 1992.

Child, John. *The Mischief of Persecution Exemplified*. 1688.

Christianson, Paul. *Reformers and Babylon: English Apocalyptic Visions from the Reformation to the Eve of the Civil War*. Toronto: University of Toronto Press, 1978.

Clarkson, Laurence. *The Lost Sheep Found*. London, 1660.

Cohn, Norman. *The Pursuit of the Millennium: Revolutionary Millenarians and the Mystical Anarchists of the Middle Ages.* London: Paladin, 1970.

Coppe, Abiezer. *A Fiery Flying Roll.* 1649.

———. *A Second Fiery Flying Roll.* 1649.

Cotton, John. *The Way of the Churches of Christ in New England.* London, 1645.

Cragg, G. R. *Puritanism in the Period of the Great Persecution, 1660–1688.* Cambridge: Cambridge University Press, 1957.

Cressy, David. "Private Lives, Public Performance, and Rites of Passage." In *Attending to Women in Early Modern England.* Edited by Betty S. Travitsky and Adele F. Seeff, 187–97. Newark: University of Delaware Press, 1994.

Crisp, Stephen. *A Journal of the Life of Stephen Crisp,* in *A Memorable Account of the Christian Experiences . . .* 1692.

Crosby, Thomas. *History of the British Baptists from the Reformation to the Beginning of the Reign of King George I.* 4 vols. 1738–42.

Danvers, Henry. *Theopolis, or the City of God, New Jerusalem, in Opposition to the City of the Nations, Great Babylon.* London, 1672.

Davis, J. C. *Fear, Myth and History: The Ranters and the Historians.* Cambridge: Cambridge University Press, 1986.

———. "Fear, Myth and Furore: Reappraising the 'Ranters.'" *Past and Present* 129 (1990): 79–103.

Davis, Natalie Zemon. *Women on the Margins: Three Seventeenth-Century Lives.* Cambridge: Harvard University Press, 1995.

De Krey, Gary S. "London Radicals and Revolutionary Politics, 1675–1683." In *The Politics of Religion in Restoration England,* edited by Tim Harris, Paul Seaward, and Mark Goldie, 133–62. Oxford: Basil Blackwell, 1990.

Delany, Paul. *British Autobiography in the Seventeenth Century.* London: Routledge & Kegan Paul, 1969.

Diehl, Huston. "Into the maze of self: the Protestant transformation of the image of the labyrinth." *Journal of Medieval and Renaissance Studies* 16 (1986): 281–301.

Dietz Moss, Jean. *"Godded With God": Hendrick Niclaes and His Family of Love.* Philadelphia: Transactions of the American Philosophical Society; new series v. 71, pt. 8, 1981.

DiSalvo, Jackie. "'The Lord's Battels': *Samson Agonistes* and the Puritan Revolution." *Milton Studies* 4 (1972): 39–62.

Dowey, Edward A. *The Knowledge of God in Calvin's Theology.* New York: Columbia University Press, 1952.

Downame, John, et al. *Annotations Upon all the Books of the New and Old Testament,* 2d ed. London, 1651.

Dryden, John. *John Dryden.* Edited by Keith Walker. Oxford and New York: Oxford University Press, 1987.

Dugdale, Clarence Eugene. "Bunyan's Court Scenes." [Texas] *Studies in English* 5 (1941): 64–78.

Dunton, John. *Dunton's Remains.* 1684.

———. *The Life and Errors of John Dunton.* 1705.

Dusinberre, Juliet. "Bunyan, and Virginia Woolf: A History and a Language of Their Own." *Bunyan Studies* 5 (1994): 15–46.

Ebner, Dean. *Autobiography in Seventeenth Century England: Theology and the Self.* The Hague: Mouton Press, 1971.

Edwards, Thomas. *Gangraena.* London, 1646.

———. *The Second Part of Gangraena.* London, 1646.

———. *The Third Part of Gangraena.* [London], 1646.

Eisenstein, Elizabeth L. *The Printing Press as an Agent of Change: Communications and Cultural Transformations in Early-Modern Europe.* 2 vols. Cambridge: Cambridge University Press, 1979.

Eliade, Mircea. *The Myth of the Eternal Return or Comos and History.* Translated by W. R. Trask. Princeton: Princeton University Press, 1954.

———. *Myth and Reality.* London: Allen & Unwin, 1964.

Ellwood, Thomas. *The History of his Life.* 1714.

Emmerson, Richard Kenneth. *Antichrist in the Middle Ages.* Manchester: Manchester University Press, 1981.

Erbery, William. *The Testimony.* 1658.

Evans, Katherine, and Sarah Chevers. *A Short Relation of the Cruel Sufferings for the Truths Sake of Katharine Evans and Sarah Chevers, in the Inquisition in the Isle of Malta.* London: Robert Wilson, 1662.

Evelyn, John. *The Diary of John Evelyn,* edited by E. S. de Beer. 6 vols. Oxford: Clarendon Press, 1955.

Fell, Margaret. *A Testimonie of the Touch-Stone.* 1656.

Ferry, Anne. *Milton's Epic Voice: The Narrator in Paradise Lost.* Chicago and London: University of Chicago Press, 1983.

Firth, Katherine R. *The Apocalyptic Tradition in Reformation Britain, 1530–1645.* Oxford: Oxford University Press, 1979.

Fish, Stanley E. *Self-Consuming Artifacts: The Experience of Seventeenth-Century Literature.* Berkeley, Los Angeles, and London: University of California Press, 1972.

Fox, George. *The Great Mistery of the Great Whore Unfolded.* 1659.

———. *Something in Answer to Lodowick Muggleton's Book.* London, 1667.

———. *The Journal of George Fox,* edited by John L. Nickalls. London: Religious Society of Friends, 1975.

French, J. Milton, ed. *The Life Records of John Milton.* 5 vols. New York: Gordian Press, 1966.

Friedman, Jerome. *Blasphemy, Immorality, and Anarchy: The Ranters and the English Revolution.* Athens: Ohio University Press, 1987.

Furlong, Monica. *Puritan's Progress.* New York: Coward, McCann & Geoghegan, 1975.

Gerhard, Kittel, et al., eds., and G. W. Bromiley trans. and ed. *Theological Dictionary of the New Testament.* 10 vols. Grand Rapids, Mich.: Eerdmans, 1967.

Gifford, John. "Pastoral Letter." In *The Minutes of the First Independent Church (now Bunyan Meeting) at Bedford, 1656–1766.* Edited by H. G. Tibbutt. Bedford: Bedfordshire Historical Record Society, 1976.

Goodwin, Thomas, et al. *An Apologeticall Narration.* London, 1643.

Gouge, William. *Of domesticall duties.* London, 1622.

Grand Jury of Devonshire, Order of. PRO SP 29/418/197. April 1682.

Greaves, Richard L. *John Bunyan*. Abingdon, Berkshire: Sutton Courtenay Press, 1969.

———. "John Bunyan and the Fifth Monarchists." *Albion* 13 (1981): 83–95.

———. "Foundation Builders: The Role of Women in Early English Nonconformity." In *Triumph Over Silence: Women in Protestant History. Contributions to the Study of Religion*. Edited by Richard Greaves. Westport, Conn., and London: Greenwood Press, 1985.

———. *Deliver Us from Evil: The Radical Underground in Britain, 1660–1663*. New York: Oxford University Press, 1986.

———. "Conscience, Liberty, and the Spirit: Bunyan and Nonconformity." In *John Bunyan: Conventicle and Parnassus: Tercentenary Essays*. Edited by N. H. Keeble, 21–43. Oxford: Clarendon Press, 1988.

———. *Enemies under His Feet: Radicals and Nonconformists in Britain, 1664–1677*. Stanford: Stanford University Press, 1990.

———. *John Bunyan and English Nonconformity*. Hambledon Press, 1992.

———. " 'Let Truth be Free': John Bunyan and the Restoration Crisis of 1667–1673." *Albion* 28, 4 (1996): 587–605.

Greaves, Richard L., and Robert Zaller, eds. *Biographical Dictionary of British Radicals in the Seventeenth Century*. 3 vols. Brighton: Harvester Press, 1982–84.

Guibbory, Achsah. *The Map of Time: Seventeenth-Century English Literature and Ideas of Pattern in History*. Urbana: University of Illinois, 1986.

Gutierrez, Donald. "The Labyrinth as Myth and Metaphor." *University of Dayton Review* 16, 3 (1983–84): 89–99.

Haller, William. *The Rise of Puritanism*. New York: Columbia University Press, 1938.

Hamilton, Alastair. *The Family of Love*. Cambridge: James Clarke, 1981.

Hammond, Brean S. "*The Pilgrim's Progress:* Satire and Social Comment." In *The Pilgrim's Progress: Critical and Historical Views*. Edited by Vincent Newey, 119–22. Liverpool: Liverpool University Press, 1980.

Harris, Tim. "Introduction: Revising the Restoration." In *The Politics of Religion in Restoration England*. Edited by Tim Harris, Paul Seaward, and Mark Goldie, 1–28. Oxford: Basil Blackwell, 1990.

Hart, A. Tindal. *William Lloyd 1627–1717*. London: S.P.C.K., 1952.

Haskin, Dayton. "The Burden of Interpretation in *The Pilgrim's Progress*." *Studies in Philology* 79 (1982): 256–78.

Hayter, Richard. *The Meaning of the Revelation*. London, 1675.

Heal, Felicity. "*Grace Abounding to the Chief of Sinners*: John Bunyan's Pauline Epistle." *Studies in English Literature* 21 (1981): 147–60.

Herbert, George. *The English Poems of George Herbert*. Edited by C. A. Patrides. London: Dent, 1991.

Hill, Christopher. *Puritanism and Revolution*. London: Secker and Warburg, 1958.

———. *Antichrist in Seventeenth-Century England*. Oxford: Oxford University Press, 1971.

———. *The World Turned Upside Down*. Harmondsworth: Penguin, 1975.

———. *Milton and the English Revolution*. London: Faber, 1979.

———. *The Experience of Defeat: Milton and Some Contemporaries*. London: Faber and Faber, 1984.

———. *A Turbulent, Seditious and Factious People: John Bunyan and His Church*. Oxford: Clarendon Press, 1988.

———. *A Tinker and a Poor Man: John Bunyan and His Church 1628–1688*. New York: Knopf, 1989.

———. *A Nation of Change and Novelty*. London: Bookmarks, 1993.

———. *The English Bible and the Seventeenth-Century Revolution*. Harmondsworth: Penguin, 1994.

Hill, Christopher, Barry Reay, and William Lamont. *The World of the Muggletonians*. London: Temple Smith, 1983.

Hillis-Miller, J. *The Linguistic Moment*. Princeton: Princeton University Press, 1985.

Hobby, Elaine. *Virtue of Necessity: English Women's Writing 1649–88*. Ann Arbor: University of Michigan Press, 1989.

Hoffman, Francis. *Pilgrim's Progress . . . Done into verse*. London, 1706.

Horton, Davies. *The Worship of the English Puritans*. Westminster, Md.: Dacre Press, 1948.

Houlbrooke, Ralph. *The English Family 1450–1700*. London and New York: Longman, 1984.

Hudson, Winthrop S. "A Suppressed Chapter in Quaker History." *Journal of Religion* 24 (1944): 108–18.

Ingle, H. Larry. "George Fox as Enthusiast: An Unpublished Epistle." *Journal of the Friends Historical Society* 55 (1989): 266–70.

———. "George Fox, Historian." *Quaker History* 82 (1993): 28–35.

Ingram, William, and Kathleen Swaim, eds. *A Concordance to Milton's English Poetry*. Oxford: Clarendon Press, 1972.

JB. *The Pilgrim's Progress From This World to that Which is to Come, The Third Part*. London: E. Millet for J. Deacon, 1693.

Jackson, John. *A Sober Word*. 1651.

———. *Strength in Weakness*. 1655.

Jacob, M. C. *The Newtonians and the English Revolution*. Hassocks, Sussex: Harvester Press, 1976.

Jardine, Lisa. "Unpicking the Tapestry: The Scholar of Women's History as Penelope among Her Suitors." In *Attending to Women in Early Modern England*. Edited by Betty S. Travitsky and Adele F. Seeff, 123–44. Newark: University of Delaware Press, 1994.

Jesse, Henry. *The Exceeding Riches of Grace Advanced by the Spirit of Grace, in an Empty Nothing Creature, viz. Mris Sarah Wight*. London: Henry Overton and Hannah Allen, 1647.

Jose, Nicholas. *Ideas of the Restoration in English Literature, 1660–71*. Cambridge: Harvard University Press, 1984.

Keach, Benjamin. *Antichrist Stormed*. London, 1689.

———. *Distressed Sion Relieved*. London, 1689.

Keeble, N. H. "Christiana's Key: The Unity of the Pilgrim's Progress." In *The Pilgrim's Progress: Critical and Historical Views*. Edited by Vincent Newey, 1–20. Liverpool: Liverpool University Press, 1980.

———. *The Literary Culture of Nonconformity in Later Seventeenth-Century England.* Leicester: University of Leicester Press; Athens: University of Georgia Press, 1987.

———, ed. *The Cultural Identity of Seventeenth-Century Woman: A Reader.* London: Routledge, 1994.

Kendall, R. T. *Calvin and English Calvinism.* Oxford: Oxford University Press, 1979.

Knollys, Hanserd. *Apocalyptical Mysteries.* 1667.

———. *The Parable of the Kingdom of Heaven Expounded.* London, 1674.

———. *An Exposition of the Eleventh Chapter of the Revelation.* 1679.

———. *Mystical Babylon Unvailed.* 1679.

———. *The World that Now Is; and the World that is to Come.* 1681.

———. *An Exposition of the Whole Book of Revelation.* London, 1689.

Knoppers, Laura L. "*Paradise Regained* and the Politics of Martyrdom." *Modern Philology* 90 (1992): 200-219.

———. *Historicizing Milton: Spectacle, Power and Poetry in Restoration England.* Athens: University of Georgia Press, 1994.

Knott, John R., Jr. *The Sword of the Spirit: Puritan Responses to the Bible.* Chicago and London: University of Chicago Press, 1980.

———. "Bunyan and the Holy Community." *Studies in Philology* 80 (1983): 200–225.

———. *Discourses of Martyrdom in English Literature, 1563–1694.* Cambridge: Cambridge University Press, 1993.

Korshin, Paul J. "Queuing and Waiting: The Apocalypse in England, 1660–1750." In *The Apocalypse in English Renaissance Thought and Culture.* Edited by C. A. Patrides and Joseph Wittreich, 240–65. Manchester: Manchester University Press, 1984.

Lamont, William. *Godly Rule: Politics and Religion, 1603–1660.* London: Macmillan, 1969.

———. *Puritans, The Millennium and the Future of Israel: Puritan Eschatology, 1600–1660.* Edited by Peter Toon. Cambridge: James Clarke, 1970.

———. *Richard Baxter and the Millennium.* London: Croom Helm, 1979.

Lieb, Michael. *Milton and the Culture of Violence.* Ithaca: Cornell University Press, 1994.

Lilburne, John. *The Resolved Man's Resolution.* London, 1647.

Loewenstein, David. "The Kingdom Within: Radical Religious Culture and the Politics of *Paradise Regained.*" *Literature & History* 3 (1994): 63–89.

Lovelace, Richard. *The Poems.* Edited by C. H. Wilkinson. Oxford: Clarendon Press, 1953.

Ludlow, Dorothy P. "Shaking Patriarchy's Foundations: Sectarian Women in England, 1641–1700." In *Triumph over Silence: Women in Protestant History. Contributions to the Study of Religion.* Edited by Richard L. Greaves, 93–123. Westport, Conn., and London: Greenwood Press, 1985.

Luxon, Thomas H. " 'Other Men's Words' and 'New Birth': Bunyan's Antihermeneutics of Experience." *Texas Studies in Literature and Language* 36 (1994): 259–90.

———. *Literal Figures: Puritan Allegory and the Reformation Crisis in Representation*. Chicago: University of Chicago Press, 1995.

M. G. Jones. *Hannah More*. Cambridge: Cambridge University Press, 1952.

MacDonald, Michael. *Mystical Bedlam: Madness, Anxiety, and Healing in Seventeenth-Century England*. Cambridge: Cambridge University Press, 1981.

Mack, Phyllis. *Visionary Women: Ecstatic Prophecy in Seventeenth-Century England*. Berkeley and Los Angeles: University of California Press, 1992.

Mackenzie, Donald. "Rhetoric *versus* Apocalypse: The Oratory of *The Holy War*." *Bunyan Studies* 2, 1 (1990): 33–45.

Madsen, Deborah L. *Rereading Allegory: A Narrative Approach to Genre*. London: Macmillan Press, 1995.

Maidwell, John. Letter to his daughter and son-in-law, from Leicester jail, 6 July 1685. Dr. Williams's Library, MS 12.63.(22)

Major, Elizabeth. *Honey on the Rod: Or, a Comfortable Contemplation for one in Affliction: with sundry Poems on several subjects*. London: Tho. Maxey, 1656.

Manners, Emily. *Elizabeth Hooton: First Quaker Woman Preacher (1600–1672)*. London: Headley Brothers, 1914.

Marsh, Christopher W. *The Family of Love in English Society, 1550–1630*. Cambridge: Cambridge University Press, 1994.

Marvell, Andrew. *The Rehearsal Transpros'd*. Edited by D. I. B. Smith. Oxford: Clarendon Press, 1971.

McGinn, Bernard. *Visions of the End: Apocalyptic Traditions in the Middle Ages*. New York: Columbia University Press, 1979.

McGregor, J. F. "Ranterism and the Development of Early Quakerism." *Journal of Religious History* 9 (1976–77): 349–63.

———. "Seekers and Ranters." In *Radical Religion in the English Revolution*. Edited by J. F. McGregor and Barry Reay, 121–39. Oxford: Oxford University Press, 1984.

McKeon, Michael. *Politics and Poetry in Restoration England: The Case of Dryden's Annus Mirabilis*. Cambridge, Mass., and London: Harvard University Press, 1975.

Milton, John. Complete Prose Works of John Milton. 8 vols. Edited by Don Wolfe et al. New Haven and London: Yale University Press, 1953–82.

———. *John Milton: Complete Poems and Major Prose*. Edited by Merritt Y. Hughes. Indianapolis: Bobbs-Merrill, 1957.

———. *The Poems of John Milton*. Edited by John Carey and Alastair Fowler. London: Longman, 1980.

Monk, Robert C. *John Wesley: His Puritan Heritage*. Nashville, Tenn.: Abingdon Press, 1966.

Moore, C. A. "John Dunton: Pietist and Imposter." *Studies in Philology* 22 (1925): 267.

Moran, Gerald F. " 'The Hidden Ones': Women and Religion in Puritan New England. " In *Triumph over Silence: Women in Protestant History, Contributions to the Study of Religion*. Edited by Richard L. Greaves, 125–49. Westport, Conn., and London: Greenwood Press, 1985.

More, Henry. *A Modest Enquiry into the Mystery of Iniquity*. London, 1664.

Morton, A. L. *The World of the Ranters: Religious Radicalism in the English Revolution*. London: Lawrence & Wishart, 1970.

Muggleton, Lodowick. *A Discourse Between John Reeve and Richard Leader*. London, 1682.

———. *The Acts of the Witnesses of the Spirit, In Five Parts*. London, 1699.

———. *The Answer to William Penn*. London, 1673.

———. *An Answer to Isaac Penington*. London, 1669.

——— to Elizabeth Dickenson, Junior, March 6, 1674. British Library Additional Manuscript 60171/134.

——— to Laurence Claxton (Clarkson), London, 25 December 1660. British Library Additional Manuscript 60168/6–7.

——— to Robert Pierce, August 2, 1680. British Library Additional Manuscript 60168/30–39.

——— to William Cleve, 1665. British Library Additional Manuscript 60171/73.

Mullett, Michael A. " 'Deprived of our Former Place': The Internal Politics of Bedford, 1660–1688." *Bedfordshire Historical Record Society* 59 (1980): 1–42.

Navone, John. *Towards a Theology of Story*. Slough, Buckinghamshire: St. Paul's, 1977.

Nedham, Marchamont. *A Short History of the English Rebellion*. London, 1661.

Ness, Christopher. *A Distinct Discourse and Discovery of the Person and Period of Antichrist*. London, 1679.

———. *A Compleat and Compendious Church-History*. London, 1681.

———. *The Signs of the Times*. London, 1681.

Newey, Vincent. " 'With the eyes of my understanding': Bunyan, Experience, and Acts of Interpretation." In *John Bunyan: Conventicle and Parnassus, Tercentenary Essays*. Edited by N. H. Keeble, 189–216. Oxford: Clarendon Press, 1988.

Nojoumian, Amir Ali. "The Representation of Space and Time in Postmodern Narrative." Master's thesis, University of Leicester, 1994.

Nuttall, Geoffrey. *Visible Saints: The Congregational Way 1640–1660*. Oxford: Basil Blackwell, 1957.

O'Malley, Thomas. " 'Defying the Powers and Tempering the Spirit': A Review of Quaker Control over Their Publications, 1672–1689." *Journal of Ecclesiastical History* 33 (1982): 72–88.

Overton, Richard. *The Araignement of Mr. Persecution*. London, 1645.

Owens, W. R., ed. "A Note on the Text." *Grace Abounding to the Chief of Sinners*. London: Penguin Classics, 1987.

———. " 'Antichrist must be Pulled Down': Bunyan and the Millennium." In *John Bunyan and His England, 1628–88*. Edited by Anne Laurence, W. R. Owens, and Stuart Sim, 77–94. London and Ronceverte: Hambledon Press, 1990.

———. "The Reception of *The Pilgrim's Progress* in England." In *Bunyan in England and Abroad: Papers Delivered at the John Bunyan Tercentenary Symposium* (Amsterdam, 1988). Edited by M. van Os and G. J. Schutte, 91–102. Amsterdam: Vrije University, 1990.

Owst, G. R. *Literature and Pulpit in Medieval England*. Repr., Oxford: Blackwell, 1966.

Pareus, David. *A Commentary upon the Divine Revelation of the Apostle and Evangelist John*. Translated by Elias Arnold. Amsterdam, 1644.

Parker, Samuel. "Preface" to *Bishop Bramhall's Vindication of Himself and The Episcopal Clergy, from the Presbyterian Charge of Popery*. London, 1670.

Parker, William Riley. *Milton: A Biography*. 2 vols. Oxford: Clarendon Press, 1968.

Parks, Stephen. *John Dunton and the English Book Trade: A Study of His Career with a Checklist of His Publications*. London: Garland Press, 1976.

Patrick, Symon. *Parable of the Pilgrim*. London, 1665.

———. *A Book for Beginners*. 12th ed. London, 1692.

Patrides, C. A. *The Grand Design of God: The Literary Form of the Christian View of History*. London: Routledge & Kegan Paul, 1972.

Patterson, Annabel. *Censorship and Interpretation: The Conditions of Writing and Reading in Early Modern England*. Madison: University of Wisconsin Press, 1990.

———. *Reading between the Lines*. Madison: University of Wisconsin Press, 1993.

Penn, William. *The New Witnesses Proved Old Hereticks*. 1672.

Perkins, William. *The Combate Betweene Christ and the Devill*. In *The Works of ... William Perkins*. 3 vols. London, 1612–1613.

Pooley, Roger. "*Grace Abounding* and the New Sense of the Self." In *John Bunyan and His England, 1628–88*. Edited by Anne Laurence, W. R. Owens, and Stuart Sim, 105–14. London and Ronceverte: Hambledon Press, 1990.

Quilligan, Maureen. *The Language of Allegory: Defining the Genre*. Ithaca and London: Cornell University Press, 1979.

Reeve, John, and Lodowick Muggleton. *A Transcendent Spiritual Treatise*. 1652.

———. *A Divine Looking-Glass*. 1661.

Ritter Dailey, Barbara. "The Visitation of Sarah Wight: Holy Carnival and the Revolution of the Saints in Civil War London." *Church History* 55 (1986): 438–55.

Rivers, Isabel. "Grace, Holiness and the Pursuit of Happiness: Bunyan and Restoration Latitudinarianism." In *John Bunyan: Conventicle and Parnassus, Tercentenary Essays*. Edited by N. H. Keeble, 45–69. Oxford: Clarendon Press, 1988.

———. *Reason, Grace, and Sentiment: a Study of the Language of Religion and Ethics in England, 1660–1780*. Cambridge: Cambridge University Press, 1991.

Ross, Aileen M. "*Paradise Regained*: The Development of John Bunyan's Millenarianism." In *Bunyan in England and Abroad: Papers Delivered at the John Bunyan Tercentenary Symposium* (Amsterdam, 1988). Edited by M. van Os and G. J. Schutte, 73–89. Amsterdam: Vrije University Press, 1990.

SM. *The Heavenly Passenger, or, The Pilgrim's Progress, From this world to that which is to come*. 1687.

Saltmarsh, John. *Sparkles of Glory or Some Beams of the Morning Star*. 1647.

Salzman, Paul. *English Prose Fiction, 1558–1700*. Oxford: Clarendon Press, 1985.

Schochet, Gordon., "From 'Persecution' to 'Toleration.' " In *Liberty Secured? Britain before and after 1688*. Edited by J. R. Jones, 122–57. Stanford: Stanford University Press, 1992.

Scholae, Ager. *The Pilgrim's Passage in Poesie*. 1697.

Sexby, Edward. *Killing Noe Murder*. London, 1659.

Sharpe, Kevin, and Steven N. Zwicker, eds. *Politics of Discourse; The Literature and History of Seventeenth-Century England*. Berkeley and Los Angeles: University of California Press, 1987.

Sharrock, Roger. "The Trial of Vices in Puritan Fiction." *Baptist Quarterly* 14 (1951): 3–12.

———. *John Bunyan*. London: Hutchinson's, 1954.

Sherman, Thomas. "The Author's Apology for his Book." *The Second Part of the Pilgrims Progress From This Present World of Wickedness and Misery To An Eternity of Holiness and Felicity*. London: Tho. Malthus, 1683.

Sherwin, William. *A Brief Representation of the Doctrine of Christs Kingdom of Power to Come upon Earth*. London, [?1671].

———. *A Plain and Evident Discovery of the Two Personal Comings of Christ*. [?1671].

———. *The True News of the Good New World (Shortly) to Come*. [?1675].

Sidney, Sir Philip. *An Apology for Poetry*. Edited by Geoffrey Shepherd. Manchester: Manchester University Press, 1965.

Sim, Stuart. *Negotiations with Paradox: Narrative Practice and Narrative Form in Bunyan and Defoe*. London: Harvester Wheatsheaf, 1990.

———. " 'Safe for Those for Whom it is to be Safe': Salvation and Damnation in Bunyan's Fiction." In *John Bunyan and His England, 1628–88*. Edited by Anne Laurence, W. R. Owens and Stuart Sim, 149–60. London and Ronceverte: Hambledon Press, 1990.

Smith, Nigel. *Perfection Proclaimed: Language and Literature in English Radical Religion, 1640–1660*. Oxford: Clarendon Press, 1989.

Smith, William, Quaker of Besthorp. *Joyfull tidings to the begotten of God*. London, 1664.

Sondergard, Sid. " 'This Giant Has Wounded Me as Well as Thee': Reading Bunyan's Violence and/as Authority." In *The Witness of Time*. Edited by Katherine Z. Keller and Gerald J. Schiffhorst, 218–37. Pittsburgh: Duquesne University Press, 1993.

Spufford, Margaret. *Small Books and Pleasant Histories: Popular Fiction and Its Readership in Seventeenth-Century England*. London: Methuen, 1981.

Spurr, John. *The Restoration Church of England, 1646–1689*. New Haven: Yale University Press, 1991.

Stachniewski, John. *The Persecutory Imagination: English Puritanism and the Literature of Religious Despair*. Oxford: Clarendon Press, 1991.

Stanwood, P. G. *The Sempiternal Season: Studies in Seventeenth-Century Devotional Writing*. New York: Peter Lang, 1992.

Sterne, Laurence, and Harold H. Kollmeier, eds. *A Concordance to the English Prose of John Milton*. Binghampton, N.Y.: Medieval & Renaissance Texts and Studies, 1985.

Stranahan, Brainerd P. "Bunyan's Satire and Its Biblical Sources." In *Bunyan in Our Time*. Edited by Robert G. Collmer, 35–60. Kent, Ohio: Kent State University Press, 1989.

Swaim, Kathleen M. *Pilgrim's Progress, Puritan Progress: Discourses and Contexts*. Urbana: University of Illinois Press, 1993.

Taylor, Edward. *Upon the Types of the Old Testament*. Edited by Charles W. Mignon. 2 vols. Lincoln: University of Nebraska Press, 1989.

Taylor, John. *Ranters of Both Sexes*. 1651.

Taylor, Thomas. *Christs Victorie Over the Dragon*. London, 1633.

———. *Truth's Innocency*. 1697.

Thickstun, Margaret Olofson. "The Preface to Bunyan's *Grace Abounding* as Pauline Epistle." *Notes and Queries* 230 (1985): 180–82.

———. "From Christiana to Stand-fast: Subsuming the Feminine in *The Pilgrim's Progress*." *Studies in English Literature, 1500–1900* 26 no. 3 (Summer 1986): 439–53.

Thompson, E. P. *The Making of the English Working Class*. New York: Vintage, 1966.

Tibbutt, H. G., ed. *The Minutes of The First Independent Church (now Bunyan Meeting) at Bedford, 1656–1766*. Bedford: Bedfordshire Historical Record Society, 1976.

Tindall, William York. *John Bunyan, Mechanick Preacher*. New York: Columbia University Press, 1934.

Tomkins, John. *Piety Promoted*. 2d ed., 3 pts. 1703–1706.

Tompkinson, Thomas, to Brethren and Sisters in Ireland, 1674. British Museum Additional Manuscript 60180/11–16.

Toplady, Augustus M. *The Works of Augustus M. Toplady*. Rev. ed. 6 vols. London: William Baynes & Son; Edinburgh: H. S. Baynes, 1825.

Travers, Rebecca. *Those that meet to worship at the Steeplehouse, called John the Evangelist, in London*. London, 1659.

Trevor-Roper, H. R. *Religion, the Reformation and Social Change*. 2d ed. London: Macmillan, 1972.

Turner, George Lyon, ed. *Original Records of Early Nonconformity Under Persecution and Indulgence*. 3 vols. London T. Fisher Unwin, 1911–14.

Turner, James. "Bunyan's Sense of Place." In *Pilgrim's Progress: Critical and Historical Views*. Edited by Vincent Newey, 91–110. Liverpool: Liverpool University Press, 1980.

Tyacke, Nicholas. "The 'Rise of Puritanism' and the Legalizing of Dissent, 1571–1719." In *From Persecution to Toleration: The Glorious Revolution and Religion in England*. Edited by Ole Peter Grell, Jonathan I. Israel, and Nicholas Tyacke, 17–49. Oxford: Clarendon Press, 1991.

Underwood, T. L. *Primitivism, Radicalism, and the Lamb's War*. New York: Oxford University Press, 1996.

Van Dyke, Carolynn. *The Fiction of Truth: Structures of Meaning in Narrative and Dramatic Allegory*. Ithaca and London: Cornell University Press, 1985.

Wall, J. N. *Transformations of the Word: Spenser, Herbert, Vaughan*. Athens: University of Georgia Press, 1988.

Walton, Robert C. *The Gathered Community*. London: Carey Press, 1946.

Walwyn, William. *A Whisper in the Eare of Mr. Thomas Edwards*. 1645.

Warren, Elizabeth. *Spiritual Thrift; or, Meditations Wherein humble Christians (as in a Mirrour) may view the verity of their saving Graces, and may see how to make a spirituall improvement of all opportunities and advantages of a pious proficiencie (or a holy Growth) in Grace and goodnesse*. London: Henry Shepherd, 1647.

Watt, Tessa. *Cheap Print and Popular Piety 1550–1640*. Cambridge: Cambridge University Press, 1991.

Watts, M. R. *The Dissenters: From the Reformation to the French Revolution.* Oxford: Clarendon Press, 1978.

Webber, Joan. *The Eloquent "I": Style and Self in Seventeenth-Century Prose.* Madison: University of Wisconsin Press, 1968.

White, B. R. "William Erbery (1604–1654) and the Baptists." *Baptist Quarterly* 23 (1969–70): 114–25.

———. "The Fellowship of Believers: Bunyan and Puritanism." In *John Bunyan: Conventicle and Parnassus, Tercentenary Essays.* Edited by N. H. Keeble, 1–19. Oxford: Clarendon Press, 1988.

———. "John Bunyan and the Context of Persecution." In *John Bunyan and His England, 1628–88.* Edited by Anne Laurence, W. R. Owens, and Stuart Sim, 51–62. London and Ronceverte: Hambledon Press, 1990.

White, J. F. *Protestant Worship: Traditions in Translation.* Louisville, Ky.: Westminster/John Knox Press, 1989.

Whitehead, George. *The Christian Quaker.* 1673.

Whitehead, George, et al., Petition to Charles II. PRO SP 29/423/15. [1683].

Whitley, W.T. *A Baptist Bibliography.* 2 vols. London: Kingsgate, 1916.

———. "The First Hymnbook in Use." *Baptist Quarterly* NS 10 (1940–41): 374.

Wilding, Michael. *Dragons Teeth: Literature in the English Revolution.* Oxford: Clarendon Press, 1987.

William Thomas of Ibley. *Christian and conjugall counsell.* London, 1661.

Wittreich, Joseph. *Interpreting Samson Agonistes.* Princeton: Princeton University Press, 1986.

Wood, William, to Lodowick Muggleton, 9 February 1692. British Library Additional Manuscript 60168/42–43.

Woolrych, Austin. "Historical Introduction." *Complete Prose Works of John Milton.* 8 vols. Edited by Don Wolfe et al. New Haven and London: Yale University Press, 1953–82. Vol. 7: 220–23.

Worden, Blair. "Milton, *Samson Agonistes* and the Restoration." In *Culture and Society in the Stuart Restoration.* Edited by Gerald MacLean, 111–36. Cambridge: Cambridge University Press, 1995.

Wright, Luella M. *The Literary Life of the Early Friends 1650–1725.* New York: Columbia University Press, 1932.

———. "John Bunyan and Stephen Crisp." *Journal of Religion* 19 (1939): 95–109.

Wright, T. R. *Theology and Literature.* Oxford: Blackwell, 1988.

Contributors

MELISSA D. AARON received her Ph.D. in English literature from the University of Wisconsin at Madison and is a graduate of Cambridge University and Indiana University. She now teaches at the University of Michigan. Her research interests focus on Renaissance drama and theatre. Her doctoral dissertation is entitled "Global Economics: An Institutional Economic History of Shakespeare's Theatrical Company and Their Texts, 1599–1642."

SHARON ACHINSTEIN is Associate Professor at the University of Maryland at College Park. Her *Milton and the Revolutionary Reader* (1994) won the Hanford award from the Milton Society of America in 1995. She is currently completing *The Dissenting Muse*, a study of Dissenting poetry and politics in Restoration England.

SUSAN COOK received her Ph.D. from the University of London in 1998. Her dissertation is entitled "*The Pilgrim's Progress* and Derivative Texts, 1678–1710." She is the author of articles on Lucy Hutchinson and is assistant editor of the Handlist of the Jack Cohen Bequest of Latin American Literature. Her research interests include women's writing and Nonconformist literature in seventeenth-century England. She is now pursuing independent research in the areas of Bunyan's influence in the eighteenth century revival and seventeenth-century spiritual autobiography.

MICHAEL DAVIES is a graduate of Keble College Oxford and is a recent graduate of the doctoral program at Leicester University, England. His dissertation is entitled *Grace-ful Reading: Theology and Narrative in the Works of John Bunyan*.

PATRICIA DEMERS, Professor of English at the University of Alberta, is the author of *Women as Interpreters of the Bible, Heaven Upon Earth, Introducing Louis Hemon's Marie Chapdelaine, The World of Hannah More*, and *P.L. Travers*, as well as numerous articles in the field of Renaissance literature.

RICHARD L. GREAVES is Robert O. Lawton Distinguished Professor of History and Courtesy Professor of Religion at Florida State University. He is the author or editor of eighteen books, including *Civilizations of the West: The Human Adventure* (1994), *Enemies under His Feet: Radicals and Nonconformists in Britain, 1664–1677* (1990), *Deliver Us from Evil: The Radical Underground in Britain, 1660–1663* (1986), *Saints and Rebels: Seven Nonconformists in Stuart England* (1985), *John Bunyan: A Reference Guide* (with James F. Forrest) (1982), *Society and Religion in Elizabethan England* (1981), among others. He is the coeditor (with Robert Zaller) of the *Biographical Dictionary of British Radicals in the Seventeenth Century* (1982–1984), and the editor of volumes 2, 8, 9, and 11 of the *Miscellaneous Works of John Bunyan*.

N. H. KEEBLE is Professor of English at the University of Stirling, Scotland. His publications on English cultural history of the early-modern period include *Richard Baxter: Puritan Man of Letters* (1982) and the *Literary Culture of Nonconformity in Later Seventeenth-Century England* (1987); editions of *Richard Baxter's Autobiography* (1974), John Bunyan's *The Pilgrim's Progress* (1984), and Lucy Hutchinson's *Memoirs of the Life of Colonel Hutchinson* (1995); an anthology illustrating *The Cultural Identity of Seventeenth-Century Woman* (1994); a tercentenary symposium, *John Bunyan: Conventicle and Parnassus* (1988); and a two-volume *Calendar of the Correspondence of Richard Baxter* (with Geoffrey F. Nuttall). He is currently working on a study of the 1660s. Professor Keeble is a Fellow of the Royal Historical Society.

JOHN R. KNOTT is Professor of English at the University of Michigan. He is the author of *Milton's Pastoral Vision* (1971), *The Sword of the Spirit: Puritan Responses to the Bible* (1981), and *Discourses of Martyrdom in English Literature, 1563–1694* (1993). He teaches seventeenth-century English literature, including Milton, and American environmental literature. He is currently working on a book on imagining wilderness in America.

W. R. OWENS is Staff Tutor and Senior Lecturer in Literature at The Open University. Previous publications on Bunyan include an edition of *Grace Abounding* and several articles. He has edited two volumes of the *Miscellaneous Works of John Bunyan*, and has coedited a volume of essays: *John Bunyan and His England, 1628–1688*. In addition to his work on Bunyan, Dr. Owens has coauthored (with P. N. Furbank) several books and many articles on the bibliography of Daniel Defoe. His most recent publication is a coedited volume on *Shakespeare, Aphra Behn and the Canon* (1996), in which he has written chapters on "Shakespeare: Theatre Poet" and "Remaking the Canon: Aphra Behn's The Rover," as well as a student edition of *The Rover*. He is currently working with P. N. Furbank on *A Critical Bibliography of the Writings of Daniel Defoe* and is coediting (with Penny Rixon) a volume entitled *Reading Shakespeare: Studying Drama*.

AILEEN ROSS is Adjunct Professor of English at Canadian University College, Red Deer, Canada. She is the author of a doctoral dissertation on the subject of Bunyan and millenarianism as well as a number of articles and conference papers on Bunyan and his era.

KEN SIMPSON teaches in the Department of English and Modern Languages at the University College of the Cariboo, Kamloops, British Columbia. He has published articles on Milton and the liturgies of nonconformity.

T. L. UNDERWOOD is Professor of History at the University of Minnesota, Morris, and Fellow of the Royal Historical Society of Great Britain. He is the author of *Primitivism, Radicalism, and the Lamb's War* and editor of volumes 1 and 4 of the *Miscellaneous Works of John Bunyan*. He is a member of the American Society of Church History and the Conference on British Studies, and of Baptist and Quaker historical societies in Britain and the United States. He is a member of the Advisory Council of the International John Bunyan Society and the Editorial Advisory Board of *Bunyan Studies*. He teaches Early Modern European and English History and is the recipient of the University of Minnesota's Morse-Alumni Award for Outstanding Contributions to Undergraduate Education.

Index

Aaron, Melissa, 21
Achinstein, Sharon, 13, 19
Act of Oblivion, 28
Act of Uniformity, 33
Adolphus, Gustavus, 83
Advocateship of Jesus Christ, The (Bunyan), 12
Allegory, Bunyan's use of, 11, 13, 53–54, 62, 68–78, 91, 105–6, 108, 113, 116, 122–25, 163, 165, 197
Alsted, Johann Heinrich, 82, 83
Anabaptist, 82, 87, 127
Andrews, St., Bishop of, 16
Anglican Church, 18, 74, 88, 175, 192, 197
Awakening word, 10, 11, 13, 19, 20

Bacon, Francis, 14
Bagshaw, Edward, 90
Bailey, Lewis, 167
Baptists, 10, 12, 13, 19, 127, 128, 129, 134, 136, 138, 159, 161, 187, 192, 193; Henry Danvers, 13; John Denne, 10; Henry Grigg, 138; Henry Jessey, 143–45; Benjamin Keach, 88, 90, 187–88, 189, 192, 197, 198; William Kiffin, 10, 15, 155, 161; Thomas Paul, 13. *See also* General Baptists
Barren Fig Tree, The (Bunyan), 117
Barth, John, 99
Baxter, Richard, 89, 119, 122, 129, 130, 135
Beaumont, Agnes, 154, 155, 160, 164, 166, 167, 196
Bedford Congregation, 10, 15, 18, 21, 37, 68, 114, 116, 124, 127, 150, 154, 159, 161, 162, 166, 169, 174–76, 183, 193; Church Book, 37, 116, 160, 172–75, 182, 193; John Gifford, 114, 115, 116, 120, 121, 167, 193; H. G. Tibbutt, 172; *A True and Impartial Narrative of Some Illegal and Arbitrary Proceedings*, 15
Bernard, Richard, 62, 65
Beverley, Thomas, 89, 90
Beza, Theodore, 101
Bible, 10, 11, 22, 75, 87, 157, 182, 183, 194–96; Geneva Bible, 195; Language of, 62; Samson, 13, 19, 68–78, 146; Old Testament, 57, 109, 155; New Testament, 109, 155, 156, 167, 195; Acts, 30, 177; 1 Corinthians, 27, 114; Daniel, 84; Ecclesiastes, 36; Exodus, 117, 194; Genesis, 157, 173; Hebrews, 118, 194; Isaiah, 56; John, 39; Judges, 70; 1 Kings, 117; Luke, 35–36; Matthew, 43, 56, 75; 1 Peter, 55; Psalms, 55; Revelation, 14, 59, 60, 77, 81, 82, 83, 85, 87, 88, 89, 117, 121, 132, 137; Romans, 182, 183; 1 Samuel, 74; 2 Thessalonians, 60; 2 Timothy, 55. *See also* Milton, John, *Samson Agonistes*
Bisbie, Elizabeth, 172
Bonner, Edmund, 33
Book of Common Prayer, 12, 16, 33, 34, 39, 119, 188
Book for Boys and Girls, A (Bunyan), 73, 197
Boyle, Sir Robert, 88
Brittain, Vera, 97
Brightman, Thomas, 82, 83
Brown, John, 9, 157, 186
Bugg, Francis, 186
Bunyan, D., 196
Bunyan, Elizabeth, 166, 167
Bunyan, John: audience, 9, 19; education, 11, 27; first wife, 167, 170; incarceration, 14, 18, 29; works: *see under individual titles*
Burder, George, 192
Burnet, Thomas, 88

Burrough, Edward. *See* Quakers
Burton, John, 11, 135, 136

Calvert, Elizabeth and Giles, 21
Calvin, John, 44, 101–4
Calvinism, 101; calvinist theology, 27, 106. *See also* election, 52–53, 57, 100–102, 104, 106, 107
Camden, Vera, 155
Cameron, Richard, 17
Capp, Bernard, 84, 86
Cargill, Donald, 17
Cary, Mary, 142
Case of Conscience Resolved (Bunyan), 12, 153, 154, 158, 159, 167, 170, 178
Catholic, Roman, 17, 39, 40, 83, 89; Anti-catholic, 21, 156; Catholic Church, 58, 197
Caton, William, 129
Chambers, A. B., 113
Charles I, 53, 83, 84
Charles II, 12, 17, 18, 85, 161
Chapbooks: literature, 192, 195–96; romances, 27, 54; *The Seven Champions of Christendom*, 58
Chevers, Sarah, 142
Christian Behaviour (Bunyan, 1663), 29, 151, 153, 160, 164
Church of England, 17, 18, 33, 43
Clarendon, Earl of, Edward Hyde, 45
Clarkson, Laurence, 129, 132
Confession of my Faith (Bunyan), 115
Congregationalists, 19; John Owen, 19
Conventicle Act, 17, 113, 116
Come, & Welcome, to Jesus Christ (Bunyan), 12
Cook, Susan, 20
Coppe, Abiezer, 130, 134
Cotton, John, 119
Cowley, Abraham, 45
Crisp, Stephen. *See* Quakers
Cromwell, Oliver, 37, 53, 76, 84, 92

Dailey, Barbara Ritter, 144
Danvers, Henry, 90
Davies, Michael, 11, 20
Davis, J. C., 130
de Certeau, Michel, 145
De Krey, Gary, 12
de l' Incarnation, Marie, 150

Defence of the Doctrine of Justification, by Faith (Bunyan), 134
Delany, Paul, 100, 103
Demers, Patricia, 20, 21
Denne, John, 10
Dent, Arthur, 167
Discourse of the Building, &c., of the House of God (Bunyan), 117, 121, 125
Dover, Joan, 21
Downame, John, 117
Dryden, John, 45, 74
Dutton, John, 186, 188, 190, 192, 194

Ebner, Dean, 100
Edwards, Thomas, 129, 136
Eisenstein, Elizabeth, 142
Election, 54, 100, 103, 107, 108, 115
Eliade, Mircea, 118, 120
Elizabeth I, 128
Ellwood, Thomas. *See* Quakers
Endogamy, 173, 174
Episcopalians, 32–34, 44
Erbery, Dorcus, 132
Erbery, William, 129, 132, 136
Evans, Katherine, 142
Evelyn, John, 45, 88, 90
Exclusion Crisis, 90
Exogamy, 174
Exposition of the First Ten Chapters of Genesis (Bunyan), 12, 58, 59, 61, 137, 161

Family of Love. *See* Familists
Familists, 19, 127–29
Fell, Margaret, 16, 129, 134
Fenne, Samuel, 18
Fifth Monarchists, 16, 39, 68, 84; Joseph Mede, 82, 83, 89, 90; Thomas Venner, 15, 68
Fish, Stanley, 69, 70, 109
Fitzharris, Edward, 17
Forrest, James F., 62, 161
Fox, George. *See* Quakers
Foxe, John, 44, 57, 60, 63, 158
Friedman, Jerome, 127, 130
Friends. *See* Quakers
Fuller, Abraham, 15

Gates, Mary, 174, 175
General Baptists, 19, 170, 160, 187;

Thomas Lamb, 170; Thomas Sherman, 187, 190, 191, 195
Gifford, John. *See* Bedford Congregation
Goodwin, Thomas, 81, 119
Gouge, William, 174
Grace, 29, 75, 78, 103, 105, 106, 109, 115, 117, 119, 121, 135, 137, 143, 145, 147, 158, 169, 182, 194
Grace Abounding to the Chief of Sinners (Bunyan), 10, 20, 29, 70, 97–110, 120, 134, 135, 143, 149, 161, 169, 193, 196
Greaves, Richard, 59, 68, 74, 84, 92, 115, 170
Grigg, Henry. *See* Baptists
Guibbory, Achsah, 197

Halifax, Marquis of, 17
Haller, William, 117
Harris, Tim, 12
Hayter, Richard, 88
Herbert, George, 157, 194
Hill, Christopher, 31, 41, 65, 69, 117, 153, 161; *A Turbulent, Seditious and Factious People: John Bunyan and His Church* (1988), 9; *The Experience of Defeat: Milton and Some Contemporaries* (1984), 13
Hobby, Elaine, 141, 145
Holme, Thomas, 15
Holy City, The (Bunyan), 12, 13, 14, 19, 21, 86, 90, 114, 115, 121, 135, 136, 170
Holy War, The (Bunyan, 1682), 13, 14, 56, 62–65, 68, 69, 72, 77, 91, 104, 135, 137, 161; (Mr.) Atheism, 135; Bloodmen, 63, 92; Boanerges, 56; Captain Credence, 63, 72; Captain Execution, 63; Captain Patience, 63; Clip-promise, 64; Conscience, 62, Conviction, 56; Diabolonians, 62, 64, 77; Diabolus, 57, 62, 63, 65, 72, 91, 92; Doubters, 63, 64, 92, 137; Emanuel, 57, 64, 65, 72, 91–92, 137, Lord Hategood, 14, 66; Lord Lasciviousness, 42; Lord Willbewill, 62; (Mr.) Lustings, 64; Mansoul, 56, 63, 64, 72, 91, 92; (Mr.) Mind, 62; (Mr.) Prejudice, 63; Secure, 57; Self-denial, 64; Self-love, 64; Shaddai, 56; (Mr.) Rashead; Understanding, 62; Zeal for God, 63
Horle, Craig, 15
House of God. *See Discourse of the Building, &c., of the House of God*
(of the) House of the Forest of Lebanon
Howgill, Francis, 129
Hubberthorne, Richard, 129
Humility, 169, 170, 177, 181, 182
Hyde, Sir Robert, Lord Chief Justice, 88

Israel's Hope Encouraged (Bunyan), 12
I Will Pray With the Spirit (Bunyan), 12, 33, 35, 39

Jackson, John, 129, 134
James II, 12, 16, 74, 90, 161
James, Duke of Ormonde, 17
Jardine, Lisa, 142
Jeffreys, Justice George, 65
Jessey, Henry. *See* Baptists
Judah leib, Glikl bas, 150

Keach, Benjamin. *See* Baptists
Keeble, N. H., 9, 12, 69
Kelyng, Sir John (Justice), 36, 40, 65
Kendall, R. T., 101
Kiffin, William. *See* Baptists
Knollys, Hanserd, 90
Knott, John, 9, 13, 14, 107

Labyrinth, 97–110
Lamb, Thomas. *See* General Baptists
Latitudinarian, 13, 41, 43, 88
L'Estrange, Roger, 32
Life and Death of Mr. Badman, The (Bunyan, 1680), 52, 160, 170, 174, 175, 188; Attentive, 176; Mr. Badman, 41, 160, 175, 177, 179, 180; Mrs. Badman, 180; Wiseman, 176, 177, 180
Lilburne, John, 76
Liturgy, 197; Nonconformist, 10, 113–25
Lloyd, William, Bishop of St. Asaph, 90
Loe, Thomas. *See* Quakers
Ludlow, Dorothy, 143
Luther, Martin, 83
Luxon, Thomas, 53, 99

INDEX

Mack, Phyllis, 141, 148
Maidwell, John, 18
Major, Elizabeth, 21, 143–51
Man, William, 173
Marriage: law, 171, manuals, 173, 174
Marsh, Christopher W., 128, 129
Marvel, Andrew, 29, 76, 77
Mason, John, 89, 90
Mather, Cotton, 171, 181
Maxie, Elizabeth, 172
McGregor, J. F., 129
Mede, Joseph, 82, 83, 89, 90
Merian, Maria Sibylla, 150
Methodists, 198
Millennium, 19, 20, 81
Millenarian [millenarianism], 19, 81–93, 178
Miller, J. Hillis, 100
Milton, John, 27–45, 76; *Areopagitica*, 76; *A Masque Presented at Ludlow Castle (Comus)*, 38; *Paradise Lost*, 31, 34, 36, 38, 39, 41; *Paradise Regained*, 27, 39; "The Readie and Easie Way to Establish a Free Commonwealth," 28, 37; *Samson Agonistes*, 37, 41, 43
Monmouth Rebellion, 133
Moore, Sir John, Lord Mayor, 17
More, Hannah, 188
More, Henry, 88, 89
Muggletonians, 19, 127–38; Lodowick Muggleton, 130, 132, 134, 135, 136, 137; Thomas Tomkinson, 134
Michael A. Mullet, 9

Naylor, James. *See* Quakers
Needham, Marchamont, 45
Ness, Christopher, 90
New Model Army, 76
Newey, Vincent, 97, 98
Newton, Sir Isaac, 88
Niclaes, Hendrick, 128, 129
North, Francis, Lord Keeper, 17
Norwood, Robert, 130
Nye, Phillip, 119

Of Antichrist, and His Ruine (Bunyan), 12, 13, 19, 60, 77, 90, 137
Offor, George, 9, 13, 69
Overton, Richard, 62, 63

Owen, John. *See* Congregationalists
Owens, W. R., 12, 19, 58

Pareus, David, 117
Parker, Samuel, 113
Patrick, Symon, Bishop of Ely, 186, 187, 188
Patterson, Annabel, 69
Paul, the Apostle, 28, 30, 55, 68, 73, 155
Pauline, 60, 62, 147, 156, 159, 160, 170, 178
Penn, William. *See* Quakers
Penitence, Public, 171
Pepys, Samuel, 45
Perkins, William, 101, 117
Pilgrim's Progress, The (Bunyan, 1678), 11, 12, 13, 14, 20, 35, 42, 52, 54, 56, 70, 105, 113–25, 170, 177; Apollyon, 54, 55, 117, 180; Attentive, 42; Beulah, 54, 115, 117, 121, 124; By-ends, 35, 41; Celestial City, 105, 115, 124; Christian, 36, 42, 52–54, 56, 57, 62, 64, 65, 105, 106–10, 115, 116, 117, 123, 124, 161, 162, 163, 164, 165, 169, 177, 178, 180, 182, 192; Civility, 41; Delectable Mountains, 86, 117, 121; Destruction, 52; Doubting Castle, 9, 109; Evangelist, 37, 36, 58, 115, 116; Faithful, 36, 42, 53, 56, 57, 60, 61, 62, 64, 69, 106, 115, 123; Formalist, 52; Giant Despair, 54, 109, 110, 116, 154; Hill Difficulty, 9, 55; Hill of Error, 52; Hopeful, 52, 54, 65, 105, 106–10, 115, 116, 124, 192; Hypocrisy, 52; Ignorance, 52; Interpreter's House, 72, 105, 108, 110, 115, 118, 122, 124; Legality, 41, 116; Lord Hategood, 36, 40, 62; Mistrust, 116; Monument to Lot's Wife, 108, 109; Palace Beautiful, 114–18, 120–22; Shepherds of the Delectable Mountains, 106–10, 115; Shining Ones, 65; Simple, Sloth and Presumption, 20, 51; Slough of Dispond, 123; Talkative, 106, 176; Timorous, 116; Vanity Fair, 9, 12, 36, 40, 42, 52, 55, 56, 57, 61–65, 181; Valley of Humiliation, 55, 180; Valley of the Shadow of Death, 10, 54, 55, 181; Watchful, 55,

120; Wicket Gate, 123; Worldly Wiseman, 41, 42, 106, 181
Pilgrim's Progress, The, Part II, (Bunyan, 1684), 20, 21, 123, 124, 153–67, 169–84, 186–98; Celestial City, 161; Christiana, 123, 124, 153, 154, 157, 161–67, 169, 174, 177, 179, 181, 182, 183; City of Destruction, 162; Beulah, 183; Bountiful, 180; Delectable Mountains, shepherds of, 183; Doubting Castle, 167; Dr. Skill, 165; (Mr.) Brisk, 41, 165, 179, 180; (Mr.) Feeblemind, 137, 167; Gaius, 178, 180, 182, 183; Gatekeeper, 177; Giant Despair, 166, 167, 181; Giant Grim, 14, 165, 179; Great-heart 51, 56, 58, 157, 162, 164, 165, 166, 167, 178, 179, 181, 183; Honest, 182; House Beautiful, 164, 165, 178, 179; House of the Interpreter, 161, 162, 164, 165, 178; James, 183; Madame Bubble, 153; Madame Wanton, 178; Mercy, 20, 51, 61, 154, 162–67, 171, 174, 177, 179–80, 181, 182; Matthew, 137, 166, 174; Phoebe, 170, 183; Prudence, 137, 165, 179, 180; (Mr.) Ready-to-hault, 167; Reliever, 163; Secret, 162; Sloth, 52, 56, 61–62; Slough of Dispond, 162; Timorous, 52, 56, 61–62; (Mrs.) Timorous, 178; Valley of Humiliation, 180; Valley of the Shadow of Death, 182; Vanity Fair, 58, 177, 181, 183; Wicket Gate, 163
Plain Man's Pathway to Heaven, The, 170
Pooley, Roger, 100
Popish Plot, 17, 68, 90, 161
Pordage, John, 130
Postmodernist writing/narrative, 9, 99
Pooley, William, 15
Practice of Piety, The, 170
Predestination, 100–104, 107, 108
Presbyterians, 10, 19, 63, 87, 129, 134
Prison Meditations (Bunyan), 29, 34, 36
Prisons, conditions of, 16, 18

Quakers, 10, 12, 14, 15, 16, 19, 20, 29, 87, 127–38, 148, 159, 170, 179, 186, 194, 195; Edward Burrough, 10, 13, 129, 134, 135, 138; Stephen Crisp, 189, 194, 195, 198; Thomas Ellwood, 29; George Fox, 16, 65, 131–32, 134, 135; Thomas Loe, 136; James Naylor, 53, 131; William Penn, 10, 42, 61, 134; William Smith, 174; Thomas Taylor, 117; John Tomkins, 129; Rebecca Travers, 21, 143–51; George Whitehead, 138
Questions About the Nature and Perpetuity of the Seventh-Day Sabbath (Bunyan), 134

Raikes, Robert, 171
Ranters, 19, 127–38, 159, 196; John Robins, 130, 136
Readers, Bunyan's, 196–98
Reeve, John, 132, 133, 134, 136, 137
Relation of my Imprisonment (Bunyan), 60, 61
Reresby, Sir John, 45
Resurrection of the Dead, The (Bunyan), 14
Restoration, 14, 16, 20, 28–45, 62, 68, 69, 71, 74, 78, 87, 88, 89, 113; government, 12
Robins, John. *See* Ranters
Rochester, Earl of, 17, 42
Ross, Aileen, 21
Rye House Plot, 15, 17, 19, 68, 74

Saints Privilege and Profit, The (Bunyan), 104
Saltmarsh, John, 129, 136
Sancroft, Archbishop, 90
Samson. *See* Bible and Milton, John, *Samson Agonistes*
Scott, Jonathan, 12
Scottish Covenanters, 16, 17
Seasonable Counsel (Bunyan), 12, 18, 36, 43, 58, 61, 68, 71, 74, 78
Seekers, 127–38
Sexby, Edward, 76
Shaftesbury, Earl of, 74
Sharrock, Roger, 9, 62, 154, 161, 172, 177, 182, 195
Sherman, Thomas. *See* General Baptists
Sherwin, William, 90
Sidney, Sir Phillip, 31
Sim, Stuart, 57, 100, 106

Simpson, John, 136
Simpson, Ken, 10
Smith, Francis "Elephant," 21, 74
Smith, Hilda, 141
Smith, Nigel, 143
Smith, William. *See* Quakers
Solomon's Temple Spiritualized (Bunyan), 12, 120
Some Gospel-Truths Opened (Bunyan), 11
Spiritual autobiography, 11, 20, 100, 101, 141–51, 166, 193
Spurgeon, Charles Haddon, 9
Stachniewski, John, 107
Stanton, John, 159, 173
Stanwood, P. G., 113
Stokes, Justice Edward, 131
Strait Gate, The (Bunyan), 121
Swaim, Kathleen, 123
Symmons, Edward, 83

Taylor, Thomas. *See* Quakers
Test Act, 12
Tibbutt, H. G. *See* Bedford Congregation
Tilney, Mary, 21, 159
Tindall, William York, 9, 84
Tomkins, John. *See* Quakers
Tomkinson, Thomas. *See* Muggletonians
Toplady, Augustus M., 187
Travers, Rebecca. *See* Quakers
True and Impartial Narrative of Some Illegal and Arbitrary Proceedings. See Bedford Congregation

Underwood, T. L., 10, 19, 153, 158, 159, 161

Venner, Thomas. *See* Fifth Monarchists
Vindication of the Book Called, Some Gospel-Truths Opened (Bunyan), 135, 136
Violence, 19, 20, 51–66, 68–78, 84, 169, 173, 179
Virgil, 28

Wall, J. N., 113
Walwyn, William, 129
Warren, Elizabeth, 142
Webb, Thomas, 130, 131
Webber, Joan, 100
Wesley, John, 188
Wharey, James Blanton, 9
White, Henry and Mary, 131
White, J. F., 113
Whitehead, George. *See* Quakers
Wight, Sarah, 21, 143–51
Wilding, Michael, 31
Wilkinson, Henry, 83
William and Mary, 90
Wilson, Henry, 189, 191
Winright, Mrs. George, 21
Wood, Tempest, 81
Wood, William, 133
Woolf, Virginia, 143
Woolrych, Austin, 37
Women: fashions, 41; role of, 20–22, 141–51, 153–67, 169–84
Worden, Blair, 37

Zemon Davies, Natalie, 145, 150